STAGE SCENERY, MACHINERY, AND LIGHTING

PERFORMING ARTS INFORMATION GUIDE SERIES

Series Editor: Louis A. Rachow, Librarian, The Walter Hampden Memorial Library, New York, New York

Also in the Performing Arts Series:

ACTORS AND ACTING—*Edited by Stephen M. Archer**

THE AMERICAN STAGE FROM 1900 TO THE 1970s—*Edited by Don B. Wilmeth**

THE AMERICAN STAGE TO 1900—*Edited by Don B. Wilmeth**

BUSINESS OF THE THEATRE—*Edited by J. Kline Hobbs**

HISTORY OF POPULAR ENTERTAINMENT—*Edited by Don B. Wilmeth**

LAW OF THE THEATRE—*Edited by Daniel Jon Strehl**

PERFORMING ARTS RESEARCH—*Edited by Marion K. Whalon*

THEATRE ARCHITECTURE—*Edited by Richard Stoddard**

THEATRICAL COSTUME—*Edited by Jackson Kesler**

*in preparation

The above series is part of the
GALE INFORMATION GUIDE LIBRARY

The Library consists of a number of separate series of guides covering major areas in the social sciences, humanities, and current affairs.

General Editor: Paul Wasserman, Professor and former Dean, School of Library and Information Services, University of Maryland

Managing Editor: Dedria Bryfonski, Gale Research Company

STAGE SCENERY, MACHINERY, AND LIGHTING

A GUIDE TO INFORMATION SOURCES

Volume 2 in the Performing Arts Information Guide Series

Richard Stoddard

Gale Research Company
Book Tower, Detroit, Michigan 48226

Library of Congress Cataloging in Publication Data

Stoddard, Richard.
    Stage scenery, machinery, and lighting.

    (Performing arts information guide series ; v. 2)
(Gale information guide library)
    Includes indexes.
    1. Theaters--Stage-setting and scenery--Bibliography.
2. Stage machinery--Bibliography. 3. Stage lighting--
Bibliography. I. Title
Z5784.S8S79   [PN2091.S8]   016.792'025   76-13574
ISBN 0-8103-1374-X

To Wendy

VITA

Richard Stoddard studied at Tufts University (B.A., 1967) and at Yale University (Ph.D., Department of Theatre History, 1971). He was assistant professor in the Department of Drama and Theatre, University of Georgia, Athens, Georgia, from 1971 to 1975. Presently he lives in New York City, where he carries on an antiquarian bookselling business specializing in rare and out-of-print performing arts materials. He has published articles in THEATRE SURVEY, EDUCATIONAL THEATRE JOURNAL, PERFORMING ARTS RESOURCES, ANTIQUES, WINTERTHUR PORTFOLIO, and other journals.

CONTENTS

Contents

INTRODUCTION

This guide is the first book-length bibliography of stage scenery, machinery, and lighting published since 1928, when the New York Public Library issued the second, enlarged edition of William Burt Gamble's THE DEVELOPMENT OF SCENIC ART AND STAGE MACHINERY. Since then, popular books and magazines have continued to reflect wide public interest in stage design, while scholarly books and articles on this subject have appeared in far greater numbers than before. A new bibliography was plainly needed.

My intention was not to supersede Gamble's valuable compilation. In fact, considerations of space made that impossible. Since this guide is intended for use by undergraduates as well as more advanced scholars, I have given first priority to sources of information that are widely available and readily usable. While Gamble included numerous foreign-language titles, I concentrated on identifying English-language sources, listing only a few dozen indispensable and unique studies in foreign languages. Nevertheless, specialists will find much that is unfamiliar to them.

The entries compiled here concern stage scenery and lighting throughout the world, from the classical Greek theatre to the theatre of the 1970s. They relate to design for drama, opera, and dance. I have included books, articles, pamphlets, some exhibition catalogs (those that pertain to influential exhibitions or contain informative essays), unpublished doctoral dissertations, and a few newspaper articles. Space restrictions prohibited the listing of all articles in THEATRE CRAFTS, THEATRE DESIGN & TECHNOLOGY, and TABS; I chose to list only historical and biographical articles in these periodicals. Articles on contemporary practice published in other journals, however, are listed.

In addition to its usefulness as a source of information, a bibliography has a certain value as an indication of progress in scholarship. It defines what has been done and suggests directions for further study. The entries compiled here reflect renewed interest in the illusionistic stage of the nineteenth century, as well as a continuing attempt to reconstruct the often mysterious workings of Renaissance and Baroque scenery. Recently, many researchers have turned their attention to the New Stagecraft and its sources: the Symbolist theatre, Appia, Craig, and the Ballets Russes.

Introduction

Much remains to be done. Biographical studies of stage designers are sorely needed. The history of American stage design, particularly in the nineteenth century, has not yet been explored in depth. The first book-length history of stage lighting in English was only recently announced for publication; more detailed national histories are wanted. And there is a need for basic reference tools: inventories of original designs in libraries and museums; indexes of published illustrations; lists of designers' productions; and, of course, bibliographies.

SOME HINTS ABOUT USING THIS GUIDE

To locate sources of information on a particular stage designer, see the Person (as Subject) Index. If the designer may have been an author (as is often the case), see also the Author Index. To locate illustrations of scenery by a particular designer, see the entries listed in the Person (as Subject) Index and the Author Index and also chapter 1, "Bibliographies and Iconographies," where several valuable listings of illustrations will be found (items 9, 12, 13, 15, 18, and 23).

Except for the comprehensive sections on Reference, Periodicals, General Histories, Classical Greece and Rome, Medieval Europe, Aesthetics, and Lighting, the organization of the guide is mainly geographical, with separate sections devoted to Czechoslovakia, England, France, Germany-Austria, Italy, Russia and the Soviet Union, Switzerland, and the United States, and one section encompassing other countries. Each country is subdivided by period: General Histories, Renaissance and Baroque, Nineteenth Century, and Twentieth Century. (I have used the term "Baroque" somewhat loosely, applying it to the whole of the eighteenth century as well as the seventeenth.) The sections on Czechoslovakia and Switzerland largely concern Josef Svoboda and Adolphe Appia, respectively. To locate entries on stage design in other countries, check the name of the country in the Subject Index.

In searching for information on scenery and machinery in a particular country, take care not to overlook the entries in chapter 4, "General Histories."

To locate sources of information on stage lighting, see part III and also the Subject Index, which lists selected references to lighting in the entries on stage scenery and machinery.

Part I

GENERAL REFERENCES

Chapter 1

BIBLIOGRAPHIES AND ICONOGRAPHIES

1. Adams, Richard G. "A Bibliography for Producing Organizations with Limited Budgets and Facilities." EDUCATIONAL THEATRE JOURNAL 7 (1955): 246-49.

    Includes citations to forty-eight articles on scenery, machinery, and lighting. Annotated.

2. Altman, George, et al. THEATER PICTORIAL: A HISTORY OF WORLD THEATER AS RECORDED IN DRAWINGS, PAINTINGS, ENGRAVINGS, AND PHOTOGRAPHS. Berkeley and Los Angeles: University of California Press, 1953. Unpaged. 516 illus.

    Most of the illustrations are stage designs and production photographs, each with brief commentary.

3. Averyt, Bennet. "Lighting for the Arena Stage." THEATRE DESIGN & TECHNOLOGY, no. 23 (December 1970): 27-29.

    A list of eighty-five books, articles, pamphlets, and unpublished theses.

4. Baker, Blanch M. THEATRE AND ALLIED ARTS: A GUIDE TO BOOKS DEALING WITH THE HISTORY, CRITICISM, AND TECHNIC OF THE DRAMA AND THEATRE. New York: Wilson, 1952. 549 p.

    "Scenic Art," pp. 293-314.

5. Botkin, Alex, et al. "Partial Index to the Russian Journal SCENIC TECHNIQUES AND TECHNOLOGY: 1965-1968." THEATRE DESIGN & TECHNOLOGY, no. 20 (February 1970): 22-23, 35. Illus.

    Title index to articles in STSENICHESKAIA TEKHNIKA I TEKHNOLOGIA, published in Moscow. Covers the years 1965-68 except for the first four issues in 1967.

6. Cheshire, D.F. BIBLIOGRAPHY OF THEATRE AND STAGE DESIGN: A SELECT LIST OF BOOKS AND ARTICLES PUBLISHED 1960-1970.

London: Commission for a British Theatre Institute, 1974.   20 p.
Paperbound.

More than 600 books and articles published in Britain, 1960–
70, on stage design, lighting, and theatre architecture. International in scope.

7.   Columbia University Dramatic Museum. A CATALOG OF MODELS AND
OF STAGE-SETS IN THE DRAMATIC MUSEUM OF COLUMBIA UNIVER-
SITY. New York: 1916. 55 p.

Describes model reconstructions of historical theatres and settings, as well as some early-twentieth-century scenic models
donated by professional scene painters. An earlier list was
published by Brander Matthews in COLUMBIA UNIVERSITY
QUARTERLY 14 (1912): 137–45.

8.   Cooperman, Gail B., and Shea, Maureen. "Index to the Journal of
the OSU Theatre Research Institute, 1954–1974." THEATRE STUDIES
20 (1973–74): 64–70.

Indexes the OSU THEATRE COLLECTION BULLETIN (later
THEATRE STUDIES), published at Ohio State University. Most
of the articles concern the history of scenery, theatre architecture, and production style.

9.   Dameron, Louise. BIBLIOGRAPHY OF STAGE SETTINGS TO WHICH
IS ATTACHED AN INDEX TO ILLUSTRATIONS OF STAGE SETTINGS.
Baltimore: Enoch Pratt Free Library, 1936. 48 p. Paperbound.
Mimeographed.

Brief list of books about scene design and stage production,
mainly twentieth century, plus an index of illustrations of
sets in forty-seven books (arranged alphabetically by name of
play and giving source and, where found, name of designer).

10. Fletcher, Ifan Kyrle, and Rood, Arnold. EDWARD GORDON CRAIG:
A BIBLIOGRAPHY. London: Society for Theatre Research, 1967.
117 p. Port.

A detailed descriptive bibliography of Craig's work: books,
articles, introductions, programs, and illustrations, as well as
the texts of plays produced by him and catalogs of exhibitions
of his work.

11. Freedley, George, ed. THEATRICAL DESIGNS FROM THE BAROQUE
THROUGH NEOCLASSICISM: UNPUBLISHED MATERIAL FROM AMERI-
CAN PRIVATE COLLECTIONS. New York: H. Bittner, 1940.

Three boxes of loose, matted plates, twenty-four per box.
Brief introduction by Freedley.

12. Gamble, William Burt. THE DEVELOPMENT OF SCENIC ART AND STAGE MACHINERY: A LIST OF REFERENCES IN THE NEW YORK PUBLIC LIBRARY. Rev., enl. ed. New York: New York Public Library, 1928. 231 p.

> An international listing, from classical Greece and Rome to the 1920s. More than 3,300 entries. Also includes an index of published illustrations of scenery "mainly since 1917," arranged by play, noting designer, theatre, and bibliographical source. Indexes of authors, persons, subjects, theatres, and stage organizations. Dated, but still very useful.

13. _____. "Stage Scenery: A List of References to Illustrations since 1900." BULLETIN OF THE NEW YORK PUBLIC LIBRARY 21 (April 1917): 239-80; (May 1917): '25-63.

> Indexes illustrations in programs, articles, and books, American and foreign, mostly published 1900-1915. Arranged by play title, with indexes of artists and theatres. Mentions a pre-1900 list that apparently was never published.

14. Gregor, Joseph, ed. MONUMENTA SCENICA. 12 vols. Vienna: National Library, [1926-1930].

> A limited edition of twelve portfolios of mounted plates (part colored) relating mainly to baroque stage design. A "new series" (one portfolio) on Giuseppe Galli da Bibiena was published in 1954 (see item 685).

15. Hammack, J. Alan. "An Index to Photographs of Scene Designs in THEATRE ARTS, 1916-1964." THEATRE DOCUMENTATION 3 (1970-71): 29-59.

> "An index to 3,158 photographs of 1,717 different titles (plays, musicals, operas, and ballets) by 550 different scene designers. The majority . . . are of actual settings, and the remainder are of sketches or models. . . . The separate indexes are: (1) titles of plays, musicals, operas, and ballets; (2) names of the scene designers; and (3) styles of scene design." An extremely valuable finding list.

16. _____. "Settings for Shakespearean Productions." PLAYERS 41 (January 1965): 96-98. Biblio.

> A survey of pictorial sources, noting various styles of Shakespeare production.

17. Hunter, Frederick J. CATALOGUE OF THE NORMAN BEL GEDDES COLLECTION, HUMANITIES RESEARCH CENTER, UNIVERSITY OF TEXAS, AUSTIN. Boston: G.K. Hall & Co., 1973. vi, 333 p. 1 illus. Biblio.

Catalog of a collection which "comprises all of the correspondence, business files, and artistic designs of Norman Bel
Geddes." Includes a fact-filled biographical sketch of his
career in the theatre, pp. 1-18, and an excellent bibliography.

18.   "Index of Illustrations." WORLD THEATRE 13 (1964-65): 271-320.

An index of photographs in WORLD THEATRE, 1950-1964,
mainly photographs of stage settings, organized by name of
playwright, composer, or choreographer. A similar index to
later volumes appears in WORLD THEATRE 16 (1967): 513-25.

19.   Larson, Orville K. "Robert Edmond Jones and His Art: A Bibliographic
Portrait." THEATRE DESIGN & TECHNOLOGY, no. 17 (May 1969):
14-24. Illus.

A list of over one hundred publications by and about Jones,
with annotations by Larson. A valuable guide. An adden-
dum listing published portrait photographs and sketches of
Jones, as well as eleven new entries, appears in THEATRE
DESIGN AND TECHNOLOGY, no. 26 (October 1971): 28-29.

20.   Miller, James H., and Rubin, Joel E[dward]. "Basic Technical
References." EDUCATIONAL THEATRE JOURNAL 4 (1952): 350-55.

An annotated bibliography of nineteen basic books on scenery,
lighting, costume, and other technical arts. Expecially useful to the amateur.

21.   Ostrom, Nicki N. "The Gordon Craig-Isadora Duncan Collection:
A Register." BULLETIN OF THE NEW YORK PUBLIC LIBRARY 76
(1972): 181-98.

A guide to approximately 400 items in the Dance Collection
of the library. "Provides insights into the development of
some of [Craig's] ideas on the theatre, information about his
activities during the period from December 1904 to 1908, and
evidence of Isadora's influence on him and his career."

22.   Powlick, Leonard. "Title Index to ACTA SCAENOGRAPHICA, Czechoslovak Magazine of Theatre Technology." THEATRE DESIGN & TECH-
NOLOGY, no. 8 (February 1967): 25-27, 29.

Index to issues published August 1962-July 1966. The original articles are in Czech, with very brief synopses in English
and other languages.

23.   Reade, Brian. BALLET DESIGNS AND ILLUSTRATIONS, 1581-1940.
London: Her Majesty's Stationery Office, 1967. 58 p. 173 pls.
Biblio.

A catalogue raisonne of ballet designs and illustrations in the Victoria and Albert Museum, South Kensington. Useful commentaries.

24. Scholz, Janos, ed. BAROQUE AND ROMANTIC STAGE DESIGN. New York: H. Bittner, 1950. 31 p. 121 illus. Biblio.

Brief introduction by A. Hyatt Mayor, catalog, and plates. Mainly Italian, early sixteenth to early nineteenth century.

25. Schoolcraft, Ralph Newman. PERFORMING ARTS BOOKS IN PRINT. New York: Drama Book Specialists/Publishers, 1973. 774 p.

"Stage and Theatre Design," pp. 367-88, 588-91.

26. Sesak, Mary M., and Cooperman, Gail. "Graduate Theses Completed at the OSU Theatre Research Institute, 1954-1974." THEATRE STUDIES 20 (1973-74): 59-63.

Lists 108 theses, of which a large number concern the history of stage design and technology.

27. Shuttleworth, Bertram. "W.J. Lawrence: A Handlist." THEATRE NOTEBOOK 8 (April-June 1954)-12 (Winter 1958).

A fourteen-part listing of William John Lawrence's publications, 1886-1939. An extraordinarily diligent and prolific researcher, Lawrence wrote often about the history of scenery, machinery, and lighting and did pioneer research in many areas. A number of his most useful articles have been listed and described individually in the present guide.

28. Teitelbaum, Robert. "Theatre Design and Technology in the Dance: A Selected, Annotated Bibliography, 1950-1969." THEATRE DESIGN & TECHNOLOGY, no. 21 (May 1970): 38-39.

Lists eighty-six books and articles on architecture, costume, lighting, management, and scene design.

29. TEN YEARS OF AMERICAN OPERA DESIGN AT THE JULLIARD SCHOOL OF MUSIC. New York: New York Public Library, 1941. 20 p. Paperbound.

"A list of the material presented to the New York Public Library by the Julliard School of Music and displayed, in part, in an exhibition." Introduction by Frederick J. Kiesler, scenic director of the school. Lists photographs and original drawings.

30. THEATRE ARTS PRINTS. Series 1. New York: John Day, 1929.

Series 2-4. 3 vols. New York: Theatre Arts Books, 1935-41.

Subtitled, respectively, "The Greeks to Our Day," "Modern Stage Design," "Shakespeare and His Times," and "Stages of the World." Each comprises from 99 to 150 plates in a box or envelope.

31. Van Brunt, Thomas. "A Selected Bibliography of Handbooks and Text-books on Procedures, Materials, and Maintenance in the Theatre Scene Shop." THEATRE DOCUMENTATION 3 (Fall 1970-Spring 1971): 61-63.

Mostly books on carpentry, woodworking, metalworking, and tools used in these crafts.

32. _____. "A Selective Bibliography of Handbooks and Textbooks on Metalworking and Plasticworking for the Theatre Scene Shop." THEATRE DESIGN & TECHNOLOGY, no. 40 (Spring 1975): 27-29, 38.

33. Watson, Leland H. "An A.E.T.A. File of Stage Lighting Theses." EDUCATIONAL THEATRE JOURNAL 6 (1954): 57-60.

Describes a project of the American Educational Theatre Association to gather a library of stage-lighting theses on microfilm. Lists sixty-one M.A. and Ph.D. theses from American universities.

Chapter 2

DICTIONARIES AND ENCYCLOPEDIAS

34.   Band-Kuzmany, Karin R.M. GLOSSARY OF THE THEATRE IN EN-
      GLISH, FRENCH, ITALIAN AND GERMAN. Amsterdam: Elsevier,
      1970. 130 p.

      Includes numerous technical terms.

35.   ENCICLOPEDIA DELLO SPETTACOLO [Encyclopedia of the performing
      arts]. 9 vols. Rome: Le Maschere, 1954–62. Supplements, 1963,
      1966. Index, 1968. Illus., part color.

      Text in Italian. A well-illustrated encyclopedia, with articles
      on scenery, machinery, lighting, and individual stage designers.
      Though the text is in Italian, the bibliographical citations at
      the end of each article often include sources in English.

36.   Lacy, Robin Thurlow. "An Encyclopedia of Scenographers, 534 B.C.
      to 1900 A.D." Ph.D. dissertation, University of Denver, 1959. 267 p.

      A biographical dictionary of scenographers and machinists from
      classical Greece to 1900, exluding Craig and Appia. Largely
      dependent on standard sources.

37.   Lounsbury, Warren C. THEATRE BACKSTAGE FROM A TO Z. Seattle:
      University of Washington Press, 1967. 200 p. Illus. Biblio.

      An illustrated glossary of technical terms relating to current
      practice (some with lengthy explanations).

38.   Southern, Richard, and Rae, Kenneth, eds. AN INTERNATIONAL
      VOCABULARY OF TECHNICAL THEATRE TERMS IN EIGHT LANGUAGES.
      Brussels: Elsevier, 1959. 139 p.

      More than 600 British terms and their equivalents in American,
      French, German, Italian, Spanish, Dutch, and Swedish.

Chapter 3

PERIODICALS

39. BUEHNENTECHNISCHE RUNDSCHAU. Stuttgart, Germany: Deutschen theatertechnischen Gesellschaft and Deutschen Sektion der Organisation International des Scenographes et Techniciens de Theatre, 1907-- . Bimonthly. Illus.

Text in German. The oldest journal of stage technology.

40. INTERSCAENA-ACTA SCAENOGRAPHICA [International supplement]. Prague, Czechoslovakia: Institute of Scenography. 1966-71. [n.s.], 1971-- . Quarterly. Illus.

Title varies: first series called INTERSCAENA. Articles in English, French, German, or Russian. Many concern advanced research in stage design and lighting in Czechoslovakia. A number of articles in English have been entered individually in the present guide.

41. THE MASK. 15 vols. Edited by Edward Gordon Craig. Florence, Italy: 1908-15, 1918-19, 1923-29. Irregular. Illus.

Craig's very personal magazine, largely concerned with stage design and theatre architecture, past and present. Craig himself contributed many illustrations and articles, often pseudonymously. (For a list of his pseudonyms, see Fletcher and Rood's bibliography [item 10 in the present guide], p. 62.)

42. PLAYERS MAGAZINE. Racine, Wis.: National Collegiate Players, 1924-- . Quarterly, later bimonthly. Illus.

Most issues have brief technical articles on scenery and lighting, and practical hints for production. (Longer articles on stage technology are entered individually in the present guide.)

43. THE SCENIC ARTIST. 1 vol. New York: United Scenic Artists Association, May 1927-April 1928. Illus.

Apparently these were the only issues published. Issued by

Local 829 of the scenic artists' union. Includes profiles and obituaries of members, editorials, reminiscences, and union news.

44.   SCENIC ARTIST NEWS. 5 issues. New York: United Scenic Artists Association, April 1931–August 1931. Illus.

Apparently these were the only issues published. Issued by Local 829 of the scenic artists' union. Notes on exhibitions by members, union news, etc.

45.   TABS. London: Strand Electric & Engineering Co., 1937-- . Illus., part color. Irregular; later three issues yearly.

Largely devoted to contemporary stage lighting and theatre architecture, with occasional articles on stage design and the history of stage technology. A few historical articles have been entered individually in the present guide.

46.   THEATRE CRAFTS. Emmaus, Pa.: Rodale Press, 1967-- . Six issues a year. Illus.

Regularly includes book reviews, notes on new products, and news of the activities of designers. Concerned with costume and theatre architecture as well as scenery and lighting. An index to the first five volumes appears in 5 (November–December 1971): 40–48; thereafter, an index is provided every two years. Historical and biographical articles have been entered individually in the present guide.

47.   THEATRE DESIGN & TECHNOLOGY. Pittsburgh: U.S. Institute for Theatre Technology, 1965-- . Quarterly. Illus.

The journal of the U.S. Institute for Theatre Technology. Regularly includes obituaries, book reviews, and notes on recent technical developments. Each issue has a list of recent publications on theatre architecture which sometimes includes publications on scenery and machinery. Historical and biographical articles have been entered individually in the present guide.

48.   THEATRE STUDIES. Columbus: Ohio State University Theatre Research Institute, 1954-- . Semiannual, 1954-56; annual, 1957-- . Illus.

Volumes 1-17 called OSU THEATRE COLLECTION BULLETIN. Largely concerned with the history of scenery, machinery, and production style. Many of the articles have been entered individually in the present guide. For an index to the first twenty years, see item 8.

Part II

SCENERY AND STAGE MACHINERY

Chapter 4

GENERAL HISTORIES
(STUDIES OF BROAD AND/OR INTERNATIONAL SCOPE)

A. VARIOUS PERIODS

49. Bablet, Denis. ESTHETIQUE DU DECOR DE THEATRE DE 1870 A 1914. Paris: Centre National de la Recherche Scientifique, 1965. 458 p. Illus. Biblio.

    An important study of naturalism and the New Stagecraft in European production style and aesthetics.

50. Beaumont, Cyril W. BALLET DESIGN PAST & PRESENT. London: Studio, 1946. 247 p. Prof. illus., part color.

    "In this volume I have combined and extended my two previous works on this subject, FIVE CENTURIES OF BALLET and DESIGN FOR THE BALLET, in an attempt to trace the evolution of design for Ballet from the Italian Renaissance to the present day" (p. xiii). More than three-quarters of the plates are devoted to twentieth-century design.

51. Berliner, Rudolf. "The Stage Designs of the Cooper Union Museum." CHRONICLE OF THE MUSEUM FOR THE ARTS OF DECORATION OF THE COOPER UNION 1, no. 8 (1941): 283-320. Illus.

    Not an iconography (as the title might suggest), but rather a survey of stage design from 1700 to the middle of the nineteenth century, mainly Italian, noting changes in style, ground plan, and subject. Well documented and well illustrated. An important study.

52. Cheney, Sheldon. STAGE DECORATION. New York: John Day Co., 1928. 160 p. Illus. 127 pls.

    A general history of stage design, machinery, and lighting, with emphasis on the reforms of the late nineteenth and early twentieth centuries.

53.   Fischel, Oskar. "Art and the Theatre." BURLINGTON MAGAZINE
        66 (January 1935): 4-14; (February 1935): 54-67. Illus.

        Relates documents of medieval and Renaissance stage history
        to medieval and Renaissance art, using both to reconstruct
        theatrical styles.

54.   Gorelik, Mordecai. NEW THEATRES FOR OLD. [New York and Los
        Angeles]: Samuel French, 1940. 570 p. Illus. Biblio.

        A critical history of stage design and production style, espe-
        cially useful in its treatment of the New Stagecraft in Ger-
        many and Russia. Extensive bibliography.

55.   Gregor, Joseph. WIENER SZENISCHE KUNST: DIE THEATERDEKORA-
        TION DER LETZTEN DREI JAHRHUNDERTE NACH STILPRINZIPIEN
        DARGESTELLT. Vol. 1. Vienna: Wiener Drucke, 1924. 148 p.
        Illus.

        Text in German. This first volume of a two-volume work
        (the second concerns costume) is an important study of stylis-
        tic development in scenery from the Renaissance to the early
        twentieth century. An English translation of the last chapter
        was published in THEATRE ARTS 17 (1933): 215-26.

56.   Hall, Roger Allan. "Neo-Classic and Romantic Destruction: Scene
        Designs of Ruins from 1700 to 1850." THEATRE STUDIES 19 (1972-73):
        7-15. Illus.

        Considers trends in European and English designs, suggesting
        that neoclassical ruins were joined by, but not replaced by,
        medieval ruins in the late eighteenth century.

57.   Hodge, Francis, ed. INNOVATIONS IN STAGE AND THEATRE DE-
        SIGN: PAPERS OF THE SIXTH CONGRESS, INTERNATIONAL FEDERA-
        TION FOR THEATRE RESEARCH . . . 1969. [New York]: American
        Society for Theatre Research and Theatre Library Association, 1972.
        165 p. Illus.

        Eleven essays on late nineteenth- and twentieth-century inno-
        vations in the United States and Europe. Those on stage de-
        sign and lighting have been entered separately in the present
        guide.

58.   Jeudwine, Wynne. STAGE DESIGNS. Feltham, Middlesex, England:
        Country Life, 1968. 64 p. Paperbound. Illus. Biblio.

        Brief illustrated history of stage design, largely Italian, from
        the Renaissance to the mid-nineteenth century.

59.   Johnson, Raoul Fenton. "United States and British Patents for Scenic

and Lighting Devices for the Theatre from 1861 to 1915." Ph.D. dissertation, University of Illinois (Urbana-Champaign), 1966. 278 p.

Study of patented lighting devices, illusionistic effects, scenery-changing apparatus, and settings, from the first patent specifically for theatrical use through the New Stagecraft.

60.   Johnson, Wallace H. "Floating the Rhinemaidens, 1869-1913." THEATRE SURVEY 7 (1966): 15-30. Illus.

A history of early methods of staging the opening scene of Wagner's DAS RHEINGOLD, in which the Rhinemaidens are seen frisking about underwater.

61.   Kernodle, George R. "Farewell to Scene Architecture." QUARTERLY JOURNAL OF SPEECH 25 (1939): 649-57.

Describes the way illusionistic perspective scenery replaced built-up "architectural" scenery in the early seventeenth century; notes a similar development in the 1920s and 1930s.

62.   Larson, Orville K. "A Commentary on the 'Historical Development of the Box Set' (THEATRE ANNUAL, 1945)." THEATRE ANNUAL 12 (1954): 28-36.

A rejoinder to an article by John H. McDowell (see item 67). Dates the "modern box set" to 1867--later than McDowell-- noting that a few isolated examples occurred earlier.

63.   Laver, James. DRAMA: ITS COSTUME & DECOR. London: Studio, 1951. 276 p. Illus. Biblio.

One of the best historical surveys available in English, with an excellent bibliography.

64.   Lawrence, W[illiam]. J[ohn]. "Art in the Theatre: Some Famous Scene-Painters." MAGAZINE OF ART 12 (1889): 41-45. Illus.

Notes on scene painters from the Renaissance to the nineteenth century.

65.   _____. "Borders: 1. Their Origins; 2. Their Decline." THE STAGE (London), 14 July 1932, p. 9; 28 July 1932, p. 13.

Discusses the origin of borders in Renaissance Italy, then traces their use up to the early twentieth century. Also discusses the development of the "horizon" (cyclorama) as an alternative.

66.   _____. "The Evolution of the Proscenium Frame." In "THE STAGE" YEAR BOOK 1928, pp. 65-78. London: Carson & Comerford, 1928. Illus.

Traces the proscenium from Renaissance Italy to the late eighteenth century, discussing various forms and decorations. Ten informative illustrations.

67. McDowell, John H. "Historical Development of the Box Set." THEATRE ANNUAL 4 (1945): 65–83. Illus.

Examines the evolution of the box set from the late eighteenth to the late nineteenth century, concluding that it developed out of the flat-wing set when new ideas of rigging were applied. For a reply, see item 62.

68. _____. "Some Pictorial Aspects of Early Mountebank Stages." PMLA 61 (1946): 84–96. Illus.

Examines iconographic evidence from the sixteenth to the early eighteenth century, noting that some mountebank stages had scenic backgrounds and even flat-wing scenery.

69. _____. "Spectacular Effects in THE TEMPEST." THEATRE STUDIES 18 (1971–72): 46–54. Illus.

Examines the use of moving panoramas, stage ships, and scenic oceans in the opening scene.

70. McNamara, Brooks. "Scene Design: 1876–1965." DRAMA REVIEW 13 (Winter 1968): 77–91. Illus.

A collection of photographs of sets, with brief comments.

71. _____. "The Scenography of Popular Entertainments." DRAMA REVIEW 18 (March 1974): 16–24. Illus.

Examines the scenic and architectural features of booth theatres, improvised theatres, melodramas, spectacles and dioramas, carnivals and amusement parks, etc.

72. Matthews, [James] Brander. "The Evolution of Scene-Painting." SCRIBNER'S 58 (July 1915): 82–94. Illus.

A good brief history, considering the sources Matthews had available, but he underestimated the impact of the New Stagecraft. Reprinted in Matthews's A BOOK ABOUT THE THEATRE (New York: Charles Scribner's Sons, 1916), pp. 127–52.

73. _____. "The Simplification of Stage Scenery." UNPOPULAR REVIEW 11 (1919): 350–63.

Discusses the development of the built-up realistic set and the reaction against it led by Craig and others.

74. Nagler, A[lois]. M. A SOURCE BOOK IN THEATRICAL HISTORY. New York: Dover Publications, 1959. 634 p. Illus.

Includes many useful accounts of scenery and stage machinery, from fifth-century Greece to the late nineteenth century.

75. Nicoll, Allardyce. THE DEVELOPMENT OF THE THEATRE. 5th ed., rev. New York: Harcourt, Brace & World, [1967]. 311 p. Illus. Biblio.

An excellent historical survey of theatre architecture and stage design from the Greeks to the twentieth century. An appendix includes a complete translation of Leone di Somi's DIALOGUES ON STAGE AFFAIRS (Mantua, c. 1565), including a discussion of scenery.

76. Oenslager, Donald M[itchell]. SCENERY, THEN AND NOW. New York: W.W. Norton & Co., 1936. 265 p. Illus.

A series of Oenslager's designs for fourteen plays, from Greek tragedy to O'Neill's THE EMPEROR JONES, with remarks on the original production milieu and on Oenslager's interpretations.

77. _____. STAGE DESIGN: FOUR CENTURIES OF SCENIC INVENTION. New York: Viking Press, 1975. 303 p. Prof. illus., part color. Biblio.

Sketch of the history of stage design from the Greeks to the Renaissance, pp. 13-25, plus a history-through-pictures of developments from the Renaissance to the present. The method of keying the text to the illustrations results in an episodic, biography-oriented history, with many gaps.

78. Palmer, John. "Gesture and Scenery in Modern Opera." MUSICAL QUARTERLY 2 (April 1916): 314-30.

Argues that Wagner's own productions and the more recent work of Gordon Craig and the Ballets Russes prove that the "total work of art" is impossible if each element is treated equally--that music must be the dominant element.

79. Peet, Alice Lida. "The History and Development of Simultaneous Scenery in the West from the Middle Ages to the Modern United States." Ph.D. dissertation, University of Wisconsin, 1961. 393 p.

Examines the use of multiple, representational settings in the Middle Ages, the Renaissance, and the late nineteenth and twentieth centuries.

80. "Research Possibilities in Scene Design." OSU THEATRE COLLECTION

BULLETIN 2 (Autumn 1955): 11-18.

Presents as an example a study of prison scenes in the eighteenth and nineteenth centuries.

81.   Ricci, Corrado. "The Art of Scenography." ART BULLETIN 10 (March
1928): 231-57. Illus.

A brief history of stage design from ancient Greece to the
early twentieth century, stressing the Italian contributions of
the Renaissance and Baroque period.

82.   Rothgeb, John Reese. "The Scenographic Expression of Nature (1545-
1845): The Development of Style." Ph.D. dissertation, Case-Western
Reserve University, 1971. 396 p.

Deals with "those innovators who redeveloped the traditional
schema to express new visions of nature more in keeping with
the changing contemporary thought" (DISSERTATION AB-
STRACTS 32, no. 8, pt. A, pp. 4762-63). Illustrates paral-
lel developments in scenery and other arts.

83.   Simonson, Lee. THE ART OF SCENIC DESIGN. New York: Harper
& Bros., 1950. 174 p. Prof. illus.

Intended to "describe and illustrate certain basic concepts of
the Renaissance, to trace their effect on the staging of plays
and the structure of the playhouse, and then to analyze the
theories and experiments of the latter part of the nineteenth
century which have become the basis of play production to-
day." Twenty of the author's productions are illustrated by
photographs and detailed working drawings.

84.   _____. THE STAGE IS SET. New York: Harcourt, Brace, and Co.,
1932. 602 p. Illus. Biblio.

A provocative (sometimes almost belligerent) history of stage
design, lighting, and production style from the classical
Greek theatre to the New Stagecraft. Includes a well-known
attack on Gordon Craig and a chapter on Adolphe Appia.
Well illustrated.

85.   Southern, Richard. THE SEVEN AGES OF THE THEATRE. New York:
Hill & Wang, 1961. 312 p. Illus. Biblio.

A broad view of the changing theatrical environment from
primitive rituals to the open stage of the twentieth century.
Includes a useful discussion of the development of changeable
scenery on the Continent and in England.

86.   "Theatre Drawings from the Donald Oenslager Collection." MINNEAP-

OLIS INSTITUTE BULLETIN 52 (March 1963): 1-47. Illus.

Catalog of an exhibition, with an introductory essay by A. Hyatt Mayor.

87. Vardac, A. Nicholas. STAGE TO SCREEN: THEATRICAL METHOD FROM GARRICK TO GRIFFITH. Cambridge, Mass.: Harvard University Press, 1949. 309 p. Illus.

The author's basic premise--that cinema was born out of an "aesthetic need"--has been disputed, but in the course of proving it, he compiled and analyzed a great deal of useful information about nineteenth- and early-twentieth-century scenery and special effects, mainly in England and the United States.

88. Winter, Marian Hannah. THE THEATRE OF MARVELS. Translated by Charles Meldon. New York: Benjamin Blom, n.d. [c. 1966]. 208 p. Illus., part color. Biblio.

A history of popular, illusionistic, spectacular theatre and ballet in Europe and America in the eighteenth and nineteenth centuries.

B. RENAISSANCE AND BAROQUE

89. Baur-Heinhold, Margarete. THE BAROQUE THEATRE. Translated by Mary Whittall. New York: McGraw-Hill Book Co., 1967. 292 p. Illus., part color. Biblio.

A splendidly illustrated book which traces the development of the baroque in European theatre architecture and stage design from the late sixteenth to the late eighteenth century. The author perceptively relates theatrical activities to the larger social and artistic context.

90. Bjurstrom, Per. "Baroque Theater and the Jesuits." In BAROQUE ART: THE JESUIT CONTRIBUTION, edited by Rudolf Wittkower and Irma B. Jaffe, pp. 99-110. New York: Fordham University Press, 1972. Illus.

Includes brief discussion of books on perspective by Jean Dubreuil and Andrea Pozzo, and a more extensive discussion of seventeenth-century altar decorations in Roman churches to celebrate the Devotion of the Forty Hours.

91. Born, Wolfgang. "Early Peep-Shows and the Renaissance Stage." CONNOISSEUR 107 (February 1941): 67-71; (April 1941): 161-64, 180. Illus.

Suggests that late sixteenth-century Viennese peep-show tableaux were influenced by Italian perspective scenery.

92. Brieger, Peter. "The Baroque Equation: Illusion and Reality." GAZETTE DES BEAUX ARTS, s. 6, 27 (1945): 143–64. Illus.

Develops the idea that the main purpose of the Baroque theatre was the "obscuring of the boundary between reality and illusion," and discusses the theatricality of many arts during the Baroque period. Considerable attention to the work of Bernini.

93. Kernodle, George R. FROM ART OF THEATRE: FORM AND CONVENTION IN THE RENAISSANCE. Chicago: University of Chicago Press, 1944. ix, 255 p. Illus. Biblio.

Traces the scenic conventions of various types of Renaissance stages to prototypes in Hellenistic, medieval, and early Renaissance painting, sculpture, and tableaux vivants.

94. Larson, Orville K. "Ascension Images in Art and Theatre." GAZETTE DES BEAUX ARTS, s. 6, 54 (October 1959): 161–76. Illus.

Renaissance ascension images "became more realistic and dramatic in painting as the manner of presentation of the ascensions and flights became more realistic and spectacular in the theatre."

95. LE LIEU THEATRAL A LA RENAISSANCE. Edited by Jean Jacquot. Paris: Centre National de la Recherche Scientifique, 1964. 542 p. Illus.

Text in French. An extremely valuable collection of articles concerning the stage and auditorium--and their functional relationship--from the late Middle Ages to the seventeenth century. Divided into three sections: the evolution of the theatrical space in Italy, 1470–1640; the nonperspective stage outside Italy; and the spread of the Italianate stage throughout Europe. Excellent illustrations. A long review was published in RENAISSANCE NEWS (see item 100).

96. Mayor, A[lpheus]. Hyatt. "Italian Sources of European Stage Design." MINNEAPOLIS INSTITUTE BULLETIN 52 (March 1963): 3–13. Illus.

Introduction to an exhibition of theatre drawings from the Donald Oenslager collection. A perceptive survey of Renaissance and Baroque scene design.

97. Nagler, A[lois]. M. "A Terminology for Sixteenth-Century Stage Forms." THEATRE RESEARCH / RECHERCHES THEATRALES 1 (1958): 30–33.

A terminology based on the terms polyscenic-monoscenic, static-dynamic, illusionistic-nonillusionistic, medieval-Renaissance-baroque.

98. Rapp, Franz. "Notes on Little-Known Materials for the History of the Theatre." THEATRE ANNUAL 3 (1944): 60-78. Illus.

Notes on periaktoi in sixteenth-century Italy; a sketchbook of drawings by Giovanni Battista Aleotti; plans for a theatre designed c. 1790-1800 by Lorenzo Quaglio; and other subjects.

99. THE RENAISSANCE STAGE. Edited by Barnard [W.] Hewitt. Coral Gables, Fla.: University of Miami Press, 1958. ix, 256 p. Illus.

Excerpts from the three most important sources of information on Renaissance stagecraft: Sebastiano Serlio's ARCHITECTURE, Book 5 (1545); Nicola Sabbattini's THE PRACTICE OF MAKING THEATRICAL SCENES AND MACHINES (1638); and Josef Furttenbach's books on architecture and technology (especially THE NOBLE MIRROR OF ART, 1663). Translated by Allardyce Nicoll, John H. McDowell, and George R. Kernodle, respectively. Illustrated with reproductions of scenery, machinery, and lighting devices from the original publications.

100. Richter, Bodo L.O. "Recent Studies in Renaissance Scenography." RENAISSANCE NEWS 19 (Winter 1966): 344-58.

Excellent review article on LE LIEU THEATRAL A LA RENAISSANCE (see item 95). A useful guide for non-French readers, though Richter does quote from the original French.

101. THEATRE ARCHITECTURE & STAGE MACHINES: ENGRAVINGS FROM THE ENCYCLOPEDIE . . . EDITED BY DENIS DIDEROT AND JEAN LE ROND D'ALEMBERT. New York: Benjamin Blom, 1969. 89 p., mostly plates.

Captions and keys to illustrations in French. A republication of the engravings of European theatres and stage machinery in various volumes of the ENCYCLOPEDIE, first published in 1762-77.

C. NINETEENTH CENTURY

SEE ALSO item 178.

102. ANATOMY OF AN ILLUSION: STUDIES IN NINETEENTH-CENTURY SCENE DESIGN. Lectures of the Fourth International Congress on Theatre Research, Amsterdam, 1965. Amsterdam: Scheltema & Holkema,

1969. 92 p. Illus.

Twelve articles (half of them in French). The lead article by
A.M. Nagler sets the tone: a renewed appreciation for the
painted illusionistic stage of the nineteenth century. The
articles in English are entered individually in the present
guide.

103. Bassett, Abe J. "The Capitol Setting for JULIUS CAESAR." OSU
THEATRE COLLECTION BULLETIN 6 (1959): 30-35. Illus.

Describes nineteenth-century English and American settings for
this Shakespearean scene.

104. Byrne, Muriel St. Clare. "Charles Kean and the Meininger Myth."
THEATRE RESEARCH / RECHERCHES THEATRALES 6 (1964): 137-53.
Illus.

Shows that many innovations (including scenic innovations)
attributed to the Duke of Saxe-Meiningen should be credited
to Charles Kean. A comment by Anthony Denning appears
in the same journal, 7 (1965): 46-47.

105. Contant, Clement, and Filippi, Joseph de. PARALLELE DES PRINCI-
PAUX THEATRES MODERNES DE L'EUROPE ET DES MACHINES THE-
ATRALES FRANCAISES, ALLEMANDES ET ANGLAISES. 1860. Reprint.
2 vols. in one. New York: Benjamin Blom, 1968. 163 p. 133 pls.

Text (in French) by Filippi, illustrations by Constant. An
extremely valuable source of information on the architecture,
scenery, stage machinery, and lighting of theatres in France,
England, Germany, Russia, Italy, Denmark, and Spain. The
section on stage machinery includes detailed drawings of the
French and German systems of stage and scenery construction.
Text includes a glossary of technical terms.

106. Fitzgerald, Percy. THE WORLD BEHIND THE SCENES. London: Chatto
and Windus, 1881. 320 p.

A rambling account of English and French theatrical life in
the second half of the nineteenth century, studded with useful
bits of information about scenery, machinery, lighting, and
special effects.

107. Hopkins, Albert A. MAGIC, STAGE ILLUSIONS AND SCIENTIFIC
DIVERSIONS. New York: Munn & Co., 1898. xii, 556 p. Illus.

In addition to explaining the tricks and illusions of conjurors,
magicians, acrobats, fire-eaters, and similar performers, Hopkins provides eight chapters on "Science in the Theatre."

108. Hunter, Jack Worth. "THE CORSICAN BROTHERS: Its History and Technical Problems Related to the Production of the Play." Ph.D. dissertation, Ohio State University, 1963. 230 p.

    Investigates major productions in England and America to identify the nature and operation of mechanical devices, especially the "Corsican trap."

109. Logan, Olive. BEFORE THE FOOTLIGHTS AND BEHIND THE SCENES. Philadelphia: Parmelee & Co.; San Francisco: H.H. Bancroft & Co., 1870. 612 p. Illus.

    A disorganized catchall of a book that fails to live up to the promise of its title. Scraps of useful information here and there. The illustrations are generally uninformative.

110. _____. "The Secret Regions of the Stage." HARPER'S NEW MONTHLY MAGAZINE 48 (April 1874): 628–42. Illus.

    A popular but informative treatment of scene-changing devices, trickwork, weather effects, and stage fires. Useful illustrations.

111. Nagler, Alois M. "The Autonomy of the Painted Stage." In ANATOMY OF AN ILLUSION (see item 102), pp. 7–12.

    Cites examples of "the emotional excitement stirred up by the marvels of the painted stage" of the nineteenth century; urges that scholars accept this stage on its own terms; and poses a number of research problems that remain to be investigated.

112. Roberts, Vera Mowry. "New Viewpoints on Nineteenth Century Scene Design." EDUCATIONAL THEATRE JOURNAL 18 (1966): 41–46.

    Suggests that a recent scholarly conference on nineteenth-century scene design (see item 102) is proof of an ongoing revaluation of the theatre of the last century. Offers a synthesis of the papers presented at the conference and indicates directions for study.

113. Sachs, Edwin O. "Stage Mechanism." JOURNAL OF THE SOCIETY OF ARTS 46 (22 April 1898): 512–28. Illus.

    Describes European stage machinery and scene-changing devices in the last quarter of the nineteenth century. Commentary by George Bernard Shaw and others.

114. Sachs, Edwin O., and Woodrow, Ernest A.E. MODERN OPERA HOUSES AND THEATRES. 1896–98. Reprint. 3 vols. New York: Benjamin Blom, 1968. Illus.

The first two volumes are architectural studies of European theatres (including Russian playhouses). Volume 3 treats theatre planning and stage construction and is illustrated with informative photographs and drawings of rigging lofts, scene-changing machinery, flying devices, hydraulic bridges (the Asphaleia system), turntables, and so on. An essential source in the study of nineteenth-century stage technology.

115. Wickman, Richard Carl. "An Evaluation of the Employment of Panoramic Scenery in the Nineteenth-Century Theatre." Ph.D. dissertation, Ohio State University, 1961. 376 p.

Traces the development of panoramas and dioramas as exhibitions in themselves, then as theatre scenery.

D. TWENTIETH CENTURY

116. Amberg, George. ART IN MODERN BALLET. [New York]: Pantheon, 1946. 115 p. 202 pls., part color.

Brief but informative history of twentieth-century ballet design, pp. 17-30, stressing the contributions of the Ballets Russes under Diaghilev. Index of Ballets, 1909-45, with full production data (including designers), pp. 35-104.

117. Bablet, Denis. "Twenty Years of Scenography." WORLD THEATRE 17 (1968): 35-57. Illus.

Stage design in Europe and America since World War II--an overview by a perceptive critic.

118. Beaton, Cecil. "Scenery and Costume Design for Ballet." In SCENE DESIGN FOR STAGE AND SCREEN (see item 1161), pp. 214-18.

Reprinted from the NEW YORK TIMES, 29 July 1956, pt. 10, p. 11. Comments on the work of a number of ballet designers, stressing their color sense.

119. Beaumont, Cyril W. "Ballet: Settings and Costumes in Recent Productions." STUDIO 117 (April 1939): 146-55. Illus., part color.

Illustrations and commentary.

120. Bickley, Francis. "Pierrot the Pessimist." BRITISH REVIEW 3 (July 1913): 92-102.

Speaks of "Pierrotic artists" who "scoff at life, hold its only use to be for the making of patterns." Discusses Leon Bakst and the Ballets Russes as the perfect expression of this spirit; shows how Gordon Craig does not fit the pattern.

121. Billeter, Erika. "The Development of Stage Design since 1950."
      GRAPHIS 20 (1964): 274-97, 342-43. Illus., part color.

      English, French, and German texts. Thoughtful commentary,
      with sixty-five illustrations of designs by European, British,
      and American artists.

122. Bourdon, Georges. "Staging in the French and English Theatre." FORT-
      NIGHTLY REVIEW 77 (January 1902): 154-69.

      Informative account of English scenery and stage machinery
      as it compares with French.

123. Bragdon, Claude. "The Artist-in-the-Theatre." AMERICAN MAGA-
      ZINE OF ART 20 (1929): 547-53. Illus.

      Discusses the transition from the illusionistic scenery of the
      late nineteenth century to the architectural, artistically-
      lighted sets of the New Stagecraft.

124. _____. "The Master of Revels." In his MERELY PLAYERS, pp. 30-39.
      New York: Alfred A. Knopf, 1929.

      Defines the task of the modern "artist in the theatre."

125. Buckle, Richard. MODERN BALLET DESIGN. New York: Macmillan,
      [1955]. 143 p. Prof. illus.

      Production photographs and designs for ballets produced in
      1945-54, mainly in London and Paris, with Buckle's brief,
      often impressionistic, remarks.

126. Carter, Huntly. THE NEW SPIRIT IN DRAMA AND ART. New York
      and London: Mitchell Kennerley, 1913. x, 270 p. Illus. Biblio.

      Survey of the early years of the New Stagecraft in England,
      France, Germany, Austria, Hungary, Poland, and Russia. In-
      teresting early reaction to the reform movement.

127. Cheney, Sheldon. "The Architectural Stage." THEATRE ARTS 11
      (1927): 478-88.

      Considers the architectural stage, or "unit set," the best
      modern arrangement for acting; describes examples from Jacques
      Copeau to Max Reinhardt and Norman-Bel Geddes.

128. _____. THE ART THEATER. Rev. and enl. ed. New York: Alfred
      A. Knopf, 1925. ix, 281 p. Illus. Biblio.

      Includes chapters on Appia and Craig and on the New Stage-
      craft in America.

129. _____. "Constructivism." THEATRE ARTS 11 (November 1927): 857-66. Illus.

> Analyzes constructivism in stage design and notes some Russian examples.

130. _____. "The International Exhibition in Amsterdam." THEATRE ARTS 6 (1922): 140-51. Illus.

> A country-by-country review of this important exhibition of stage designs.

131. _____. THE NEW MOVEMENT IN THE THEATRE. New York: Mitchell Kennerley, 1914. 309 p. Illus.

> An early study of the New Stagecraft in Europe and in America. Considers both drama and stage design.

132. _____. "The Painter in the Theatre." THEATRE ARTS 6 (1922): 191-99.

> Concerns the role of the stage designer in creating productions in which all elements are synthesized.

133. _____. "The Space Stage." THEATRE ARTS 11 (1927): 762-74. Illus.

> Explores productions in which actors and set pieces are picked out of a void with light.

134. Cole, Wendell. "Current Trends in European Stage Design." EDUCATIONAL THEATRE JOURNAL 5 (1953): 27-32.

> Notes a return to painted perspective scenery and to "simultaneous settings which employ such devices as scrims, skeleton constructions, and projections."

135. COSTUMES AND CURTAINS FROM THE DIAGHILEV AND DE BASIL BALLETS. 2 vols. in 1. New York: Viking Press, 1972. xxxvii, [181], 129 p. Illus., part color.

> Limited edition (750 copies). Reprinted auction catalogs from Sotheby & Co., 1968-69. Introduction by Richard Buckle. Excellent illustrations.

136. Davis, Jed Horace, Jr. "The Art of Scenic Design and Staging for Children's Theatre." Ph.D. dissertation, University of Minnesota, 1958. 365 p.

> Examines designs for children's theatre since 1900, then formulates principles of design for children.

137. deShong, Andrew [Walter III]. "MAGIC/Magic Lantern/LANTERN."
     YALE / THEATRE 3 (Fall 1970): 38-50. Illus.

     A brief history of live action/film integration in the theatre,
     from Erwin Piscator and Georg Grosz in Germany to E.F.
     Burian and Alfred Radok in Czechoslovakia. Also includes an
     interview with Bohumil Svoboda, another Czech designer ac-
     tive in developing these techniques.

138. DESIGN IN THE THEATRE. Edited by Geoffrey Holme. London: Stu-
     dio, 1927. viii, 31 p. 120 pls., part color.

     Essays by George Sheringham (on British and American design)
     and James Laver (on Continental design), plus brief contribu-
     tions by Gordon Craig, Charles B. Cochran, and Nigel Play-
     fair.

139. Eaton, Walter Prichard. "The Man of Letters and the New Art of the
     Theater." CENTURY 87 (December 1913): 284-89.

     Remarks on the techniques of the New Stagecraft and their
     significance to the dramatist.

140. _____. "The New Stagecraft." AMERICAN MAGAZINE 74 (May
     1912): 104-113. Illus.

     Perceptive comments on the significance of Reinhardt's produc-
     tion of SUMURUN, Craig's HAMLET, and the Irish Players's
     productions in New York.

141. Exposition internationale des arts decoratifs et industriels modernes,
     Paris, 1925. RAPPORT GENERAL. Vol. 10: THEATRE, PHOTO-
     GRAPHIE ET CINEMATOGRAPHIE. Paris: Larousse, 1929. 106 p.
     Illus., part color.

     Text in French. The report on theatre arts, pp. 11-45, sum-
     marizes the development of the New Stagecraft in Europe and
     comments briefly on each country's exhibition. (The United
     States was not represented.) This text is followed by fifty-
     eight uncommon reproductions of scene and costume designs
     (some beautifully colored) and production photographs.

142. Fern, Dale Edward. "Ballet Design in Perspective." DANCE MAGA-
     ZINE 33 (December 1959): 80-87. Illus.

     Review of a ballet design exhibition.

143. Fischel, Oskar, ed. DAS MODERNE BUEHNENBILD. Berlin: E. Was-
     muth, 1923. 142 p. Prof. Illus., part color.

     Brief introduction (in German) and 155 illustrations of set and costume designs. Many of the artists are German, but the selection is international.

144. Fuerst, Walter Rene, and Hume, Samuel J. XXTH CENTURY STAGE DECORATION. 2 vols. London: Alfred A. Knopf, 1928. Illus., part color. Biblio.

Volume 1 (text) has an introduction by Adolphe Appia; an extensive list of designers, identifying their most important productions; and an excellent bibliography. Volume 2 (plates) includes almost 400 illustrations. Essential for research on the New Stagecraft. (A recent reprint by Blom, 1967, has a new index of plays and lists of illustrations.)

145. Genauer, Emily. "Modern Art and the Ballet." THEATRE ARTS 35 (October 1951): 16-17, 75-77. Illus.

Explains a trend away from the use of distinguished artists as ballet designers.

146. George, Waldemar. "The 1933 Ballets and the Spirit of Contemporary Art." FORMES, no. 33 (1933): 377-79. Pls., part color.

Illustrations of designs by Andre Derain, Christian Berard, Pavel Tchelitchew, and Emilio Terry, with commentary.

147. Goodman, G.E. "Twenty-Five Years of Decor." DANCING TIMES, October 1935, pp. 45-48. Illus.

An historical review of ballet design since 1910. (This is one of numerous brief articles on ballet design contributed by Goodman to DANCING TIMES in the 1930s, usually under the title "Notes on Decor.")

148. Gorelik, Mordecai. "The Conquest of Stage Space." THEATRE ARTS 18 (1934): 213-18. Illus.

Describes a trend in stage design away from illusionistic "reminiscence" towards immediate theatricality, paralleling a trend away from individualism towards communalism in society. Reprinted, without illustrations, in SCENE DESIGN FOR STAGE AND SCREEN (item 1161), pp. 274-79.

149. _____. "Epic Scene Design." THEATRE ARTS 43 (October 1959): 75-80. Illus.

A useful survey of design for "Epic Theatre" from Piscator and Brecht to Mielziner and Gorelik himself. Reprinted, without illustrations, in SCENE DESIGN FOR STAGE AND SCREEN (item 1161), pp. 280-91.

150.   . Some Observations on the New Stagecraft." ARTS (New York) 9 (1926): 193–97.

A critique of the excesses of the New Stagecraft, particularly the work of Gordon Craig.

151. Hainaux, Rene, ed. STAGE DESIGN THROUGHOUT THE WORLD, 1970–1975. New York: Theatre Arts Books, 1976. 159 p. Illus., part color. Biblio.

A record of 179 "non-traditional" productions in twenty-seven countries. Introductory essay. on some new trends.

152. Hainaux, Rene, and Bonnat, Yves, eds. STAGE DESIGN THROUGH-OUT THE WORLD SINCE 1935. New York: Theatre Arts Books, 1956. 222 p. Illus., part color.

Essays on scene design in twenty-three different countries, 1935–55, by such authorities as Raymond Cogniat on French design, Edmund Stadler on Switzerland, and Charles Elson on the United States. Includes 159 pages of illustrations, indexed by designer, composer, playwright, and choreographer.

153.   . STAGE DESIGN THROUGHOUT THE WORLD SINCE 1950. New York: Theatre Arts Books, 1964. 276 p. Illus., part color.

Concerns design from 1950 to the early 1960s. Includes an essay on new methods and materials, with commentary by designers from around the world. There are no country-by-country essays, as in the first volume, but the illustrations depict productions in fifteen countries not covered in the first volume. A new feature is a "Stage Designers' Who's Who."

154.   . STAGE DESIGN THROUGHOUT THE WORLD SINCE 1960. New York: Theatre Arts Books, 1973. 239 p. Illus., part color. Biblio.

The third volume in this series, with emphasis on experimental and nontraditional designs. Unlike the country-by-country arrangement of the previous volumes, the organization here is by playwright, from Aeschylus to recent playwrights such as Stoppard and Sondheim. More than 500 production photographs and designs. Useful bibliography of works published since 1960.

155. Hale, Edward E. "Modern Ideas on Stage Setting." DIAL 55 (16 December 1913): 520–23.

A complacent, traditionalist view of the New Stagecraft.

156. Hamilton, Clayton. "The New Art of Stage Direction." BOOKMAN

(New York) 35 (July 1912): 481–88.

Remarks on Max Reinhardt's production of SUMURUN, comparing it to H.G. Fiske's production of KISMET, and discussion of the theories of Gordon Craig.

157. Hays, David. "Painters in the Theatre." CHRYSALIS 6, no. 3–4 (1953): 3–15. Illus.

Perceptive comments on the stage work of Marc Chagall, Georges Rouault, Eugene Berman, and Christian Berard, plus an added note on Fernand Leger by Baird Hastings, pp. 16–17.

158. Hunningher, Benjamin. "Makers of a New Theatre." In ANATOMY OF AN ILLUSION (see item 102), pp. 56–59.

A brief investigation of the anti-naturalist revolt at the turn of the century: Gordon Craig and Adolphe Appia in stage design, Ibsen and Strindberg in drama, and their interrelationships.

159. Komisarjevsky, Theodore, and Simonson, Lee. SETTINGS AND COSTUMES OF THE MODERN STAGE. Edited by Geoffrey Holme. London and New York: Studio, 1933. 132 p. Prof. illus., part color.

Essays by Komisarjevsky on European stage design and by Simonson on American, plus numerous well-selected illustrations of designs and production photographs (often hard to find elsewhere).

160. Krempel, Daniel. "The Theatre of the Absurd and the Art of Scene Design." PLAYERS 40 (December 1963): 72–75. Illus.

Evaluates "assemblages" and similar avant-garde works of art as sources of absurdist stage design.

161. Laban, Juana de. "Scenery for the Dance." DANCE OBSERVER 9 (April 1942): 48–49: (May 1942): 62. Illus.

Discusses the contributions of Craig and Appia to modern dance design and defines challenges to be met.

162. Leeper, Janet. "Wadsworth Athenaeum: the Diaghilev Era, 1909–1929." APOLLO, n.s. 88 (December 1968): 482–87. Illus., one in color.

Brief text about the designers who worked for Diaghilev; fifteen illustrations.

163. McDowell, John H. "Shakespeare and Modern Design." JOURNAL OF ENGLISH AND GERMANIC PHILOLOGY 46 (1947): 337–47.

Examines numerous twentieth-century stage designs for Shakespearean plays, dividing them into five types: selective realism, platforms and steps, curtains, painted sets, and architectural stages.

164.   Macgowan, Kenneth.   "The Living Scene."   THEATRE ARTS 11 (1927):
444-54. Illus.

Discusses the New Stagecraft and its revolt against painted
illusionism, then analyzes the principles of modern stage design.

165.   _____. THE THEATRE OF TOMORROW. New York: Boni and Liveright, 1921. 302 p. Illus., part color.

Considers in detail the three sources of the New Stagecraft--
Appia, Craig, and the Ballets Russes--as well as experiments
in expressionism and cubism.

166.   Macgowan, Kenneth, and Jones, Robert Edmond. CONTINENTAL
STAGECRAFT. New York: Harcourt, Brace, and Co., 1922. 249 p.
Illus., part color.

"A record of impressions gained from ten weeks of travel
through the theaters of France, Sweden, Germany, Czecho-
Slovakia, and Austria during April, May, and June, 1922."
Evocative illustrations by Jones. Indispensable to an understanding of the New Stagecraft in Europe. Particularly informative about developments in Germany.

167.   Marshall, Francis. "The Artist and the Ballet." STUDIO 144 (December 1952): 161-67. Illus., part color.

General comments on painters' and sculptors' work for the
stage in the twentieth century.

168.   Moderwell, Hiram K. THE THEATRE OF TODAY. New York: Lane
Publishing Co., 1914. 322 p. Illus.

One of the first books that brought early-twentieth-century
European innovations to the attention of American readers.
Discusses Appia, Fuchs, Craig, Reinhardt, Bakst, and other
sources of the New Stagecraft, as well as American designers
working in experimental styles.

169.   Moussinac, Leon. THE NEW MOVEMENT IN THE THEATRE: A SUR-
VEY OF RECENT DEVELOPMENTS IN EUROPE AND AMERICA. Fore-
word by Gordon Craig. Introduction by R.H. Packman. London:
B.T. Batsford, 1931. xi, 24 p. 128 pls., part color. Biblio.

Packman's introduction discusses the aesthetics of the new movement.

Splendidly illustrated (in many cases the plates reproduce all
the costume and set designs for a particular production, as
well as one or more photographs of the production).

170. Penrose, A.P.D. "The Art of the Theatre." In REPORTS ON THE
      PRESENT POSITION AND TENDENCIES OF THE INDUSTRIAL ARTS
      AS INDICATED AT THE INTERNATIONAL EXHIBITION OF MODERN
      DECORATIVE AND INDUSTRIAL ARTS, PARIS, 1925, pp. 173-82.
      London: Dept. of Overseas Trade, [1927].

      Surveys the theatrical exhibits country-by-country and general-
      izes about stage design since World War I. Ten illustrations.

171. PRAZSKE QUADRIENNALE JEVISTNIHO VYTVARNICTVI A DIVADELNI
      ARCHITEKTURY 1967 (PRAGUE QUADRENNIAL OF THEATRE DESIGN
      AND ARCHITECTURE 1967). Edited by Vera Ptackova and Vladimir
      Jindra. [Prague: Theatre Institute, 1967]. 336 p. 72 p., illus.
      Paperbound.

      Text in Czech, French, and English. Sections on the exhibi-
      tions of each of the participating countries, with biographical
      notes on the designers.

172. PRAZSKE QUADRIENNALE JEVISTNIHO VYTVARNICTVI A DIVADELNI
      ARCHITEKTURY 1971 (PRAGUE QUADRENNIAL OF THEATRE DESIGN
      AND ARCHITECTURE 1971). Edited by Vladimir Jindra. Prague:
      Theatre Institute, 1971.

      Text in Czech, French, and English. A collection of twenty-
      four unbound booklets, of which twenty are devoted to indi-
      vidual countries exhibiting in the Quadrennial, and the re-
      maining to introductory material, a survey of exhibits of the-
      atre architecture, a group of illustrations, and a supplement.
      The booklets range from seven to seventy-seven pages in length
      and contain much biographical material about stage designers.

173. Ricketts, Charles. "Stage Decoration." FORTNIGHTLY REVIEW 98
      (December 1912): 1083-91.

      A penetrating discussion of stage design--principles and prac-
      tice--touching on the work of Richard Wagner, Adolphe Appia,
      Gordon Craig, and Leon Bakst. Reprinted, with a few changes,
      in his book PAGES ON ART (1913).

174. Rischbieter, Henning, comp., with Storch, Wolfgang. ART AND THE
      STAGE IN THE 20TH CENTURY; PAINTERS AND SCULPTORS WORK
      FOR THE THEATER. Translated by Michael Bullock and Andreas
      Schroeder. Greenwich, Conn.: New York Graphic Society, n.d.
      [c. 1968]. 306 p. Prof. illus., part color.

      Compiled by Rischbieter, documented by Storch. An important book, introduced by a valuable sketch of the history of stage design since the Renaissance, with commentary on its relation to the other arts and discussion of the theory and practice of twentieth-century stage design. The illustrations are accompanied by numerous "documents" by the artists and by critics. Ranges from the Symbolist productions of the fin de siecle to Op Art and Happenings. Catalog of productions, with bibliographical references.

175. Rouche, Jacques. L'ART THEATRAL MODERNE. Paris: E. Cornely, 1910. 79 p. Illus., part color.

Text in French. An influential book that brought wide attention to the work of Appia, Craig, Fritz Erler, Georg Fuchs, Meyerhold, and Stanislavsky.

176. Rowell, Kenneth. STAGE DESIGN. New York: Reinhold Book Corp.; London: Studio Vista, 1968. 96 p. Paperbound. Illus., part color. Biblio.

Succinct and well-illustrated review of twentieth-century stage design and an analysis of recent trends.

177. Simonson, Lee, ed. THEATRE ART. 1934. Reprint. New York: Cooper Square Publishers, 1969. 68 p. 73 pls.

Originally published as the catalog of the International Exhibition of Theatre Art at the Museum of Modern Art, New York. Includes brief essays by various authors on Inigo Jones, the Drottningholm Theatre in Sweden, and modern stage design in Germany, Russia, and the United States.

178. Smith, Marjorie Marie. "Expressionism in Twentieth Century Stage Design." Ph.D. dissertation, University of Michigan, 1960. 283 p.

Primarily concerned with German developments, 1890-1917.

179. Smith, Oliver. "Ballet Design." DANCE NEWS ANNUAL 1953, pp. 92-103. New York: Alfred A. Knopf, 1953. Illus.

Comments on modern designers for the ballet--both painters and professional scenic artists--and brief remarks on his own work for ballet.

180. Stravinsky, Igor, and Craft, Robert. "Some Painters of the Russian Ballet." ATLANTIC 202 (August 1958): 65-68. Illus.

Stravinsky recalls his collaboration with Leon Bakst, Giacomo Balla, Alexandre Benois, Andre Derain, Alexander Golovine, Michel Larionov, Henri Matisse, Nicholas Roerich, and Pablo Picasso.

181. Taylor, Mildred A.K. "The New Stagecraft: Its Relation to Easel Painting." Ph.D. dissertation, Stanford University, 1953. 213 p.

    Finds that the aims of the New Stagecraft and modern movements in painting (after 1906) were the same.

182. Thompson, James Robert. "Twentieth-Century Scene Design: Its History and Stylistic Origins." Ph.D. dissertation, University of Minnesota, 1957. 211 p.

    Defines changing styles in stage design and examines their relation to developments in the other arts.

183. Unruh, Walther. "Types of Adaptable Fore-Stage." WORLD THEATRE 3, no. 4 (1954): 35-47.

    Notes renewed interest in the forestage; discusses machinery for moving forestages, framing elements, and decorative details.

184. Van Vechten, Carl. INTERPRETERS AND INTERPRETATIONS. New York: Alfred A. Knopf, 1917. 368 p.

    "The Problem of Style in the Production of Operas," pp. 175-220, attacks the hackneyed sets at the Metropolitan Opera House, New York, and indicates sources of new ideas, such as Appia's production of ORFEO at Hellerau, Germany.

185. _____. MUSIC AFTER THE GREAT WAR AND OTHER STUDIES. New York: G. Schirmer, 1915. 168 p.

    Includes farsighted essays on the scenery and costumes of the Ballets Russes; on scenery "as a fine art"; and on Gordon Craig and Adolphe Appia.

186. _____. "Shall We Realize Wagner's Ideals?" MUSICAL QUARTERLY 2 (July 1916): 387-401. Illus.

    Criticizes the staging of Wagner's operas at the Metropolitan Opera House, New York, and elsewhere. Suggests new sources of production techniques: Appia, Craig, and the Ballets Russes. Reprinted in Van Vechten's MUSIC AND BAD MANNERS (1916).

187. Vaughan, David. "Diaghilev/Cunningham." ART JOURNAL 34, no. 2 (Winter 1974-75): 135-40. Illus.

    Discusses Diaghilev's policy of commissioning ballet designs from progressive artists outside the theatre and compares it to Merce Cunningham's similar policy in more recent times.

188. Victoria and Albert Museum, South Kensington. INTERNATIONAL
      THEATRE EXHIBITION. [London]: 1922. 102 p. Illus. Biblio.

      Catalog of an influential exhibition of the New Stagecraft.

189. Villiers, Andre. "'Interscena 66' at Prague." WORLD THEATRE 15
      (1966): 159–63.

      Report on the first international symposium on scenography.

190. Wedwick, Daryl Melvin. "United States and British Patents of Scenic
      and Illusionistic Devices and Effects for the Theatre, 1916–1970."
      Ph.D. dissertation, Bowling Green State University, 1972. 197 p.

191. Whitworth, Geoffrey. THEATRE IN ACTION. London and New York:
      Studio, [1938]. 128 p. Prof. illus.

      More than 200 illustrations of stage designs of the 1930s in
      sixteen different countries, including several Eastern European
      countries and Palestine.

192. Williams, Peter. "Talking about Design." DANCE AND DANCERS 14
      (April 1963): 26–27; (May 1963): 29–31. Illus.

      Suggests how ballet designers should train themselves; discusses
      the scenic demands of ballet.

193. Williamson, Audrey. "Art and the Ballet." DANCING TIMES, Septem-
      ber 1943, pp. 551–54. Illus.

      Asserts that ballet decor should provide a background for the
      dancers; thus it suits the methods of easel painters. For a
      rebuttal of this view, see Richard Seddon's article in DANC-
      ING TIMES, January 1944, pp. 155–57.

194. Yeats, William Butler. "The Theater of Beauty." HARPER'S WEEKLY
      55 (11 November 1911): 11. Illus., port.

      "An address delivered before the Dramatic Club of Harvard
      University." Condemns illusionistic perspective and painted
      shadows onstage; discusses recent reforms intended to eliminate
      them.

Chapter 5

CLASSICAL GREECE AND ROME

195. Arnott, Peter D. GREEK SCENIC CONVENTIONS IN THE 5TH CEN-
      TURY B.C. Oxford: Clarendon Press, 1962. ix, 147 p. Biblio.

      A history of fifth-century production style tempered by the
      author's experiences in staging the plays.

196. Beare, William. THE ROMAN STAGE. 3d ed., rev. London:
      Methuen, 1964. 410 p. Illus. Biblio.

      "The Stage and the Actors' House," pp. 176-83, describes
      the stage used during the Republic. Appendices deal with
      the Roman stage curtain and with the question of scenery on
      the Greek and Roman stage.

196a. _____. "Side Entrances and Periaktoi in the Hellenistic Theatre."
       CLASSICAL QUARTERLY 32 (1938): 205-10.

       Scholarly discussion of the use of periaktoi to indicate scene
       changes in the Greek theatre.

196b. Bieber, Margarete. THE HISTORY OF THE GREEK AND ROMAN
       THEATER. 2d ed., rev. and enl. Princeton: Princeton University
       Press, 1961. 357 p. Illus. Biblio.

       Includes chapters on the development of Greek and Roman
       theatre architecture; a chapter on Greek scenery and mechani-
       cal devices (pp. 74-79); and some notes on Renaissance adap-
       tations of classical scenic devices.

197. Dawson, Christopher. ROMANO-CAMPANIAN MYTHOLOGICAL
      LANDSCAPE PAINTING. Yale Classical Studies, vol. 9. New Haven,
      Conn.: Yale University Press, 1944. 249 p. 25 pls. Biblio.

      Chapter 6: "The Relationship of the Mythological Landscapes
      to the Theatrical Performances of the Early Empire."

198. Exon, Charles. "A New Theory of the Ekkyklema." HERMATHENA 11

(1900-1901): 132-43. Illus.

Suggests a pivoted, revolving platform rather than a rolling wagon.

199. Flickinger, Roy. THE GREEK THEATER AND ITS DRAMA. 4th ed. Chicago: University of Chicago Press, 1936. 413 p. Illus.

See especially chapter 5, "The Influence of Physical Conditions."

200. Friend, A.M., Jr. "The Portraits of the Evangelists in Greek and Latin Manuscripts, Part II." ART STUDIES 7 (1929): 3-29. Illus.

Stimulating study of the relationship between Hellenistic stage scenery and the architectural backgrounds in portraits of the Evangelists from the early Christian period.

201. Gardner, Percy. "The Scenery of the Greek Stage." JOURNAL OF HELLENIC STUDIES 19 (1899): 252-64.

Dated, but still useful.

202. Hourmouziades, Nicolaos C. PRODUCTION AND IMAGINATION IN EURIPIDES: FORM AND FUNCTION OF THE SCENIC SPACE. Athens: Greek Society for Humanistic Studies, 1965. Greek Society for Humanistic Studies, Second Series, Essays and Researches, no. 5. x, 180 p. Biblio.

Scholarly study of scenic conventions in Euripides's plays, including consideration of machinery and changeable scenery. An important contribution.

203. Kernodle, George R. "The Fifth-Century Skene: A New Model." EDUCATIONAL THEATRE JOURNAL 20 (1968): 502-5.

Suggests that the fifth-century stage house was the "supporting structure for niches or thrones of the gods."

204. Little, Alan M.G. ROMAN PERSPECTIVE PAINTING AND THE ANCIENT STAGE. Wheaton, Md.: Distribution by the author, 1971. 50 p. Illus. Biblio.

205. _____. "A Roman Sourcebook for the Stage." AMERICAN JOURNAL OF ARCHAEOLOGY 60 (1956): 27-33, pls. 20-27.

Scholarly investigation of the relation between Roman wall paintings at Pompeii and elsewhere, and scenery in the Hellenistic and Roman theatre.

206. _____. "Scaenographia." ART BULLETIN 18 (1936): 407-18. Illus.

Scenery on the Hellenistic and Roman stage.

207. Pickard-Cambridge, Arthur W. THE THEATRE OF DIONYSUS IN ATHENS. Oxford: Clarendon Press, 1946. 303 p. Illus. Biblio.

The standard scholarly study, requiring knowledge of Greek and Latin to be fully appreciated. Discusses the staging of the extant plays, painted scenery and machinery, and the evidence from wall paintings at Pompeii, Boscoreale, and elsewhere.

208. Pollux, Iulius. "Pollux on Scenes, Machines, and Masks." In A SOURCE BOOK IN THEATRICAL HISTORY (see item 74), pp. 7-15.

The only readily accessible translation of this chapter on the Greek theatre in Pollux's second-century A.D. encyclopedia, ONOMASTIKON.

209. Six, J. "Agatharcos." JOURNAL OF HELLENIC STUDIES 40 (1920): 180-89. Illus.

Scholarly investigation of the scene-painting techniques Agatharcus may have employed.

210. Vitruvius Pollio. ON ARCHITECTURE. Edited and translated by Frank Granger. 2 vols. London: William Heinemann; New York: G.P. Putnam's Sons, 1931-34. Illus. Biblio.

Latin and English texts. Volume 1, book 5, includes Vitruvius's immensely influential remarks on the architecture and scenery of Greek and Roman theatres.

211. Webster, Thomas B.L. "Classical Antiquity: The Theatre and the Artist." APOLLO, n.s. 86 (August 1967): 94-101. Illus.

Discusses scenery in the Greek and Roman theatre. Illustrated with photographs of wall paintings, vases, sculpture, and masks.

212. _____. GREEK THEATRE PRODUCTION. 2d ed. London: Methuen, 1970. 231 p. Illus.

A standard study. See especially part I, "Athens: Theatre, Scenery, and Stage Machinery," pp. 1-28. Also considers "Scenery in the Fourth Century" in Sicily and Italy, pp. 101-110.

213. _____. "Staging and Scenery in the Ancient Greek Theatre." BULLETIN OF THE JOHN RYLANDS LIBRARY 42 (1959-60): 493-509.

Traces the development of the stage and machinery of the
Theatre of Dionysus in Athens in the fifth and fourth centuries
B.C., in the light of Menander's rediscovered play DYSKOLOS.

Chapter 6

MEDIEVAL EUROPE

SEE ALSO item 270.

214. Cameron, Kenneth, and Kahrl, Stanley J. "Staging the N-Town Cycle."
THEATRE NOTEBOOK 21 (1966–67): 152–65.

> The second part of a two-part article. This part identifies
> scenic localities, pageants, and properties needed to stage
> the English N-Town plays.

215. Chambers, Edmund K. THE MEDIAEVAL STAGE. 2 vols. Oxford:
Clarendon Press, 1903.

> The standard study, more useful for background information
> than for information on scenery and machinery.

216. Cohen, Gustave. HISTOIRE DE LA MISE EN SCENE DANS LE THE-
ATRE RELIGIEUX FRANCAIS DU MOYEN AGE. Rev. ed. Paris:
Champion, 1951. 410 p. Illus. Biblio.

> Text in French. The standard history of scenery and produc-
> tion style in the medieval French theatre.

217. Collins, Fletcher, Jr. THE PRODUCTION OF MEDIEVAL CHURCH
MUSIC-DRAMA. Charlottesville: University Press of Virginia, 1971.
369 p. Illus., part color.

> Describes the staging requirements of sixteen European music-
> dramas from c. 1100–1275, discussing set pieces, properties,
> costumes, and lighting effects necessary for production.

218. Evans, M[arshall]. Blakemore. THE PASSION PLAY OF LUCERNE.
New York: Modern Language Association of America; London: Oxford
University Press, 1943. xi, 245 p., 29 p. of music inserted between
pp. 68–69. Illus. Biblio.

> Chapters 7 and 8 discuss the stage, costumes, and properties.
> Much of the text Is In German.

219. _____. "The Staging of the Donaueschingen Passion Play." MODERN
LANGUAGE REVIEW 15 (1920): 65-76, 279-97.

A scholarly study of the mansions, props, costumes, and effects required by the text or indicated in a sketch attributed
to a production of the play.

220. Galante Garrone, Virginia. L'APPARATO SCENICO DEL DRAMMA
SACRO IN ITALIA. [The scenic apparatus of Italian religious drama].
Turin: V. Bona, 1935. 129 p. Illus. Biblio.

Text in Italian. A scholarly monograph on the staging of
liturgical drama, mystery plays, and religious festivals in
medieval Italy.

221. Hashim, James. "Notes Towards a Reconstruction of LE MYSTERE DES
ACTES DES APOTRES as Presented at Bourges, 1536." THEATRE RE-
SEARCH / RECHERCHES THEATRALES 12 (1972): 29-73.

Considers staging, costumes, scenic "mansions," and special
effects in this spectacular production.

222. Hosley, Richard. "Three Kinds of Outdoor Theatre Before Shakespeare."
THEATRE SURVEY 12 (1971): 1-33. Illus.

Place and scaffolds theatre, pageant wagons, and booth stages.

223. Kernodle, George R. "The Medieval Pageant Wagons of Louvain."
THEATRE ANNUAL 2 (1943): 58-62, 13 pls. Reprinted in THE-
ATRE ANNUAL 10 (1952): 71-75. Pls.

Reproduces thirteen illustrations of the dramatic procession in
Louvain, Belgium, in 1594, with commentary.

224. Loomis, Laura H. "Secular Dramatics in the Royal Palace, Paris, 1378,
1389, and Chaucer's 'Tregetoures.'" SPECULUM 33 (1958): 242-55.
Illus.

Drawing on accounts in the fourteenth-century CHRONIQUE
DE CHARLES V and Jean Froissart's CHRONIQUES, Loomis discusses performances employing ships, towers, and other elaborate set pieces to reenact the sieges of Jerusalem and Troy.
Chaucer's FRANKLIN'S TALE may refer to these performances.

225. Penn, Dorothy. THE STAGING OF THE "MIRACLES DE NOSTRE DAME
PAR PERSONNAGES" OF MS. CANGE. New York: Institute of
French Studies, Columbia University, 1933. 95 p. Illus. Biblio.

Includes reconstructions of polyscenic stages.

226. Salter, Frederick M. MEDIEVAL DRAMA IN CHESTER. Toronto:

University of Toronto Press, 1955. xi, 138 p.

Discusses the cost and construction of pageant wagons.

227. Schmitt, Natalie Crohn. "Was There a Medieval Theatre in the Round?"
THEATRE NOTEBOOK 23 (1968–69): 130–42; 24 (1969–70): 18–25.
Illus.

An attempt to refute Richard Southern's interpretation of the
staging of THE CASTLE OF PERSEVERANCE (see item 233),
and a skeptical view of iconographic evidence that suggests
medieval staging in the round.

228. Sharp, Thomas. A DISSERTATION ON THE PAGEANTS OR DRAMATIC
MYSTERIES ANCIENTLY PERFORMED AT COVENTRY. Coventry: Mer-
ridew and Son, 1825. 226 p. Illus.

Discusses the form and decoration of pageant wagons. Includes
a frequently reproduced "reconstruction" of such a wagon.

229. Shiley, Robert A. "A Chappelle in the MIRACLES DE NOSTRE DAME."
MODERN LANGUAGE NOTES 58 (1943): 493–97. Illus.

Suggests that a chappelle lowered in the MIRACLE DE LA
MERE DU PAPE was really a catafalque or funeral canopy.

230. _____. "The Staging of the MIRACLES DE NOSTRE DAME." Ph.D.
dissertation, Yale University, 1939.

231. Shoemaker, William Hutchinson. THE MULTIPLE STAGE IN SPAIN
DURING THE FIFTEENTH AND SIXTEENTH CENTURIES. Princeton,
N.J.: Princeton University Press, 1935. xi, 150 p. Biblio.

232. Shull, Virginia. "The Stagecraft of the Medieval English Drama."
Ph.D. dissertation, Yale University, 1941.

233. Southern, Richard. THE MEDIEVAL THEATRE IN THE ROUND: A
STUDY OF THE STAGING OF "THE CASTLE OF PERSEVERANCE" AND
RELATED MATTERS. Rev. and enl. ed. New York: Theatre Arts
Books, 1975. 285 p. Illus.

234. Stuart, Donald Clive. STAGE DECORATION IN FRANCE IN THE
MIDDLE AGES. New York: Columbia University Press, 1910. ix,
230 p.

Out of date, but still the only book-length study of the subject in English. Considers scenery for both religious and secular plays.

235. _____. "The Stage Setting of Hell and the Iconography of the Middle Ages." ROMANIC REVIEW 4 (1913): 330-42.

   Discusses various forms of the Hell mansion and their relation to medieval painting and sculpture.

236. Wickham, Glynne. THE MEDIEVAL THEATRE. New York: St. Martin's Press, 1974. 245 p. Illus. Biblio.

   A broad view of the European theatre between the tenth and the sixteenth centuries, with some account of scenery, good illustrations, and an excellent bibliography.

237. _____. "The Staging of Saint Plays in England." In THE MEDIEVAL DRAMA, edited by Sandro Sticca, pp. 99-119. Binghamton, N.Y.: State University of New York Press, 1971.

238. Young, William Donald. "Devices and FEINTES of the Medieval Religious Theatre in England and France." Ph.D. dissertation, Stanford University, 1960. 262 p.

Chapter 7

CZECHOSLOVAKIA

A. EIGHTEENTH AND NINETEENTH CENTURIES

239.   Bartusek, Antonin.   "Castle and School Theatres in Czech Lands."
INTERSCAENA 4 (Summer 1970): 1-23. Illus.

Includes data on surviving eighteenth-century scenery and
machinery at the Cesky-Krumlov castle theatre, among others.

240.   Prochazka, Vladimir.   "Bohemia and Scenery: First Half of the Nineteenth Century." In ANATOMY OF AN ILLUSION (see item 102),
pp. 35-38, 82-84. Illus.

Discusses and illustrates early nineteenth-century scenery that
has survived in several remote castle theatres in Czechoslovakia.

241.   Sarlos, Robert K.   "Two Outdoor Opera Productions of Giuseppe Galli
Bibiena." THEATRE SURVEY 5 (1964): 27-42. Diags.

ANGELICA, VINCITRICE DI ALCINA, at the Viennese imperial summer residence, 1716; and COSTANZA E FORTEZZA
in Prague, 1723.

242.   Vadlejchova, Ivana.   "The Theatre at the Kacina Chateau (1821-23)."
INTERSCAENA-ACTA SCAENOGRAPHICA 3 (Summer 1973): 20-26.
Illus.

Discusses the scenery and stage machinery preserved in this
early nineteenth-century Czech theatre.

B. TWENTIETH CENTURY

SEE ALSO items 22, 40.

243.   Bablet, Denis.   "Joseph Swoboda: Technician and Artist."   ENCORE

(London) 11 (July–August 1964): 37–41.

Survey of his methods, based on an interview.

244. Burian, Jarka M. "Czechoslovakian Stage Design and Scenography, 1914–38: A Survey." THEATRE DESIGN & TECHNOLOGY, no. 41 (Summer 1975): 14–23, 35; no. 42 (Fall 1975): 23–32. Illus.

A valuable survey, with information on the work of Vlastislav Hofman, Bedrich Feuerstein, Antonin Heythum, Josef Capek, Frantisek Muzika, Frantisek Troester, and Miroslav Kouril. Numerous illustrations.

245. _____. "Josef Svoboda's American University Tour, 1972." THEATRE DESIGN & TECHNOLOGY, no. 33 (May 1973): 7–12. Illus.

Includes excerpts from Svoboda's lectures.

246. _____. THE SCENOGRAPHY OF JOSEF SVOBODA. Middletown, Conn.: Wesleyan University Press, 1971. 224 p. Illus. Biblio.

A comprehensive study of Svoboda's productions to 1971, including a short biography, a statement of his aesthetic principles, illustrations of representative work, and a register of his productions.

247. Casson, Hugh. "Conversation with Svoboda." JOURNAL OF THE ROYAL INSTITUTE OF BRITISH ARCHITECTS 74 (May 1967): 202–3. Illus.

248. DECORATEURS DE THEATRES TCHECOSLOVAQUES 1960–1970 (DESIGNERS OF THE CZECHOSLOVAK THEATRES 1960–1970). Prague: Theatre Institute, 1971. 35 p. text, 62 p. illus. Paperbound.

Text in French and English. Brief introduction and an alphabetical list of designers, with date of birth and a few biographical facts on each; plus the illustrations.

249. Gillar, Jaroslav. "Miroslav Kouril and Scenography D34-D41." INTER-SCAENA 3 (Spring 1969): 1–25. Illus.

Discusses E.F. Burian's productions at the D Theatre in Prague, 1934–41, with scenery by Miroslav Kouril, J. Novotny, and Josef Raban.

250. Heymann, Henry. "Josef Svoboda and His Czech Scenographic Milieu." THEATRE DESIGN & TECHNOLOGY, no. 20 (February 1970): 4–11. Illus.

A survey of Svoboda's work, with biographical notes, a list of productions, a brief bibliography, and nineteen illustrations.

251. Jindra, Vladimir. WHO IS JOSEF SVOBODA? Translated by Marian Wilbraham. Prague: Orbis, 1968. 30 p. Paperbound. Illus.

252. Kouril, Miroslav. "The Prague Scenographic Institute." WORLD THEATRE 14 (1965): 303-6. Illus.

    Brief description of the activities at this "scenic laboratory."

253. Loney, Glenn [M]. "Josef Svoboda Retires?" THEATRE CRAFTS 5 (January-February 1971): 26-31, 30-40. Illus.

    An interview with Svoboda, referring particularly to his not-altogether-successful technology for THE IDIOT in London and THE MAGIC FLUTE in Munich.

254. "Notes on the Slovak Scenographer Ladislav Vychodil." THEATRE DESIGN & TECHNOLOGY, no. 20 (February 1970): 20. Illus.

    Very brief survey of the career of this contemporary Czech stage designer.

255. Svoboda, Josef. "Designing for the Stage." OPERA 18 (August 1967): 631-36. Illus.

    An interview with Svoboda conducted by Charles Spencer. Stress on his designs for opera.

256. _____. "New Ways in Czechoslovakia." WORLD THEATRE 12 (1963): 32-44. Illus.

    Comments on new materials, projection techniques, and experimentation with light. Eighteen illustrations.

257. "Theatre Art in Czechoslovakia." THEATRE ARTS 21 (1937): 976-79, 991. Illus.

    Brief discussion of progressive theatre in Czechoslovakia, with three production photographs.

258. Veber, Vaclav. "History of the Institute of Scenography." INTER-SCAENA-ACTA SCAENOGRAPHICA 2 (Summer 1972): 5-18.

    Sketch of the fifteen-year history of this remarkable Czech center of training and research.

259. Vychodil, Ladislav, and Gaiser, Gary. "A Short Course in Scenography, University of California, Santa Barbara." THEATRE DESIGN & TECHNOLOGY, no. 38 (October 1974): 23-26, 37. Illus.

    The course was based on the principles of scenographic study in Czechoslovakia, which are described here. Illustrated with designs by Vychodil.

Chapter 8

ENGLAND

A. GENERAL HISTORIES

260. Blanchard, E.L. "Scenery and Scene-Painters." ERA ALMANACK, 1871, pp. 34-37. London: The Era, 1871.

A brief but fact-filled history of scene design in England, preceded by a few largely mistaken remarks on Greek and Renaissance scenery.

261. Harker, Joseph. STUDIO AND STAGE. 1924. Reprint. New York: Benjamin Blom, 1972. 283 p. Illus.

Autobiography of a scene painter. Mostly devoted to reminis-cences about actors, managers, scene painters, and playwrights. Two interesting chapters present various opinions about the New Stagecraft, with which Harker was unsympathetic.

262. "Historical Sketch of the Rise and Progress of Scene-Painting in England." LIBRARY OF THE FINE ARTS 1 (May 1831): 321-29.

Mentions scene painters active in the Restoration, the eigh-teenth century, and the early nineteenth century.

263. Lawrence, W[illiam]. J[ohn]. "A Forgotten State Conventionality." ANGLIA 26 (1903): 447-60.

Traces the history of proscenium doors on the London stage.

264. Leacroft, Richard. THE DEVELOPMENT OF THE ENGLISH PLAYHOUSE. London: Eyre Methuen, 1973. 367 p. Prof. illus. Biblio.

Traces the development of the playhouse from medieval halls and churches to the elaborately equipped theatres of the early twentieth century. Includes extensive discussion of scenery and stage machinery. The author's ingenious isometric re-constructions of the theatres are valuable aids to understanding scenic equipment.

265. Rosenfeld, Sybil. A SHORT HISTORY OF SCENE DESIGN IN GREAT
BRITAIN. Oxford: Basil Blackwell, 1973. 232 p. Illus. Biblio.

A valuable book, the only general survey of the subject yet
published. Ranges from the Middle Ages to the present.
Well-chosen illustrations (though too few) and a useful bibliography.

266. "A Sketch of the History of Scene Painting." BUILDER 17 (1859):
353-54.

Mainly concerns scenery in England from the seventeenth to
the mid-nineteenth century.

267. Southern, Richard. CHANGEABLE SCENERY: ITS ORIGIN AND DE-
VELOPMENT IN THE BRITISH THEATRE. London: Faber and Faber,
1952. 411 p. Illus.

The best general history of scenery and stage machinery in
Britain, late sixteenth to late nineteenth century.

268. _____. "The Curtain Drops for Scene-Change." LIFE & LETTERS
TO-DAY 33 (April 1942): 32-41.

Traces the visible scene change from its Renaissance origin
to its demise in the late nineteenth century, with particular
attention to the British theatre.

269. _____. "The 'Houses' of the Westminster Play." THEATRE NOTE-
BOOK 3 (1948-49): 46-52. Illus.

Discusses scenery used for Latin plays at Westminster School
from the sixteenth to the twentieth century, suggesting that
the "houses" flanking the sides of the stage were first used
in the sixteenth or even the fifteenth century.

270. Wickham, Glynne. EARLY ENGLISH STAGES, 1300 TO 1600. 3 vols.
London: Routledge and Kegan Paul; New York: Columbia University
Press, 1959-72. Illus. Biblio.

The second and third volumes are numbered volume 2, parts 1 and
2. A fourth volume, called volume 3, is planned. Volume 1,
1300 to 1576, includes scattered references to the scenery and
machinery of medieval productions. Volume 2, part 1, chapters
6 and 7 are concerned with emblematic scenic devices and perspective scenery during the sixteenth and seventeenth centuries.

271. Withington, Robert. ENGLISH PAGEANTRY: AN HISTORICAL OUT-
LINE. 2 vols. Cambridge, Mass.: Harvard University Press, 1918.
Illus. Biblio.

Includes information on scenery, set pieces, and props for masques, royal entries, Lord Mayor's shows, historical folk plays, etc., from the Middle Ages to the early twentieth century in England. Includes a chapter on American pageants in the nineteenth and twentieth centuries. Extensive bibliography.

B. RENAISSANCE

272. Adams, John C. THE GLOBE PLAYHOUSE: ITS DESIGN AND EQUIP-MENT. Cambridge, Mass.: Harvard University Press, 1942. x, 420 p. Illus.

   Mainly architectural.

273. Archer, William. "The Elizabethan Stage." QUARTERLY REVIEW 208 (April 1908): 442-71. Illus.

   Review article on six books about Shakespeare's stage.

274. Beckerman, Bernard. SHAKESPEARE AT THE GLOBE, 1599-1609. New York: Macmillan, 1962. 270 p.

   Chapter 3 considers stage properties and the design of the stage.

275. Campbell, Lily B. SCENES AND MACHINES ON THE ENGLISH STAGE DURING THE RENAISSANCE. Cambridge: Cambridge University Press, 1923. x, 302 p. Illus.

   To provide a background to English practice, the author first traces the development of perspective scene painting in Italy, then she examines stage decoration in England in the sixteenth and seventeenth centuries. Dated, but still useful.

276. Chambers, Edmund K. THE ELIZABETHAN STAGE. 4 vols. Oxford: Clarendon Press, 1923. Illus.

   Once the standard study, now somewhat dated. Volume 3 considers staging at court and in the public theatres.

277. Feuillerat, Albert, ed. DOCUMENTS RELATING TO THE OFFICE OF THE REVELS IN THE TIME OF QUEEN ELIZABETH. Louvain: A. Uystpruyst, 1908. 529 p. DOCUMENTS RELATING TO THE REVELS AT COURT IN THE TIME OF KING EDWARD VI AND QUEEN MARY. Louvain: A. Uystpruyst, 1914. 354 p.

   Including records of payments for scenery, properties, and costumes.

278. Freehafer, John. "Inigo Jones's Scenery for THE CID." THEATRE

NOTEBOOK 25 (1970-71): 84-92. Illus.

Attributes one of Jones's surviving designs to a production of THE CID at the Cockpit-in-Court Theatre, 1639. For a rejoinder, see THEATRE NOTEBOOK 26 (1971-72): 89-91. And for Freehafer's reply, see the same journal 27 (1972-73): 98-113, an article that attempts to show that perspective scenery was used in the private playhouses before 1642.

279. Gotch, J. Alfred. INIGO JONES. 1928. Reprint. New York: Benjamin Blom, 1968. xi, 271 p. Illus.

A biography that considers Jones's work on court masques as well as his architectural activities.

280. Hawley, James Abgriffith. "Inigo Jones and the New English Stagecraft." Ph.D. dissertation, Ohio State University, 1967. 154 p.

By analyzing libretti and surviving stage designs, the author traces Jones's technique from the use of large set pieces behind shutters to the full flat wing and shutter system.

281. Hodges, Cyril Walter. THE GLOBE RESTORED. 2d ed. London: Oxford University Press, 1968. 192 p. Illus. Biblio.

See especially chapter 5, "The Stately-Furnished Scene."

282. Hotson, Leslie. SHAKESPEARE'S WOODEN O. London: Rupert Hart-Davis, 1959. 335 p. Illus.

Suggests that Elizabethan plays were staged in the round, with "transparent" mansions (frameworks, sometimes curtained) at the ends of the stage.

283. Isaacs, Jacob. PRODUCTION AND STAGE MANAGEMENT AT THE BLACKFRIARS THEATRE. London: Published for the Shakespeare Association, Oxford University Press, 1933. 28 p. Paperbound.

Brief consideration of scenery and lighting.

284. King, Thomas James. SHAKESPEAREAN STAGING, 1599-1642. Cambridge, Mass.: Harvard University Press, 1971. xii, 163 p. Illus.

An analysis of the staging requirements (entrances, large properties, doors or hangings, upper stage, etc.) for 276 plays.

285. Lawrence, W[illiam]. J[ohn]. THE ELIZABETHAN PLAYHOUSE AND OTHER STUDIES. Philadelphia: J.B. Lippincott Co.; Stratford-upon-Avon: Shakespeare Head Press, 1912. 265 p. Illus. Biblio.

Includes essays on stage curtains, proscenium doors, "title

and locality boards" on the pre-Restoration stage, and the
staging of court masques.

286. _____. THE ELIZABETHAN PLAYHOUSE AND OTHER STUDIES.
SECOND SERIES. Stratford-upon-Avon: Shakespeare Head Press, 1913.
261 p. Illus. Biblio.

Includes essays on windows on the pre-Restoration stage, the
origin of the English "picture stage," and "light and darkness
in the Elizabethan theatre."

287. _____. "Oxford as Scenic Pioneer." NEW YORK DRAMATIC MIRROR,
23 March 1907, p. 13.

Movable scenery in Oxford productions, 1605, 1618, and
1636.

288. McCalmon, George. "A Study of Some of the Renaissance and Baroque
Factors in the Theatre Style of Inigo Jones." Ph.D. dissertation, Case-
Western Reserve University, 1946. 852 p.

289. McDowell, John H. "Conventions of Medieval Art in Shakespearian
Staging." JOURNAL OF ENGLISH AND GERMANIC PHILOLOGY 48
(1948): 215-29. Illus.

Shows how medieval painting and sculpture throw light on
Elizabethan stage conventions such as multiple settings, fore-
stage, methods of revealing interiors, form of set pieces such
as caves and tombs, etc.

290. _____. "Tudor Court Staging: A Study in Perspective." JOURNAL
OF ENGLISH AND GERMANIC PHILOLOGY 44 (1945): 194-207.

Examines Tudor drama, court staging methods, and the Tudor
attitude towards scientific perspective to explain why Italian
perspective staging was not introduced during the Tudor period
in England.

291. McManaway, James G. "Notes on Two Pre-Restoration Stage Curtains."
PHILOLOGICAL QUARTERLY 41 (1962): 270-74. Illus.

Commentary on an illustration in English editions of John
Ogilby's FABLES OF AESOP (1651, 1668, and 1673); and
an illustration in Jan Amos Komenski's ORBIS SENSUALIUM
PICTUS (1659). Both show a stage with a front curtain drawn
back into festoons.

292. Miller, William E. "PERIAKTOI in the Old Blackfriars." MODERN
LANGUAGE NOTES 74 (1959): 1-3. Biblio.

Cites a marginal note in Abraham Fleming's translation of
Vergil's GEORGICS (1589) as evidence of periaktoi at the
Blackfriars Theatre. Miller further defends his hypothesis in
SHAKESPEARE QUARTERLY 15 (Winter 1964): 61–65.

293.   Nagler, A[lois]. M. SHAKESPEARE'S STAGE. Translated by Ralph
Manheim. New Haven, Conn., and London: Yale University Press,
1958. ix, 117 p.

Includes a concise summary of evidence about scenery on the
Elizabethan–Jacobean stage, as well as a good case for "pa-
vilion" staging of discovery scenes.

294.   Nicoll, Allardyce. STUART MASQUES AND THE RENAISSANCE STAGE.
London and Toronto: G.G. Harrap, 1937. 223 p. Illus. Biblio.

A study of the staging of court masques in England during the
reigns of James I and Charles I. Nicoll sets the masques in
the context of royal patronage, emblem literature, and the
Italian sources from which Inigo Jones drew his scenic techniques.

295.   Orgel, Stephen, and Strong, Roy. INIGO JONES: THE THEATRE OF
THE STUART COURT. 2 vols. London: Sotheby Parke Bernet; Berkeley
and Los Angeles: University of California Press, 1973. Prof. illus.,
part color.

Limited edition. Reproduces and describes all of Jones's theatrical drawings for the Stuart court masques, as well as the
texts of the masques and, where identified, Jones's Italian
sources.

296.   Presley, Horton Edward. "O Showes, Showes, Mighty Showes: A
Study of the Relationship of the Jones-Jonson Controversy to the Rise
of Illusionistic Staging in Seventeenth-Century British Drama." Ph.D.
dissertation, University of Kansas, 1966. 308 p.

297.   Reynolds, George F. THE STAGING OF ELIZABETHAN PLAYS AT
THE RED BULL THEATER, 1605-1625. New York: Modern Language
Association of America; London: Oxford University Press, 1940. 203 p.
Illus.

Includes a chapter on stage effects.

298.   Richards, Kenneth R. "Changeable Scenery for Plays on the Caroline
Stage.." THEATRE NOTEBOOK 23 (1968-69): 6-20.

A well-reasoned argument concluding that changeable painted
scenery was used only "on special occasions, before exclusive

audiences, and in private and aristocratic venues." A post-
script appears in THEATRE NOTEBOOK 23 (1968-69): 114-15.

299. Simpson, Percy, and Bell, C.F., eds. DESIGNS BY INIGO JONES
FOR MASQUES & PLAYS AT COURT. Oxford: Printed for the Walpole
and Malone Societies at the University Press, 1924. 158 p. 51 pls.
Colored frontispiece.

Useful introduction on the scenery and costumes of the masques,
plus a descriptive catalog of designs.

300. Smith, Irwin. SHAKESPEARE'S BLACKFRIARS PLAYHOUSE: ITS HIS-
TORY AND DESIGN. New York: New York University Press, 1964.
597 p. Illus. Biblio.

Mostly architectural, but includes brief consideration of
changeable scenery in the private theatres.

301. _____. SHAKESPEARE'S GLOBE PLAYHOUSE: A MODERN RECON-
STRUCTION IN TEXT AND SCALE DRAWINGS. New York: Charles
Scribner's Sons, 1956. 263 p. Illus., part color. Biblio.

Brief treatment of scenery and traps.

302. Southern, Richard. "Davenant, Father of English Scenery." LIFE &
LETTERS TO-DAY 32 (February 1942): 114-26.

Examines Davenant's theatrical activities before, during, and
after the Commonwealth.

303. _____. "He, Also, Was a Scene Painter." LIFE & LETTERS TO-DAY
23 (December 1939): 294-300.

Explains a Revels Office account of payments for scene
painting by William Lyzarde in 1572.

304. _____. "Inigo Jones and FLORIMENE." THEATRE NOTEBOOK 7
(1952-53): 37-39. Illus.

Discusses some of the surviving designs for FLORIMENE, ampli-
fying his remarks in CHANGEABLE SCENERY.

305. _____. "Observations on Lansdowne MS. No. 1171." THEATRE
NOTEBOOK 2 (1947-48): 6-19. Illus.

Reproduces, page by page, this highly important collection
of scenic drawings attributed to Inigo Jones and John Webb,
with detailed commentary.

C. RESTORATION AND EIGHTEENTH CENTURY

SEE ALSO item 363.

306. Allen, Ralph G. "Capon's Scenes for Melodrama." THEATRE RE-
SEARCH / RECHERCHES THEATRALES 8 (1966): 7-17.

Examines William Capon's Gothic and "Saxon" scenes for
melodramas at Drury Lane, c. 1796-1801.

307. _____. "A CHRISTMAS TALE, or, Harlequin Scene Painter." TEN-
NESSEE STUDIES IN LITERATURE 19 (1974): 149-161.

A reconstruction of the scenery and lighting effects by P.J.
De Loutherbourg for this pantomime produced at Drury Lane
in 1773.

308. _____. "De Loutherbourg and Captain Cook." THEATRE RESEARCH /
RECHERCHES THEATRALES 4 (1962): 195-211.

A detailed examination of P.J. De Loutherbourg's scenery for
the pantomime OMAI, produced at Covent Garden in 1785.

309. _____. "The Eidophusikon." THEATRE DESIGN & TECHNOLOGY,
no. 7 (December 1966): 12-16. Illus.

An account of P.J. De Loutherbourg's scenic spectacle (first
shown in 1781), based on contemporary sources.

310. _____. "Kemble and Capon at Drury Lane, 1794-1802." EDUCA-
TIONAL THEATRE JOURNAL 23 (March 1971): 22-35.

Sketches William Capon's career as a stage designer and antiquarian, suggesting that Capon, "in collaboration with Kemble,
may be said to have invented the antiquarian style" of Shakespeare production.

311. _____. "The Stage Spectacles of Philip James De Loutherbourg."
D.F.A. dissertation, Yale University, 1960. 368 p.

Reconstructs thirty-one productions, describing De Loutherbourg's
innovations in scenery and lighting and tracing his sources.

312. _____. "Topical Scenes for Pantomime." EDUCATIONAL THEATRE
JOURNAL 17 (1965): 289-300.

Describes five scenes designed by P.J. De Loutherbourg for
insertion into Drury Lane productions, 1773-1780. Based on
recent newsworthy events, the scenes were characterized by
realism and accuracy.

313. _____. "THE WONDERS OF DERBYSHIRE: A Spectacular Eighteenth-Century Travelogue." THEATRE SURVEY 2 (1961): 54-66.

Describes P.J. De Loutherbourg's scenery for this harlequinade produced in 1779 at Drury Lane, and interprets the scenes in the light of contemporary taste.

314. Barker, Kathleen M.D. "Michael Edkins, Painter." THEATRE NOTE-BOOK 16 (1961-62): 39-55.

Excerpts from the ledger of an artist who worked at the Theatre Royal, Bristol, 1768-86.

315. Barlow, Graham. "Sir James Thornhill and the Theatre Royal, Drury Lane, 1705." In ESSAYS ON THE EIGHTEENTH-CENTURY ENGLISH STAGE, edited by Kenneth Richards and Peter Thomson, pp. 179-193. London: Methuen, 1972. Illus.

Attributes certain Thornhill designs to a Drury Lane production of ARSINOE in 1705; infers from them and other evidence that the generally accepted sectional drawing of Drury Lane ought to be rejected in favor of another drawing by Wren.

316. Boswell, Eleanore. THE RESTORATION COURT STAGE (1660-1702). Cambridge, Mass.: Harvard University Press, 1932. 388 p. Illus.

Well-documented study of theatres and staging in the Restoration English court, with a detailed examination of the production of John Crowne's CALISTO in 1675.

317. Burnim, Kalman A. DAVID GARRICK, DIRECTOR. Pittsburgh: University of Pittsburgh Press, 1961. [xiv], 234 p. Illus. Biblio.

Chapters 4 and 5, pp. 62-102, include valuable information on scenic practices at Drury Lane under Garrick's management.

318. _____. "Eighteenth-Century Theatrical Illustrations in the Light of Contemporary Documents." THEATRE NOTEBOOK 14 (1959-60): 45-55. Illus.

Draws on promptbooks and other documents to illuminate iconographic evidence of staging and scenic practices in eighteenth-century England.

319. _____. "Some Notes on Aaron Hill and Stage Scenery." THEATRE NOTEBOOK 12 (1957-58): 29-33.

Discusses slanted wings used in a production of Hill's MEROPE in 1749 and suggests that two earlier productions of Hill's plays may have employed angle perspectives.

320. Croft-Murray, Edward. JOHN DEVOTO: A BAROQUE SCENE
PAINTER. London: Society for Theatre Research, 1953. 16 p. 12 pls.

Devoto was active in the London theatre of the first half of
the eighteenth century.

321. Dobson, Austin. "Loutherbourg, R.A." In his AT PRIOR PARK AND
OTHER PAPERS, pp. 94-127. London: Chatto & Windus, 1912.

An early study of P.J. De Loutherbourg's career as a stage
designer and easel painter. Still useful, and engagingly
written. See also, in this edition, the appendix, pp. 277-81.

322. Donohue, Joseph W., Jr. "Kemble's Production of MACBETH (1794):
Some Notes on Scene Painters, Scenery, Special Effects, and Costumes."
THEATRE NOTEBOOK 21 (1966-67): 63-74. Illus.

Identifies the painters who worked on the production and describes the scenery in detail.

323. Fawcett, Trevor. "Scene-Painting at the Norwich Theatre, 1758-
1799." THEATRE NOTEBOOK 26 (1971-72): 15-19.

Discusses the work of William Williams, James Bunn, and
others.

324. Gage, John. "Loutherbourg: Mystagogue of the Sublime." HISTORY
TODAY 13 (May 1963): 332-39. Illus.

Survey of the career of P.J. De Loutherbourg emphasizing his
"Eidophusikon" and its influence.

325. Highfill, Philip H., Jr.; Burnim, Kalman A.; and Langhans, Edward
A[llen]. A BIOGRAPHICAL DICTIONARY OF ACTORS, ACTRESSES,
MUSICIANS, DANCERS, MANAGERS, & OTHER STAGE PERSONNEL
IN LONDON, 1660-1800. 4 vols. (ABACO-DYNION). Carbondale
and Edwardsville: Southern Illinois University Press, 1973-75. Illus.

The first four of a projected twelve or more volumes. Includes scene painters and machinists. (See, for example,
the informative article on P.J. De Loutherbourg in vol. 4,
pp. 300-314.)

326. Jackson, Allan Stuart. "The Perspective Landscape Scene in the English Theatre, 1660-1682." Ph.D. dissertation, Ohio State University,
1962. 211 p.

Discusses extant designs, evidence from plays, easel painting,
and eyewitness accounts in order to identify the kinds of
landscape scenes used in this period.

327. _____. "Restoration Scenery, 1656-1680." RESTORATION AND
EIGHTEENTH-CENTURY THEATRE RESEARCH 3 (November 1964): 25-
38. Illus.

Examines the use of practical set pieces, types and styles of
designs, and scene painters' sources.

328. Keith, William Grant. "The Designs for the First Movable Scenery
on the English Public Stage." BURLINGTON MAGAZINE 25 (April
1914): 29-33; (May 1914): 85-98. Illus.

Discusses John Webb's designs for Davenant's THE SIEGE OF
RHODES, stressing the influence of Inigo Jones.

329. Kern, Ronald C. "Two Designs by the Elder Thomas Greenwood in
1777." THEATRE NOTEBOOK 15 (1960-61): 31-32. Illus.

330. Langhans, Edward Allen. "Staging Practices in the Restoration Theatres,
1660-1682." Ph.D. dissertation, Yale University, 1955. 544 p.

Equipment and staging practices at the five main public theatres in Restoration London.

331. Lawrence, W[illiam]. J[ohn]. "Art in the Theatre: The Pioneers of
Modern English Stage Mounting: William Capon." MAGAZINE OF
ART 18 (1895): 289-92. Illus.

A sketch of Capon's career, stressing his antiquarian settings
for Drury Lane Theatre in the 1790s.

332. _____. "A Century of Scene-Painting." GENTLEMAN'S MAGAZINE
264 (March 1888): 282-94.

A survey of English scene painting in the eighteenth century,
stressing the reforms made by P.J. De Loutherbourg.

333. _____. "Stage Scenery in the Eighteenth Century." MAGAZINE OF
ART 18 (1895): 385-88. Illus.

Particular attention to John Inigo Richards and P.J. De Loutherbourg.

334. McDowell, John H. "Scenery and Special Effects in Satirical Prints."
OSU THEATRE COLLECTION BULLETIN 3 (Fall 1956): 9-25. Illus.

Examines eighteenth- and early-nineteenth-century English
prints as sources of information on scenery, machinery, and
lighting.

335. Miesle, Frank Leland. "The Staging of Pantomime Entertainments on

the London Stage, 1715-1808." Ph.D. dissertation, Ohio State University, 1955. 376 p.

Discusses literary and performance aspects as well as scenery and machinery.

336. Nicoll, Allardyce. "Doors and Curtains in Restoration Theatres." MODERN LANGUAGE REVIEW 15 (1920): 137-42.

Argues for two doors on each side of the stage at the Theatre Royal, Drury Lane, during the Restoration; discusses the use of the curtain on the Restoration stage. W.J. Lawrence comments on this article in the same volume, pp. 414-20; and Montague Summers adds his comments in 16 (1921): 66-71.

337. _____. "Scenery in Restoration Theatres." ANGLIA 44 (1920): 217-25.

A brief survey, drawing largely on evidence in published plays.

338. Oliver, Anthony, and Saunders, John. "De Loutherbourg and PIZARRO, 1799." THEATRE NOTEBOOK 20 (1965-66): 30-32. Illus.

Attributes a glass painting of a scene in Sheridan's PIZARRO to De Loutherbourg. For a reply, see THEATRE NOTEBOOK 20 (1965-66): 160.

339. Preston, Lillian E. "Loutherbourg's Letters to Garrick." DRAMA CRITIQUE 9 (Winter 1966): 42-44.

Translations of two letters concerning his work as supervisor of scenery at Drury Lane Theatre.

340. _____. "Philippe Jacques de Loutherbourg: Eighteenth Century Romantic Artist and Scene Designer." Ph.D. dissertation, University of Florida, 1957. 315 p.

A survey of his career and an assessment of his contributions to the theatre.

341. Price, Cecil. THEATRE IN THE AGE OF GARRICK. Totowa, N.J.: Rowman & Littlefield, 1973. 212 p. Illus.

Includes an informative chapter, "The Attraction of Spectacle," pp. 61-83, discussing scenery by Jean Servandoni and P.J. De Loutherbourg.

342. Quinn, James Taylor. "Antiquarianism as Moral Theory on the London Stage from 1794 to 1817: A Study of the Interrelationships between the Arts of Poetry and Painting in the Theatrical Productions of John Philip Kemble." Ph.D. dissertation, Ohio University, 1972. 235 p.

343. Rosenfeld, Sybil. "The EIDOPHUSIKON Illustrated." THEATRE NOTE-
BOOK 17 (1963–64): 52–54. Illus.

Reproduces and discusses the only known illustration of P.J.
De Loutherbourg's Eidosphusikon.

344. _____. "Landscape in English Scenery in the Eighteenth Century."
In ESSAYS ON THE EIGHTEENTH–CENTURY ENGLISH STAGE, edited
by Kenneth [R.] Richards and Peter Thomson, pp. 171–78. London:
Methuen, 1972. Illus.

Discusses the work of George Lambert, John Inigo Richards,
P.J. De Loutherbourg, and others.

345. _____. "Scene Designs by William Capon." THEATRE NOTEBOOK
10 (1955–56): 118–22. Illus.

Describes and illustrates rediscovered designs by Capon; summarizes his career.

346. _____. "Scene Painters at the London Theatres in the 18th Century."
THEATRE NOTEBOOK 20 (1965–66): 113–18.

An appendix to the checklist compiled by Rosenfeld and
Edward Croft–Murray (see item 348). A compilation by year
and by London theatre, indicating who worked where, 1704–
1800.

347. _____. "A Transparency by Thomas Greenwood the Elder." THEATRE
NOTEBOOK 19 (1964–65): 21–22. Illus.

Reproduces and discusses an engraving showing Greenwood's
scenery for a spectacle produced in 1779.

348. Rosenfeld, Sybil, and Croft–Murray, Edward. "A Checklist of Scene
Painters Working in Great Britain and Ireland in the 18th Century."
THEATRE NOTEBOOK 19 (1964–65)–20 (1965–66). Illus.

A six–part series providing biographical information, names
and dates of productions, locations of extant designs, and
bibliographical sources.

349. Saxon, A[rthur]. H. "Capon, the Royal Circus, and THE DESTRUCTION
OF THE BASTILLE." THEATRE NOTEBOOK 28 (1974): 133–35. Illus.

Attributes to William Capon the scenery shown in an engraving on a sheet of writing paper, 1789.

350. Southern, Richard. "Aphra Draws Off a Scene." LIFE & LETTERS
TO-DAY 31 (November 1941): 106–14.

Examines the stage directions in Aphra Behn's SIR PATIENT

FANCY (1678) for information about Restoration scenic practices.

351. _____. "Lediard and Early 18th Century Scene Design." THEATRE NOTEBOOK 2 (1947-48): 49-54. Illus.

Reproduces seven engraved illustrations of scene designs by Thomas Lediard (1684-1743) for musical and operatic performances in Hamburg and London, 1725-32. Discusses the significance of these engravings, particularly with reference to transparent scenery. (This issue of THEATRE NOTEBOOK also includes a biographical sketch of Lediard, by Sybil Rosenfeld, and a bibliographical description of seven of his books, by I.K. Fletcher.)

352. _____. "An Old Bristol Theatre: The Puzzle of the Sloat." LIFE & LETTERS TO-DAY 22 (September 1939): 426-33.

Examines an eighteenth-century mechanism for raising drops and set pieces from under the stage.

353. _____. "The Stage Groove and the Thunder Run." ARCHITECTURAL REVIEW 95 (May 1944): 135-36.

Machinery at the Theatre Royal, Bristol.

354. Thomas, Russell. "Contemporary Taste in the Stage Decorations of London Theaters, 1770-1800." MODERN PHILOLOGY 42 (1944): 65-78.

An informative investigation of many aspects of scene painting in the late-eighteenth-century theatre, noting an increasing taste for romantic realism.

355. Watters, Don Albert. "The Pictorial in English Theatrical Staging, 1773-1833." Ph.D. dissertation, Ohio State University, 1954. 388 p.

Examines changes in scenery and theatre architecture resulting from the taste for "picturesqueness" in theatrical productions.

356. Wells, Mitchell. "Spectacular Scenic Effects of the Eighteenth-Century Pantomime." PHILOLOGICAL QUARTERLY 17 (1938): 67-81.

D. NINETEENTH CENTURY

SEE ALSO items 334, 342, and 355.

357. Adelsperger, Walter. "Aspects of Staging ADELGITHA." OSU THEATRE COLLECTION BULLETIN 7 (1960): 14-34. Illus.

A reconstruction of the scenery used in a production of
Matthew G. Lewis's ADELGITHA at Covent Garden in 1818.

358. Allen, Walter J. "The Art Decoration of the Stage." BUILDING
NEWS 36 (1879): 286-87.

Mainly concerns nineteenth-century scenery in England.

359. Archer, William. "Art in the Theatre: The Limitations of Scenery."
MAGAZINE OF ART 19 (1896): 432-36.

Defends illusionistic scenery as suitable to proscenium theatres,
but condemns productions that rely wholly on elaborate scenery.

360. _____. "Scene-Painter and Actor." MAGAZINE OF ART 6 (1883):
314-16.

"Thespis' cart has become a furniture van." Shakespearean
productions require simplicity; the producer must avoid "ir-
relevant and distracting splendour."

361. Armstrong, William A. "Madame Vestris: A Centenary Appreciation."
THEATRE NOTEBOOK 11 (1956-57): 11-18. Illus.

Largely concerned with her innovations in scenery and costume.

362. _____. "Peter Nicholson and the Scenographic Art." THEATRE
NOTEBOOK 8 (1953-54): 91-96. Illus.

Summarizes and comments on an article about scenery written
by Nicholson for Abraham Rees's CYCLOPAEDIA (see item 412).

363. Arnott, J.F. "Two Drawings by Alexander Nasmyth." THEATRE NOTE-
BOOK 13 (1958-59): 18-20. Illus.

Discusses and reproduces designs by Nasmyth for Scottish theatres in 1792 and 1820.

364. "The Art Movement: Act Drops by Mr. A.J. Black in the New Metropolitan Theatres." MAGAZINE OF ART 24 (1900): 519-21. Illus.,
one in color.

Brief text and illustrations of six designs for act drops for
theatres in and around London.

365. THE ART OF SCENE PAINTING. By practical scenic artists. London:
Samuel French, 1879. 24 p.

A scarce practical guide intended primarily for amateurs.

366. Bangham, [P.] Jerald. "Samuel Phelps: Producer of Shakespeare at Sadler's Wells." OSU THEATRE COLLECTION BULLETIN 6 (1959): 9–20. Illus.

Provides information on the scenery and effects in Phelps's productions, 1844–62. Illustrations from four promptbooks.

367. Benwell, Henry N. "Practical Scene Painting for Amateurs." AMATEUR WORK 4 (December 1884)–7 (November 1888). Illus.

An informative thirty-one part series by a professional scene painter concerning tools, materials, perspective and painting techniques, definitions of technical terms, etc. Applicable, on the whole, to the professional as well as the amateur theatre. Excellent illustrations. This series is discussed by Richard Southern in THEATRE NOTEBOOK 1 (1945–47): 61–62.

368. Berry, Douglas M. "William Telbin's Theories of Scene Painting: The Aesthetic of Romantic Realism." THEATRE STUDIES 21 (1974–75): 52–60. Illus.

Interprets a series of articles that Telbin the Younger (d. 1931) wrote for the MAGAZINE OF ART, 1889–1895.

369. Blakely, Clyde. "A Reconstruction of the Masque Scene from Charles Kean's THE TEMPEST." OSU THEATRE COLLECTION BULLETIN 13 (1966): 38–45. Illus.

Concerns Kean's production at the Princess's Theatre, London, 1857. Illustrations from promptbooks.

370. Bogusch, George E. "Clarkson Stanfield, R.A.: Scene Painter, Artist, Gentleman, and Friend." QUARTERLY JOURNAL OF SPEECH 56 (1970): 245–55.

A study of this English scene painter's career, with particular attention to his association with William Charles Macready.

371. Buckle, J[ames]. G[eorge]. THEATRE CONSTRUCTION AND MAINTENANCE. London: "The Stage" Office, 1888. 157 p. Illus.

"The Stage and Its Appurtenances," pp. 31–46; "Gas Lighting," pp. 72–79; "Electric Lighting," pp. 79–82.

372. Butler, James H. "Early Nineteenth-Century Stage Settings in the British Theatre." THEATRE SURVEY 6 (1965): 54–64. Illus.

Examines frontispiece etchings and engravings in published plays, 1800–1850, for evidence about scenery and properties, especially ceiling pieces and box sets.

373. Byrne, Muriel St. Clare. "Early Multiple Settings in England." THE-
ATRE NOTEBOOK 8 (1953-54): 81-86. Illus.

Discusses early-nineteenth-century settings that permitted the
audience to see action in more than one room of a building.
For a short rejoinder, see THEATRE NOTEBOOK 9 (1954-55): 15.

374. Cundall, H.M. "Charles Kean, F.S.A., and Theatrical Scenery." ART
JOURNAL (1903): 199-206. Illus.

Describes a collection of stage designs newly acquired by the
Victoria and Albert Museum. All were executed for Kean's
productions at the Princess's Theatre, London, in the 1850s.
Twelve illustrations.

375. Dircks, Henry. THE GHOST! AS PRODUCED IN THE SPECTRE DRAMA
. . . BY THE APPARATUS CALLED THE DIRCKSIAN PHANTASMAGORIA
. . . . London: Spon, 1863. 102 p. Illus.

Describes an optical illusion invented by the author and exhibited under the name "Pepper's Ghost."

376. Fitzgerald, Percy. "On Scenic Illusion and Stage Appliances." JOUR-
NAL OF THE ROYAL SOCIETY OF ARTS 35 (18 March 1887): 456-66.

Explains the working of some special effects (thunder, lightning,
traps, etc.), then describes, unsympathetically, the recent
transition from flats and wings to built-up scenery illuminated
with colored light.

377. _____. "What is 'The Scene'?" LIVING AGE 215 (23 October 1897):
274-79.

Criticizes faults in the prevailing system of spectacular realism
and proposes suggestive scenery--perhaps a return to drops and
wings--to provide a generalized background. (Reprinted from
GENTLEMAN'S MAGAZINE.)

378. Forsyth, Gerald. "Wilhelm: A Noted Victorian Theatrical Designer."
THEATRE NOTEBOOK 11 (1956-57): 55-58. Illus.

Summary of the career of William John Charles Pitcher (1858-
1925), who designed scenery and costumes in England under
the name "Wilhelm." Informative illustrations of four scenic
models for pantomimes, which were his specialty.

379. Godwin, Edward W. "The Architecture and Costume of Shakespeare's
Plays." ARCHITECT 12 (31 October 1874)-13 (26 June 1875).

A thirty-part series devoted to the "archaeology" of settings
and costumes for Shakespeare's plays. An excellent example

(perhaps the best) of Victorian antiquarianism in Shakespeare production.

380. Hamblin, Junius N. "The Artistic Approach of the Grieve Family to Selected Problems of Nineteenth-Century Scene Painting." Ph.D. dissertation, Ohio State University, 1966. 332 p.

An attempt to define the Grieve style.

381. Harbron, Dudley. THE CONSCIOUS STONE: THE LIFE OF EDWARD WILLIAM GODWIN. London: Latimer House, 1949. 208 p. Illus.

Includes two chapters largely concerned with Godwin's theatrical work.

382. Harris, Augustus. "Art in the Theatre: Spectacle." MAGAZINE OF ART 12 (1889): 109-13. Illus.

Notes improvements in the production of spectacles in London theatres. Illustrations of scenery by Wilhelm and T.E. Ryan.

383. Hatton, Joseph. "A Propos of the Lyceum FAUST." ART JOURNAL (1886): 24-28, 57-61. Illus.

Henry Irving's production, with scenery by Hawes Craven, William Telbin, and others. The illustrations include an engraving after one of Craven's scenic models.

384. Hawley, James A. "Touring with Benson." OSU THEATRE COLLECTION BULLETIN 6 (1959): 25-30. Illus., diags.

Examines Frank R. Benson's promptbooks to identify the scenic practices of his touring company in the late nineteenth century.

385. Herkomer, Hubert von. "Art in the Theatre: The Pictorial Music-Play: 'An Idyl.'" MAGAZINE OF ART 12 (1889): 316-24. Illus.

Concerns his experiments with "pictorial music-plays," in which he attempted integration of music, song, scenery, lighting, and action.

386. _____. "Scenic-Art." MAGAZINE OF ART 15 (1892): 259-64, 316-21. Port.

First presented as a lecture at the Lyceum Theatre, London. Promotes carefully arranged lighting (including instruments placed in the auditorium), abolition of footlights, an adjustable proscenium, and projected images.

387. Herman, Henry. "Art in the Theatre: The Stage as a School of Art

and Archaeology." MAGAZINE OF ART 11 (1888): 332-37. Illus.

Condemns common errors in historical accuracy and urges the use of the stage for archaeological instruction.

388. Hewitt, Barnard [W.]. "Herkomer: Forerunner of Gordon Craig." PLAYERS 18 (May 1942): 6, 23-24.

Describes Herkomer's experiments with scenery and lighting at his private theatre, beginning in 1889.

389. Hunter, Jack W[orth]. "The Rise of Realism on the Eighteenth- and Nineteenth-Century Stage." OSU THEATRE COLLECTION BULLETIN 5 (1958): 27-39.

Mainly concerned with the development of enclosed settings (box sets) in England in the nineteenth century.

390. _____. "Some Research Problems in a Study of THE CORSICAN BROTHERS." OSU THEATRE COLLECTION BULLETIN 9 (1962): 6-22. Illus.

Examines the construction and operation of the "Corsican trap" used for the ghost's appearance in this nineteenth-century play.

391. Huston, Hollis W. "Macready's RICHELIEU Promptbooks: Evolution of the Enclosed Setting." THEATRE STUDIES 21 (1974-75): 41-51. Illus.

Draws on promptbooks and George Scharf's RECOLLECTIONS to show that W.C. Macready used enclosed settings in his 1839 production of the play at Covent Garden.

392. Jackson, Allan S[tuart]., and Morrow, John C[harles]. "Aqua Scenes at Sadler's Wells Theatre, 1804-1824." OSU THEATRE COLLECTION BULLETIN 9 (1962): 22-47. Illus.

Describes the water tank built under the stage at Sadler's Wells; discusses scenery and special effects in the "aquadramas" produced there.

393. Kernodle, George R. "Stage Spectacle and Victorian Society." QUAR-TERLY JOURNAL OF SPEECH 40 (1954): 31-36.

Suggests that crowd scenes and spectacular effects were integral parts of dramatic structure in some Victorian plays.

394. Kilburn, Michael. "Nineteenth-Century Timber Stage Machinery at the Theatre Royal [Bristol]." ARCHITECTURAL REVIEW 153 (February 1973): 131. Illus.

395. Lancaster, Harry. "Stage Scenery, Decoration, Upholstery, Furniture, and Effects." FURNITURE GAZETTE, n.s. 3 (10 April 1875)-n.s. 5 (19 February 1876).

An informative series of articles by a practicing scene painter. Mainly a practical guide; also includes historical data and anecdotes about nineteenth-century English scene painters and productions.

396. Lawrence, W[illiam]. J[ohn]. "Scenery and Scenic Artists." GENTLE-MAN'S MAGAZINE 266 (June 1889): 608-14.

Miscellaneous notes and anecdotes about nineteenth-century scene painting in England, with a few remarks about the inferior work produced by scenic studios in the United States.

397. _____. "Scenery on Tour." MAGAZINE OF ART 19 (1896): 476-79. Illus.

Fears that the decline of provincial stock companies in England will lead to wide use of scenery from American-style scenic studios producing mechanical work.

398. _____. "Some Stage Effects: Their Growth and History." GENTLE-MAN'S MAGAZINE 265 (July 1888): 83-95.

Moving panoramas, multiple settings, gauzes for clouds, and other effects. Refers mainly to nineteenth-century productions in England.

399. "The Limits of Scenic Effect." GRAPHIC 1 (4 December 1869): 11.

An early protest against built-up scenery and realistic box sets, suggesting that they destroy a desirable romantic effect.

400. Lloyds, Frederick. PRACTICAL GUIDE TO SCENE PAINTING AND PAINTING IN DISTEMPER. London: George Rowney & Co., [1875]. vi, 97 p. Illus., part color.

A valuable documentation of nineteenth-century techniques by a well-known professional scene painter. Straightforward, practical instructions for painting landscapes, architectural scenes, and "fairy scenes" for pantomimes; explanations of technical processes such as glazing and scumbling; some notes on the placing of lights. Illustrated with colored lithographs showing progressive stages in painting a scene, and with pasted-down paint swatches showing colors wet and dry.

401. Marker, Frederick J. "The First Night of Charles Kean's THE TEMPEST --from the Notebook of Hans Christian Andersen." THEATRE NOTE-BOOK 25 (1970-71): 20-23. Illus.

Andersen provides details of Kean's scenery and mechanical effects, among which was a collapsible ship made of inflated canvas.

402. Marlis, Alan Philip. "Augustus Welby Northmore Pugin's Influence in Theatre." Ph.D. dissertation, City University of New York, 1974. 339 p.

A study of the little-known theatre work of a skillful designer and mechanic whose scenery for theatres in London and Paris was influential in promoting the Gothic style.

403. Mayer, David III. HARLEQUIN IN HIS ELEMENT: THE ENGLISH PANTOMIME, 1806-1836. Cambridge, Mass.: Harvard University Press, 1969. 417 p. Illus. Biblio.

Text includes discussion of scenery and machinery; appendix transcribes, with illustrations, "the only extant document from the early nineteenth century that discusses the construction and operation of pantomime trickwork."

404. Merchant, W. Moelwyn. "On looking at THE MERCHANT OF VENICE." In ESSAYS ON NINETEENTH CENTURY BRITISH THEATRE, edited by Kenneth [R.] Richards and Peter Thomson, pp. 171-78. London: Methuen, 1971.

Discusses historical accuracy in London productions of the play, especially the ideas of Edward W. Godwin.

405. "Modern Stage Mechanism." SCIENTIFIC AMERICAN 81 (7 October 1899): 232-33. Illus.

Electric motors and hydraulic power to lift sections of the stage at Drury Lane Theatre.

406. Morrow, John Charles. "The Staging of Pantomime at Sadler's Wells Theatre, 1828-1860." Ph.D. dissertation, Ohio State University, 1963. 393 p.

Emphasizes scenery, special effects, and acting. Reconstructs two pantomimes, drawing on promptbooks and pictorial sources.

407. "Moving (Dioramic) Experiences." ALL THE YEAR ROUND 17 (1867): 304-7.

A humorous account of exhibitions of moving dioramas in England, including some useful information about methods of operation and audience behavior.

408. "A New Stage Stride." ALL THE YEAR ROUND 10 (1863): 229-34.

Informative description of the Continental system of scenery (wing-chariots and flown drops) installed at the Lyceum Theatre, London, under the supervision of the actor Charles Fechter.

409. "On Cosmoramas, Dioramas, and Panoramas." PENNY MAGAZINE 11 (1842): 363-64.

Brief descriptions of each, mentioning some notable examples.

410. Phillabaum, Corliss E. "Chambers' Prompt Book with Hawes Craven Designs." OSU THEATRE COLLECTION BULLETIN 6 (1959): 35-41. Illus.

Craven's designs from an 1895 production of ROMEO AND JULIET may have been adapted for another production in the 1930s.

411. _____. "Panoramic Scenery at Sadler's Wells." OSU THEATRE COLLECTION BULLETIN 6 (1959): 20-25. Illus.

Moving panoramas in Samuel Phelps's productions of PERICLES (1854), TIMON OF ATHENS (1851 or 1856), and THE TEMPEST (1849).

412. Rees, Abraham. THE CYCLOPAEDIA; OR, UNIVERSAL DICTIONARY OF ARTS, SCIENCES, AND LITERATURE. 39 vols., 6 vols. pls. London: Longman, Hurst, Rees, Orme & Brown, 1819-20.

Volume 12 (1819) includes a valuable six-page article, "Dramatic Machinery," concerning stage construction, traps, systems of wing-changing at Covent Garden and at the Theatre Royal, Glasgow, and machinery for flying a chariot, making waves, and effecting magical transformations. All these techniques are illustrated in two plates labeled "Miscellanies," in volume 3 of the plates (1820). Volume 31 (1819) includes a five-page article, "Scenography," by Peter Nicholson, concerning theatrical perspective painting. Volume 4 of the plates (1820) includes diagrams to illustrate Nicholson's remarks. William A. Armstrong discusses Nicholson's article in THEATRE NOTEBOOK 8 (1953-54): 91-96.

413. Rohrig, Gladys May. "An Analysis of Certain Acting Editions and Promptbooks of Plays by Dion Boucicault." Ph.D. dissertation, Ohio State University, 1956. 208 p.

Examines promptbooks of Boucicault's plays to identify production and playwriting practices in England and the United States, 1841-74.

414.　Rosenfeld, Sybil.　"The Grieve Family."　In ANATOMY OF AN IL-
LUSION (see item 102), pp. 39–44, 85–86.　Illus.

Excellent study of the careers of John Henderson Grieve, his
sons Thomas and William, and Thomas's son, Thomas Walford
Grieve.

415.　_____.　"Neo-Classical Scenery in England:　A Footnote to the Exhibition of 'The Age of Neo-Classicism.'"　THEATRE NOTEBOOK 27
(1972–73):　67–71.　Illus.

Provides a useful list of characteristics of neoclassical scene
designs; discusses some English examples; and reproduces photographs of six designs.

416.　_____.　"A Sadler's Wells Scene Book."　THEATRE NOTEBOOK 15
(1960–61):　57–62.　Illus.

Concerns designs by Robert C. Andrews, Luke Clint, and John
Henderson Grieve.

417.　_____.　"Scene Designs by Hodgins the Younger."　THEATRE NOTE-
BOOK 27 (1972–73):　22–25.　Illus.

Survey of the career of a scene painter who worked at Covent
Garden from 1796 to 1826; reproductions of five surviving
designs.

418.　"Scenery and Decorations of Theatres."　BUILDER 5 (1847):　216–17.

Report on a paper read by Mr. Dwyer at a meeting of the
Decorative Art Society, London.　Dwyer suggested that wings
should be slanted, borders abolished, and perspective effects
improved.

419.　S[charf]., G[eorge].　RECOLLECTIONS OF THE SCENIC EFFECTS OF
COVENT GARDEN THEATRE DURING THE SEASON 1838-9.　London:
James Pattie, 1839.

Issued in fourteen parts, each with its own paper wrapper, and
each with three engraved sketches.　The productions are HAM-
LET, OTHELLO, WERNER, VIRGINIUS, MACBETH, KING
LEAR, THE LADY OF LYONS, CORIOLANUS, THE TWO
FOSCARI, ION, THE TEMPEST, WILLIAM TELL, RICHELIEU,
and HENRY V.　A valuable record of William C. Macready's
productions.

420.　Southern, Richard.　"Interesting Matter Relating to the Scenery, Decoration, Etc., of the Theatre Royal at Ipswich."　ARCHITECTURAL REVIEW
100 (August 1946):　41–44.　Illus.

Notes on a manuscript compiled in the late nineteenth century
by a manager of the Ipswich Theatre, H.S. Eyre, who described its scenery and stage machinery.

421. _____. "The Problem of A.B.'s Theatre Drawings." THEATRE NOTE-
BOOK 4 (1949-50): 58-62. Illus.

Concerns sixteen drawings of English theatre interiors (all reproduced) by an unidentified artist of the 1860s. All show
scenery onstage in some detail.

422. _____. "Scenery at the Book League." THEATRE NOTEBOOK 5
(1950-51): 35-38. Illus.

An album of designs from Drury Lane, early nineteenth century; a design in a promptbook from 1834; and an album of
designs by John O'Connor for the Shakespeare Memorial Theatre, 1879.

423. _____. "Trick-Work in the English Nineteenth Century Theatre."
LIFE & LETTERS TO-DAY 21 (May 1939): 94-101.

A popular treatment, mainly about various kinds of traps.

424. _____. THE VICTORIAN THEATRE: A PICTORIAL SURVEY. New
York: Theatre Arts Books, 1970. 112 p. Prof. illus. Biblio.

Mainly illustrations with explanatory captions. Most of them
depict scenery and machinery. Among the chapters are "How
Victorian Stages Worked" and "Victorian Scene-painting."

425. Southern, Richard, et al. "A Bristol Theatre Royal Inventory." In
STUDIES IN ENGLISH THEATRE HISTORY, pp. 98-113. London:
Society for Theatre Research, 1952.

Transcription of an 1829 inventory of scenery, machinery,
properties, lights, and furnishings, with commentary.

426. Spanabel, Robert R. "Charles Kean's HENRY THE FIFTH." OSU
THEATRE COLLECTION BULLETIN 17 (1970): 6-19. Illus.

Includes reproductions of seven designs for this production,
from the collection at the Victoria and Albert Museum.

427. Speaight, George. "An English Scene Painter in America." THEATRE
NOTEBOOK 10 (1955-56): 122-24.

Brief summary of the career of Luke Clint, who worked at
Sadler's Wells, 1813-18, then emigrated to Savannah, Georgia.

428. Spielmann, M.H. "Art in the Theatre: The Development of Spectacle, as Exemplified in the Ballet of FAUST." MAGAZINE OF ART 19 (1896): 25-28. Illus.

   Praise of the unity of style in this production designed by Wilhelm.

429. _____. "Art in the Theatre: II. A Shakespearean Revival: 'Macbeth.'" MAGAZINE OF ART 12 (1889): 98-100. Illus.

   Discusses the historical research undertaken for a forthcoming revival by Henry Irving, with scenery by Hawes Craven.

430. Stokes, John. RESISTIBLE THEATRES. London: Paul Elek, 1972. 203 p. Illus. Biblio.

   Chapters on Edward W. Godwin's "aesthetic theatre" and Hubert von Herkomer's "pictorial music-plays," as well as discussion of experiments with "color music" by A. Wallace Rimington and others.

431. Strange, Edward F. "The Scenery of Charles Kean's Plays and the Great Scene-Painters of His Day." MAGAZINE OF ART 26 (1902): 454-59, 514-18. Illus.

   Describes a collection of designs newly acquired by the Victoria and Albert Museum.

432. Telbin, William [the Younger]. "Art in the Theatre: Act Drops." MAGAZINE OF ART 18 (1895): 335-40. Illus.

   Discusses styles of painting act drops: architecture, allegory, landscapes, and painted draperies.

433. _____. "Art in the Theatre: I. Scenery." MAGAZINE OF ART 12 (1889): 92-97. Illus.

   Miscellaneous comments on scenic practices in England, defending Irving-style realism and commenting on the work of his father.

434. _____. "Art in the Theatre: The Painting of Scenery." MAGAZINE OF ART 12 (1889): 195-201. Illus.

   Discusses the preparation of scenery, from the first conference to model making, construction, painting, and lighting. Good illustrations.

435. _____. "Art in the Theatre: The Question of Reform." MAGAZINE OF ART 17 (1894): 44-48. Illus.

   A response to Hubert von Herkomer's articles in the MAGA-

ZINE OF ART (see item 386). Agrees that traditional auditorium style and sky borders are deplorable, but sees no alternatives. Defends footlights and argues against an adjustable proscenium.

436. _____. "The Painting of Panoramas." MAGAZINE OF ART 24 (1900): 555-58. Illus.

Largely refers to nineteenth-century British panoramas.

437. Tree, Herbert Beerbohm. "The Staging of Shakespeare." FORTNIGHTLY REVIEW 74 (July 1900): 52-66.

A defense of the archaeological, splendidly upholstered style of Shakespeare production. For replies, see FORTNIGHTLY REVIEW 74 (September 1900): 504-12, and WESTMINSTER REVIEW 154 (October 1900): 427-31.

438. Turner, Godfrey. "Scenery, Dresses and Decoration." THEATRE (London), n.s. 3 (1 March 1884): 126-34.

A chatty survey of scenery and effects in England since the early nineteenth century, particularly in Shakespeare productions.

439. Von Hagen, Victor Wolfgang. FREDERICK CATHERWOOD ARCHT. New York: Oxford University Press, 1950. 196 p. Illus. Biblio.

Includes two chapters on Catherwood's activities as a panoramist in London and New York, plus an excellent brief bibliography of panoramas.

440. Watson, Ernest Bradlee. SHERIDAN TO ROBERTSON: A STUDY OF THE NINETEENTH-CENTURY LONDON STAGE. Cambridge, Mass.: Harvard University Press, 1926. 504 p. Illus. Biblio.

441. Weeks, Lyman H. "Scenic Art in Mr. Irving's 'Faust.'" In THE DRAMATIC YEAR: 1887-88, edited by Edward Fuller, pp. 42-51. Boston: Ticknor and Co., 1889.

Praises the historical accuracy, subtle color, and harmony of the scenery, costumes, and lighting of this famous Henry Irving production.

442. Wilde, Oscar. "Shakespeare and Stage Costume." NINETEENTH CENTURY 17 (May 1885): 800-818.

Mainly concerns historical accuracy in costumes, but includes some perceptive general observations on production style. Defends archaeological research as necessary to create illusion.

Revised and published as "The Truth of Masks" in Wilde's
INTENTIONS (London: Osgood, McIlvaine, 1891), pp. 217-
58.

443.   Wilhelm, C.   "Art in the Theatre: Art in the Ballet."   MAGAZINE
OF ART 18 (1895):   12-16, 48-53.   Illus.

"C. Wilhelm" was the professional name of William John
Charles Pitcher, an English stage designer.   Here he reviews
current trends in costume design for ballet and pantomime,
criticizes typical lighting practices of the day, and describes
his method of harmonizing colors in costumes and scenery.

444.   Wilson, M[ardis]. Glen, Jr.   "The Box Set in Charles Kean's Productions of Shakespearean Tragedy."   OSU THEATRE COLLECTION BUL-
LETIN 5 (1958):   7-26.   Illus.

Examines seven tragedies staged at the Princess's Theatre, London, in the 1850s.

445.   _____.   "OSU Theatre Collection Studies on Charles Kean, with Notes
on a Scene from Kean's 'Henry VIII.'"   OSU THEATRE COLLECTION
BULLETIN 13 (1966):   27-37.   Illus.

Concerns Kean's scenery for act 3, scene 1 of HENRY VIII.

446.   _____.   "THE WIFE'S SECRET: History of a Victorian Play."   THE-
ATRE STUDIES 20 (1973-74):   9-23.   Illus.

Discusses the staging of Charles Kean's revivals of this play
by George Lovell, at the Princess's Theatre, London, in the
1850s.   The illustrations include designs by Frederick Lloyds
and W. Gordon.

447.   Woodrow, Ernest A.E.   "Theatres."   BUILDING NEWS 64 (10 February
1893):   188-89; (10 March 1893):   330-31; (24 March 1893):   398-99;
65 (22 September 1893):   366-68; (29 September 1893):   426-27.   Illus.

Parts of a series of articles mainly concerned with theatre
architecture.   These five parts describe the construction of the
stage floor, stage bridges, traps, gridiron, scene-painting studio, and carpenter's shop.   Good illustrations.

E. TWENTIETH CENTURY

SEE ALSO items 122, 410.

448.   Abbott, Claude C., and Bertram, Anthony, eds.   POET AND PAINTER:

BEING THE CORRESPONDENCE BETWEEN GORDON BOTTOMLEY
AND PAUL NASH, 1910-1946. London and New York: Oxford University Press, 1955. 295 p. Illus.

Numerous references to Nash's stage designs.

449. Amery, Colin. "'How to Lower a Cloud with Persons in It.'" ARCHITECTURAL REVIEW 152 (December 1972): 354-56. Illus.

Illustrates and discusses John Bury's flying machinery for a 1972 production of Monteverdi's RETURN OF ULYSSES at Glyndebourne.

450. Ayrton, Michael. "The Decor of Sadler's Wells Ballets, 1939-1946." In BALLET ANNUAL 1947, pp. 74-81. London: A. & C. Black, 1947. Illus., part color.

Remarks on the work of a dozen designers.

451. Bablet, Denis. EDWARD GORDON CRAIG. Translated by Daphne Woodward. New York: Theatre Arts Books, n.d. [c. 1966]. ix, 207 p. Illus.

"An account of his development and a description of the landmarks in his career." A serious study by a perceptive scholar.

452. Battersby, Martin. "Claud Lovat Fraser, 1890-1921." ART AND ARTISTS 4 (November 1969): 38-41. Illus.

Sketch of his career, with reproductions of four stage designs.

453. Baughan, E.A. "The Background of Drama." NINETEENTH CENTURY AND AFTER 61 (1907): 256-64.

Condemns elaborate spectacle in Shakespeare productions such as those of H. Beerbohm Tree; promotes "impressionistic suggestion rather than inartistic reality."

454. Beaton, Cecil. "Designing for Ballet." DANCE INDEX 5 (1946): 184-204. Illus.

Recollections of Diaghilev's ballets and discussion of the scenic requirements of ballet.

455. _____. THE WANDERING YEARS: DIARIES, 1922-1939. London: Weidenfeld & Nicholson, 1961. 387 p. Illus.

The first of a series of diaries.

456. Beaumont, Cyril W. "'The Emperor and the Nightingale': Michael Martin-Harvey's Costumes and Settings for His Operetta." STUDIO 127

(January 1944): 13-17. Illus., part color.

457. _____. "Hugh Stevenson: Designer for the Theatre." STUDIO 127 (April 1944): 122-26. Illus., part color.

458. Bertram, Anthony. PAUL NASH: THE PORTRAIT OF AN ARTIST. London: Faber and Faber, 1955. 336 p. Illus. Biblio.

"Designs for the Theatre: 1911-1927," pp. 123-28. Excellent bibliography.

459. Billington, Michael, and Waterhouse, Robert. "The Designer Talks." PLAYS AND PLAYERS 17 (October 1969)-18 (December 1970).

A series of brief, illustrated profiles of contemporary stage designers, including the following British artists (in alphabetical order): Jocelyn Herbert (September 1970), Ralph Koltai (November 1969), Christopher Morley (January 1970), Timothy O'Brien (October 1969), Julia Trevelyan Oman (July 1970), Patrick Robertson (April 1970), Carl Toms (December 1970), and Tony Walton (February 1970).

460. Bland, Alexander. "Recent Ballet Design." In BALLET ANNUAL 1963, pp. 58-62. London: A. & C. Black, 1963.

Refers to ballet in Britain.

461. Bottomley, Gordon. "Charles Ricketts, R.A." THEATRE ARTS 16 (1932): 377-95. Illus.

An informative biographical sketch illustrated with a portrait photograph and seven excellent production photographs.

462. _____. "The Theatre Work of Paul Nash." THEATRE ARTS 8 (1924): 38-48. Illus.

463. Boys, Arthur. "Oliver Messel--English Designer." SOUVENIRS DE BALLET, no. 1 (1949): 28-39. Illus.

Describes Messel's work on designs for SLEEPING BEAUTY.

464. Browne, Van Dyke [pseud]. SECRETS OF SCENE PAINTING AND STAGE EFFECTS. London: George Routledge & Sons; New York: E.P. Dutton & Co., n.d. [c. 1913]. 75 p. Illus., part color.

Practical discussion of tools, materials, and techniques of scene painting, scene changing, and effects such as thunder and rain. Primarily intended for amateurs.

465. Browse, Lillian, ed. LESLIE HURRY: SETTINGS & COSTUMES FOR

SADLER'S WELLS BALLETS. [London]: Published for the Shenval Press by Faber and Faber, [1946]. 72 p. Illus., one in color.

Sketch of his career and an assessment of his contributions, by Cyril Beaumont, pp. 5-15, and fifty illustrations.

466.   Buckle, Richard. "Sophie Fedorovitch." BALLET ANNUAL 1954, pp. 58-61. London: A. & C. Black, 1954. Illus.

A tribute and commentary.

467.   Bulloch, J.M. "New Theory of Stage Production." LAMP 27 (August 1903): 23-27. Illus., port.

A discussion of Gordon Craig's early productions in London. One of the first articles on Craig to appear in an American periodical.

468.   Byles, R.S. "Concerning Diagonal Curtain Tracks." THEATRE NOTE-BOOK 8 (1953-54): 11-15. Illus.

Explains and illustrates a system of diagonal curtains used in the 1953 Old Vic production of HENRY V.

469.   Cheney, Sheldon. "Gordon Craig, the Theatre's Chief Revolutionary." THEATRE ARTS 11 (1927): 919-26.

Recollections of a recent talk with Craig and an appreciation of his contributions to the theatre.

470.   Child, Harold. "'Attila' and the Art of Stage Production." BURLING-TON MAGAZINE 12 (1907): 3-6.

Describes some of the obstacles in the way of stage reform, then discusses Charles Ricketts's designs for Binyon's ATTILA at Her Majesty's Theatre, London.

471.   "Conversation: Nicholas Georgiadis and Ralph Koltai." DRAMA (London), no. 95 (Winter 1969): 44-58. Illus.

Two British designers talk about their work and about some of the problems of the contemporary designer.

472.   Cooper, Courtney Ryley. "Gordon Craig--Genius?" GREEN BOOK ALBUM 6 (August 1911): 388-93.

A sympathetic survey of Craig's achievements, particularly his work with screens and stage lighting.

473.   Corathiel, Elisabethe H.C. "The Creative Artist in the Theatre." THE-ATRE WORLD 45 (November 1949)-61 (December 1965).

Two series of brief, illustrated profiles of contemporary stage
designers, including the following British artists (in alphabetical order): Michael Annals (April 1964), James Bailey (Jan-
uary 1956), Henry Bardon (August 1965), Martin Battersby
(April 1962), Cecil Beaton (June 1965), John Bury (February
1964), Joseph Carl (December 1949), Hugh Casson (July 1955),
Nicholas Georgiadis (February 1961), Barbara Hepworth (April
1955), Leslie Hurry (May 1953), Disley Jones (February 1962),
Sean Kenny (October 1961), George Kirsta (November 1949),
Ralph Koltai (September 1963), Osbert Lancaster (June 1954),
Oliver Messel (May 1950), Tanya Moiseiwitsch (February 1963),
Motley (October 1962), Richard Negri (January 1963), Thea
Neu (January 1957), Timothy O'Brien (February 1965), Gower
Parks (March 1950), John Piper (July 1953), Malcolm Pride
(September 1964), Peter Rice (May 1956), Kenneth Rowell
(November 1960), Loudon Sainthill (April 1954), Hutchinson
Scott (March 1963), Yolanda Sonnabend (December 1965),
Alix Stone (April 1965), N.H. ("Toni") Stubbing (January
1958), Carl Toms (January 1964), John Truscott (September
1965), Tony Walton (June 1963), and Michael Whittaker (Sep-
tember 1959).

474. Cournos, John. "Gordon Craig and the Theatre of the Future." PO-
ETRY AND DRAMA 1 (September 1913): 334-40.

A sympathetic commentary on Craig's work.

475. Craig, Edward [Anthony]. "Gordon Craig and Bach's ST. MATTHEW
PASSION." THEATRE NOTEBOOK 26 (1971-72): 147-51. Illus.

The author describes the evolution of his father's project for
a setting for the PASSION. Illustrated with four photographs
and a drawing of Craig's model as reconstructed by the author.

476. _____. "Gordon Craig and Hubert von Herkomer." THEATRE RE-
SEARCH / RECHERCHES THEATRALES 10 (1969-70): 7-16. Illus.

An important account of Craig's youth and of the considerable
influence Herkomer had on him. The author reconstructs the
scenery and lighting of Craig's production of DIDO AND
AENEAS, 1900.

477. _____. GORDON CRAIG: THE STORY OF HIS LIFE. New York:
Alfred A. Knopf, 1968. 398 p. Illus. Biblio.

An indispensable biography by Craig's son.

478. Craig, Edward Gordon. INDEX TO THE STORY OF MY DAYS. London: Hulton Press, 1957. vii, 308 p. Illus.

Craig's memoirs, incomplete (to 1907 only) and often frustrat-
ingly impressionistic, but fascinating nonetheless.

479.   . ON THE ART OF THE THEATRE. London: William Heinemann,
1924. 318 p. Illus.

Craig's best known book (first published in shorter form in
1905), in which he explains his theory of theatrical production. This and later editions include a new preface in which
Craig clarifies his ideas about the "Super-marionette."

480.   . A PRODUCTION: BEING THIRTY-TWO COLLOTYPE PLATES
OF DESIGNS PROJECTED OR REALISED FOR "THE PRETENDERS" OF
HENRIK IBSEN AND PRODUCED AT THE ROYAL THEATRE COPEN-
HAGEN 1926. London: Oxford University Press, 1930. Folio. 21 p.
32 pls., part color.

481.   . SCENE. London: Oxford University Press, 1923. xi, 27 p.
Illus., 19 pls.

Craig reviews the history of theatre architecture and stage
design, then discusses his "Scene," a simplified system of
stage setting composed of movable elements "shaped like
screens--angular--plain." The plates illustrate the system.

482.   . THE THEATRE--ADVANCING. Boston: Little, Brown and
Co., 1919. vii, 298 p.

A collection of essays on stage design, marionettes, copyright,
acting, and many other topics.

483.   . TOWARDS A NEW THEATRE: FORTY DESIGNS FOR STAGE
SCENES WITH CRITICAL NOTES BY THE INVENTOR, EDWARD GOR-
DON CRAIG. London and Toronto: J.M. Dent & Sons, 1913. 106 p.
Illus.

Eleven-page introductory essay; thirty-nine illustrations by
Craig and one by Giovanni Maria Galli da Bibiena, with
Craig's comments on each.

484. Craven, Arthur Scott. "Modern Scenic Art." In "THE STAGE" YEAR
BOOK 1914, pp. 17-26. Pls.

An informative article about the New Stagecraft in England,
with excerpts from letters by Albert Rothenstein, Norman
Wilkinson, Gordon Craig, Conrad Tritschler, R.C. McCleery,
and Joseph Harker, as well as some biographical notes on
W.T. Hemsley. Illustrations of scenery by, and portraits of,
all these designers.

485. Crossley, Dorothy. "Stage Designers—IV: Edward Burra." BALLET 7 (January 1949): 18-24. Illus.

486. Drinkwater, John, and Rutherston, Albert. CLAUD LOVAT FRASER. New York: Alfred A. Knopf, 1923. 39 p. Pls., part color.

   Limited edition (450 copies). Includes a memoir by Drinkwater, pp. 1-23, and an essay on Fraser's art by Rutherston, pp. 25-39. The plates include a number of stage designs.

487. Easton, Malcolm. "THE BOY DAVID: Augustus John and Ernst Stern." APOLLO, n.s. 82 (October 1965): 318-25. Illus.

   A detailed study of the scenery and costumes of James Barrie's THE BOY DAVID as produced in Edinburgh and London in 1936. During the preparations, John's inadequate designs were altered by Stern.

488. "Eleven Designers Answer." PLAYS AND PLAYERS 10 (November 1962): 21-26. Illus.

   Commentary on stage design in England by eleven British designers.

489. Epstein, John, et al. THE BLACK BOX: AN EXPERIMENT IN VISUAL THEATRE. London: Latimer Press, 1970. 71 p. Illus.

   A record of a multimedia production titled CHANGE, adapted from a story by Hermann Hesse and produced by a group of painters in a London warehouse in 1970.

490. Ffolkes, David. "Westward Look: An English Designer on Broadway." THEATRE ARTS 31 (January 1947): 27-29. Illus.

   Brief comparison between American and English practices, and a few autobiographical notes by this English designer.

491. Fitzgerald, Percy. "Shakespearean Representations, Their Laws and Limits." GENTLEMAN'S MAGAZINE 294 (April 1903): 323-45.

   Condemns Shakespeare productions presented in the built-up antiquarian style, in blazing light; discusses the staging of supernatural effects, battles, and other scenes in Shakespeare's plays; calls for a return to flats and wings and low lighting.

492. Flanagan, Hallie. SHIFTING SCENES OF THE MODERN EUROPEAN THEATRE. New York: Coward-McCann, 1928. 280 p. Illus.

   Includes a chapter on Gordon Craig, pp. 64-80. She met him in Copenhagen during his work on THE PRETENDERS.

493. Fleet, Simon. "Cecil Beaton as Ballet Designer." In BALLET ANNUAL 1950, pp. 78-81. London: A. & C. Black, 1950. Illus.

494. _____. "Sophie Fedorovitch as Ballet Designer." In BALLET ANNUAL 1948, pp. 71-79. London: A. & C. Black, 1948. Illus.

    A critical survey of her career.

495. _____, ed. SOPHIE FEDOROVITCH: TRIBUTES AND ATTRIBUTES. [Bolton, England]: Printed for private circulation, 1955. 69 p. Illus.

    Includes a twenty-page biographical sketch.

496. Fletcher, Ifan Kyrle. "Charles Ricketts and the Theatre." THEATRE NOTEBOOK 22 (1967-68): 6-23. Illus.

    A thorough and sensitive discussion of Ricketts's work as a stage designer, with a chronological list of productions, 1906-1931.

497. "Franciszka Themerson's Stage Designs." STUDIO INTERNATIONAL 172 (August 1966): 104-5. Illus.

    Designs for Jarry's UBU ROI and Brecht's THREEPENNY OPERA.

498. Frankfurter, Alfred. "Controversial Noguchi Sets for LEAR." ART NEWS 54 (December 1955): 42-43. Illus.

    Isamu Noguchi's designs for KING LEAR at the Shakespeare Memorial Theatre, Stratford-upon-Avon.

499. Fraser, Grace Lovat. CLAUD LOVAT FRASER. London: Victoria and Albert Museum, 1969. 40 p. Illus., one in color.

    Exhibition catalog including an informative short biography, pp. 5-22, by the artist's wife.

500. _____. "The Visual Interpretation of Music." STUDIO 122 (November 1941): 137-40. Illus.

    Sympathetic comments on Ernst Stern's scenic projects for interpreting opera, and a condemnation of Disney's FANTASIA.

501. FRENCH'S CATALOGUE OF SCENERY, ETC. [London: Samuel French, c. 1920?]. 32 p. Paperbound. Illus., mostly color.

    Scarce catalog of lithographed paper scenery meant for mounting on canvas for amateur productions.

502. Furst, Herbert. "Charles Ricketts and His Stage Work." APOLLO 1

(June 1925): 329-34. Illus., one in color.

A summary of his career as a stage designer, quoting an interesting letter he wrote to Furst.

503. GEORGE W. HARRIS. London: Nisbet & Co., 1930. 23 p. 44 pls., part color.

Recollections of Harris by St. John Irvine and Lascelles Abercrombie; a biographical note by Basil Dean; Harris's essay "The Function of the Scenic Designer"; and excellent reproductions of stage designs by Harris.

504. Goffin, Peter. "Designing for Gilbert and Sullivan." STUDIO 149 (June 1955): 161-67. Illus., part color.

505. Grossman, Harvey. "Gordon Craig and the Actor." CHRYSALIS 6, nos. 7-8 (1953): 3-14. Illus.

506. Guthrie, John. CHAMBER DRAMA. Flansham, Sussex, England: Pear Tree Press, 1930. 6 p. 12 color pls.

Limited edition (sixty copies). Guthrie briefly describes, then illustrates, his system of simplified, "symbolic" scenery.

507. _____. FIRST DESIGNS FOR THE THEATRE. [Flansham, Sussex, England: Pear Tree Press, 1923].

Limited edition (fifty-five copies). Twenty colored designs for scenery and costumes.

508. _____. TEN DESIGNS FOR "TWO GENTLEMEN OF VERONA." [Flansham, Sussex, England: Pear Tree Press, 1925].

Limited edition (fifty copies). Ten loose colored plates of stage designs, with a brief note of explanation.

509. Haehnel, Siegfried. "The Need to Supersede Nineteenth-Century Scenic Tradition." In ANATOMY OF AN ILLUSION (see item 102), pp. 50-55.

A useful summary of Gordon Craig's theories (especially as they were expressed in his early productions) and comments on their relation to society at large.

510. Hamilton, Clayton. "Seen on the Stage." VOGUE 45 (15 March 1915): 61-63, 98. Illus.

A review of Granville-Barker's New-Stagecraft-style productions, suggesting that they effect a compromise between the conventions of the apron stage and those of the picture-frame stage.

511.   . "Shakespeare and Gordon Craig." ENGLISH JOURNAL 18 (April 1929): 280-87.

Somewhat long-winded review of George C. Tyler's production of MACBETH in New York in 1928, with designs by Gordon Craig.

512.   Harshbarger, Karl. "Edward Gordon Craig." PLAYERS 41 (January 1965): 103-4, 108.

An explication of Craig's designs in terms of his attitude towards death.

513.   Herf, Estelle. "Peter Farmer." BALLET TODAY 18 (July-August 1970): 16-17. Illus.

Informative sketch of Farmer's career as a stage designer.

514.   Herstand, Theodore. "Edward Gordon Craig's Theory of 'The Art of the Theatre of the Future.'" Ph.D. dissertation, University of Illinois (Urbana-Champaign), 1963. 193 p.

An analysis of Craig's aesthetics of the theatre: the artist, his materials, and the object of art.

515.   Hewitt, Barnard [W.]. "Gordon Craig and Post-Impressionism." QUARTERLY JOURNAL OF SPEECH 30 (1944): 75-80.

Craig shares with post-Impressionist painters a concern with creating formal relationships; this is the key to understanding his theoretical writings.

516.   Hitchman, Percy J. "THE FAIRY QUEEN at Nottingham." THEATRE NOTEBOOK 14 (1959-60): 92-99. Illus.

Describes and illustrates a 1959 production of Purcell's opera at the University of Nottingham, done in a period style, with wings-in-grooves scenery, movable dragons, and elaborate transformations.

517.   . "KING ARTHUR in Nottingham: A Notable Revival." THEATRE NOTEBOOK 11 (1956-57): 121-28. Illus.

Concerns a period-style revival of an opera by Dryden and Purcell. Cf. item 516.

518.   H[oppe]., E.O. "The Art of the Theatre: The Designs of W. Bridges Adams." INTERNATIONAL STUDIO 69 (1919-20): 156-59. Illus., part color.

519.   . "The Art of the Theatre--Mr. C. Lovat Fraser's Designs for
'As You Like It.'" INTERNATIONAL STUDIO 68 (August 1919): 63-
67. Illus., part color.

520.   . "The Art of the Theatre--Mr. Norman MacDermott's Settings."
INTERNATIONAL STUDIO 69 (1919-20): 65-69. Illus., part color.

521. Horton, Percy. "Henry Bird--Painter and Designer." STUDIO 137
(1949): 114-17. Illus.

Biographical sketch and reproductions of two stage designs.

522. Hubbard, Hesketh, and Whittington, Marjory. "Stage Decor and Costume in 1935." ART REVIEW (London), 1935, pp. 53-58. Illus.,
part color.

A survey of British stage design during 1935.

523. Hyllested, Mogens. "THE PRETENDERS: Copenhagen 1926." THEATRE
RESEARCH / RECHERCHES THEATRALES 7 (1966): 117-22. Illus.

Describes and illustrates Gordon Craig's scenery for this production, noting that it was not wholly successful.

524. Jackson, Peter. "Success on a Shoe-String." PLAYS AND PLAYERS 8
(January 1961): 8-9. Illus.

Surveys the career of stage designer Hutchinson Scott.

525. Johnstone, Alick. "Scene Painting." ARTIST 44 (November, December
1952): 65-67, 77-79. Illus., part color.

Description of the activities of a professional scene painter
who executes the work of designers.

526. Kenny, Sean. "The Building or the Theatre." THEATRE CRAFTS 2
(January-February 1968): 30-35. Illus.

Urges a new direction for the theatre, freed from traditional
restraints.

527.   . "Designing OLIVER." TABS 18 (September 1960): 7-12.
Illus.

528.   . "Must Scenery Go?" PLAYS AND PLAYERS 8 (April 1961):
6-7. Illus.

In an interview Kenny talks about his designs and his work as
a stage architect.

529.   _____ . "A Plea for Simplicity." WORLD THEATRE 12 (1963): 45–48. Illus.

   "We should stop using costumes now" and "light should take the place of our cleverness for sets."

530.   Kramer, William Case. "Gordon Craig, Ueber-Director: Major Influences on Craig's Theory and Practice." Ph.D. dissertation, Ohio State University, 1974. 285 p.

   Examines the influence of Edward W. Godwin, Ellen Terry, and Henry Irving; traces some of Craig's ideas to Maeterlinck and Wagner. Appendix includes interviews with four artists who worked with Craig on THE PRETENDERS in 1926.

531.   Lancaster, Karen. "John Piper as a Designer for the Theatre." ADELPHI 29, no. 1 (1952): 19–25.

532.   Lancaster, Osbert. "At Work in Opera, 3: The Designer." OPERA 13 (February 1962): 80–85. Illus.

   General discussion of the problems of the opera designer.

533.   Laver, James. "Designing for the Theatre: Continental Methods at the Slade School." STUDIO 108 (December 1934): 261 bis – 66 bis. Illus., part color.

   Vladimir Polunin's classes in stage design. Illustrated with designs by students.

534.   _____ . "George Ramon." STUDIO 134 (September 1947): 70–73. Illus.

   Survey of the career of this Hungarian-born designer, active in England.

535.   _____ . "Peter Goffin--Man of the Theatre." STUDIO 162 (July 1961): 16–19. Illus., part color.

536.   Leeper, Janet. EDWARD GORDON CRAIG: DESIGNS FOR THE THEATRE. Harmondsworth, England: Penguin Books, 1948. 48 p. 40 pls., part color.

   A good brief biography, unusual for its color plates.

537.   _____ . "Stage Designers--II: Rex Whistler." BALLET 5 (June 1948): 40–48. Illus.

538.   MacFall, Haldane. THE BOOK OF LOVAT CLAUD FRASER. London: J.M. Dent & Sons, 1923. 183 p. Illus., part color.

A sensitive biography by a critic who was Fraser's close
friend and mentor. Illustrated with Fraser's designs for THE
THREE STUDENTS, as well as numerous nontheatrical illustrations.

539. _____. "Some Thoughts on the Art of Gordon Craig, with Particular
Reference to Stage-Craft." STUDIO 23 (September 1901): 246-57.
Illus., part color.

An early and perceptive appreciation, with particular remarks
on Craig's DIDO AND AENEAS.

540. Marks, Claude. "Calling on Craig." THEATRE ARTS 41 (September
1957): 78-82. Illus.

A charming portrait of Gordon Craig, based on an interview.

541. Marshall, Herbert. "Are Designers Necessary?" PLAYS AND PLAYERS
10 (November 1962): 18-20.

A review of English stage design since World War II.

542. Messel, Oliver. STAGE DESIGNS AND COSTUMES. London: John
Lane, The Bodley Head, 1933. 37 p. 71 illus., part color.

Informative sketch of Messel's career by James Laver, pp. 11-
37. The illustrations are mostly of costumes and masks.

543. Miles, Bernard. "Sean Kenny." PLAYS AND PLAYERS 20 (August
1973): 16-19. Illus.

A tribute, with reminiscences.

544. Miller, Charles James. "An Analytical and Descriptive Study of the
Contributions of Edward Gordon Craig to Modern Theater Art." Ph.D.
dissertation, University of Southern California, 1957.

545. Miller, Harry Tatlock, ed. LOUDON SAINTHILL. London: Hutchinson, 1973. 64 p. Illus., part color.

Biographical notes and appreciation, plus thirty-eight pages
of plates (stage designs).

546. Moiseiwitsch, Tanya. "Problems in Design." DRAMA SURVEY 3 (May
1963): 113-16. Illus.

The author responds to questions about her methods.

547. Morrison, Hugh. "Stages and Settings Today." DRAMA (London), n.s.
no. 75 (Winter 1964): 35-37.

Brief discussion of trends in British design: sets for open and arena stages, use of new materials.

548. Myers, Norman. "Early Recognition of Gordon Craig in American Periodicals." EDUCATIONAL THEATRE JOURNAL 22 (1970): 78-86.

A study of articles on Craig published in the years 1901-14, noting that qualified enthusiasm gave way to considerable skepticism about his theories on the art of the theatre.

549. Myerscough-Walker, Raymond. STAGE AND FILM DECOR. London: Sir Isaac Pitman & Sons, 1940. 192 p. Illus., part color.

Historical sketch of the development of stage design followed by a discussion of the art and practice of contemporary design for theatre and film. A final section describes the work of Ernst Stern, Gordon Craig, Oliver Messel, and three film designers.

550. Nash, George. EDWARD GORDON CRAIG. London: Her Majesty's Stationery Office, 1967. 66 p. Paperbound. Illus.

Sixteen-page survey of Craig's career plus an excellent selection of sixty-three illustrations.

551. Nash, Paul. "The Artist Outside the Theatre." ENGLISH REVIEW 35 (1922): 147-53. Illus.

Brief remarks on his work in the theatre and his experiments in stage design outside it.

552. "A New MACBETH: Gordon Craig Designs a Production for George Tyler." THEATRE ARTS 12 (1928): 804-13. Illus.

Brief text and eleven illustrations of Craig's only American production, 1928.

553. Newquist, Roy. "Tanya Moiseiwitsch." In his SHOWCASE, pp. 276-86. New York: William Morrow and Co., 1966.

An interview about her work at the Guthrie Theatre, Minneapolis.

554. "Nicholas Georgiadis." DANCE AND DANCERS 17 (July 1966): 32-34. Illus.

An interview in which Georgiadis discusses ballet design.

555. Norman, Gertrude. "Edward Gordon Craig: A New Stage Genius." THEATRE (New York) 5 (June 1905): 147-49. Illus., port.

One of the earliest notices of Craig in an American periodical.

556. O'Brien, Timothy. "Matching the Action." ENCORE (London) 8 (November-December 1961): 32-36. Illus.

Critical review of English stage design, 1956-61, by a designer.

557. Osanai, Kaoru. "Gordon Craig's Production of HAMLET at the Moscow Art Theatre." Translated by Andrew T. Tsubaki. EDUCATIONAL THEATRE JOURNAL 20 (1968): 586-93.

Osanai, a Japanese Craig enthusiast and stage director, saw Craig's HAMLET in Moscow and later published this careful, scene-by-scene account of it.

558. Pilbrow, Richard. "Stages and Scenery." TWENTIETH CENTURY 169 (1961): 118-28.

Description and evaluation of stage design, lighting equipment, and machinery in contemporary London theatres.

559. Poel, William. SHAKESPEARE IN THE THEATRE. London: Sidgwick & Jackson, 1913. vii, 247 p. Illus., port.

A collection of periodical articles on various aspects of Shakespeare production, including some remarks on Gordon Craig's work, pp. 222-27.

560. Polunin, Vladimir. THE CONTINENTAL METHOD OF SCENE PAINTING. Edited by Cyril W. Beaumont. London: Beaumont, 1927. 98 p. Illus., one in color.

Both anecdotal and technical, including a practical discussion of the technique of painting on the floor, as well as remarks on his work for the Ballets Russes and other companies.

561. Rambert, Marie. "Sophie Fedorovitch." DANCE AND DANCERS 4 (March 1953): 8-9. Illus.

A tribute, with reminiscences.

562. Reuling, Karl F. "Gifts of a Greek." OPERA NEWS 37 (May 1973): 12-15. Illus.

Interview with Nicholas Georgiadis, active mainly in England as a designer for films, opera, and ballet.

563. Ricketts, Charles. SELF-PORTRAIT: TAKEN FROM THE LETTERS & JOURNALS OF CHARLES RICKETTS, R.A. Compiled by T. Sturge

Moore. Edited by Cecil Lewis. London: Peter Davies, 1939. 459 p. Illus.

Excerpts were published in BALLET 2 (June 1946): 13-18.

564. Rood, Arnold. "'After the Practise the Theory': Gordon Craig and Movement." THEATRE RESEARCH / RECHERCHES THEATRALES 11 (1971): 81-101. Illus.

Analyzes a fundamental element in Craig's designs: movement of scenery, of performers, of light.

565. _____, comp. EDWARD GORDON CRAIG: ARTIST OF THE THEATRE, 1872-1966. New York: New York Public Library, 1967. 57 p. Illus.

An exhibition catalog first published in the BULLETIN OF THE NEW YORK PUBLIC LIBRARY 71 (1967): 431-67, 524-41. Donald Oenslager's introduction summarizes Craig's career and comments on his significance. Arnold Rood's catalog is a chronological survey of Craig's life and work, with biographical commentary and quotations by Craig and his contemporaries.

566. Rose, A. SCENES FOR SCENE PAINTERS. London: George Routledge & Sons; New York: E.P. Dutton & Co., 1925. 59 p. Illus.

Line drawings of scenes and details suitable for amateur productions, with suggested colors: "Old London Street," "Dungeon," "Aboard a Ship," etc.

567. _____. STAGE EFFECTS: HOW TO MAKE AND WORK THEM. London: George Routledge & Sons, [1926]. 60 p. Illus.

Thunder and wind machines, moon box, etc. Intended primarily for amateurs.

568. Rose, Enid. GORDON CRAIG AND THE THEATRE: A RECORD AND AN INTERPRETATION. London: Sampson Low, Marston & Co., [1931]. ix, 250 p. Illus. Biblio.

The earliest and least useful biography of Craig.

569. Ross, Douglas. "The Craig-Shakespeare MACBETH." DRAMA 19 (December 1928): 69-70. Illus. pp. 68, 71-75.

Ross, director of Gordon Craig's only American production, gives his account of his work with Craig.

570. Rosse, Herman. "The 'New Theatre' of Gordon Craig." CHAPTER ONE 9 (Autumn 1962): 1-2, 5-8. Illus.

A commentary on Craig's career, setting it in the context of the progressive architecture of his day.

571. Rutherston, Albert. "Decoration in the Art of the Theatre." MONTHLY CHAPBOOK 1 (August 1919): 1-28. Pls.

> A lecture delivered in February 1915 at Leeds University. Promotes simplicity and integration of all elements of production.

572. _____. SIXTEEN DESIGNS FOR THE THEATRE. London: Oxford University Press, 1928. 16 p. 16 pls., part color.

> Brief introduction by Rutherston, remarking on the problems of the artist who takes up stage design.

573. "Sean Kenny and His Philosophy of Anti-Theatre." STUDIO 165 (January 1963): 2-7. Illus., part color.

574. Sheren, Paul. "Edward Gordon Craig and MACBETH." Ph.D. dissertation, Yale University, 1974. iv, 219 p.

> A study of Craig's many ideas, projects, and designs relating to MACBETH--and what they reveal about him as an artist and a man.

575. _____. "Gordon Craig's Only American Production." PRINCETON UNIVERSITY LIBRARY CHRONICLE 29 (Spring 1968): 163-29. Illus.

> A detailed study of the preparation and production of MACBETH in New York in 1928, with designs by Craig. Drawn largely from unpublished sources. Excellent illustrations.

576. _____. "A Note on Ellen Terry, Gordon Craig, and Screens." YALE / THEATRE 3 (Fall 1970): 4-6 and cover photograph.

> Discusses Craig's conception of and first experiments with screens; reproduces a little-known photograph of screens built for an unrealized production in 1909.

577. Sheringham, George. "Scene Design in England." THEATRE GUILD MAGAZINE 8 (May 1931): 12-15. Illus.

> Useful comments on twentieth-century design in England.

578. Shipp, Horace. "The Path of Decoration in the English Theatre." APOLLO 3 (May 1926): 282-86. Illus.

> Notes on the New Stagecraft in England.

579. Simonson, Lee. "The Case of Gordon Craig." THEATRE GUILD MAGAZINE 8 (February 1931): 18-23; 8 (March 1931): 28-33. Illus.

> A hostile view of Craig's work, similar to that in Simonson's THE STAGE IS SET.

580. Southern, Richard. "The Permanent Set in Theatrical Design." ATELIER 1 (April 1931): 248–51. Illus., one in color.

     Southern discusses his permanent set for Andreyev's THE THOUGHT at the Festival Theatre, Cambridge.

581. Speaight, Robert. WILLIAM POEL AND THE ELIZABETHAN REVIVAL. London: William Heinemann, 1954. 302 p. Illus. Biblio.

     Describes Poel's neo–Elizabethan production style.

582. "The Spectacular Element in Drama." LIVING AGE 231 (12 October 1901): 73–85.

     A thoughtful discussion, concluding that "an essential part of poetic tragedy is spectacle." Reprinted from EDINBURGH REVIEW.

583. "Stage Bridges at the Covent Garden Opera House, London, England." SCIENTIFIC AMERICAN SUPPLEMENT 52 (21 September 1901): 21511–12. Illus.

     Describes Edwin O. Sachs's electrical machinery for lifting sections of the Covent Garden stage.

584. Stevenson, Florence. "A Desmond Heeley Scrapbook." OPERA NEWS 36 (29 January 1972): 21–23. Illus.

     Six illustrations of Heeley's designs for Debussy's PELLEAS ET MELISANDE at the Metropolitan Opera House, New York, with brief commentary.

585. _____. "Love Affair." OPERA NEWS 34 (4 April 1970): 13. Illus., port.

     Interview with British designer Desmond Heeley.

586. Sutton, Denys. "Jacques Copeau and Duncan Grant." APOLLO, n.s. 86 (August 1967): 138–41. Illus.

     Grant designed several productions for Copeau, 1914–18.

587. _____. "A Neglected Virtuoso: Charles Ricketts and His Achievements." APOLLO, n.s. 83 (Feburary 1966): 138–47. Illus.

     Useful survey of his career, mainly about his nontheatrical work, but with some discussion of his theory of stage design.

588. Symons, Arthur. "A New Art of the Stage." In his STUDIES IN SEVEN ARTS, pp. 349–67. New York: Dutton, 1906.

     Penetrating commentary on the early work of Gordon Craig.

589. Talley, Paul M. "Architecture as Craig's Interim Symbol: Ruskin and Other Influences." EDUCATIONAL THEATRE JOURNAL 19 (1967): 52–60.

    Suggests that Craig's frequent references to architecture are "interim symbols" of his theories--visual analogies that lead to more practical conceptions.

590. Terry, Ellen. "Some Ideas on Stage Decoration." MCCLURE'S MAGAZINE 36 (January 1911): 289–94.

    Defends antiquarian realism in scenery, if intelligently carried out.

591. Trench, Herbert. "Shakespeare and Modern Staging." SATURDAY REVIEW (London) 110 (13 August 1910): 198–99.

    Suggests symbolic scenery and modulated lighting.

592. Tutaev, David. "Gordon Craig Remembers Stanislavsky: A Great Nurse." THEATRE ARTS 46 (April 1962): 17–19.

    Based on an interview in which Craig recalled his production of HAMLET in Moscow.

593. Tweddell, George. "The Scene Painter's Progress." ERA 76 (11 January 1913): 13.

    Last of a series of articles by a veteran English scene painter. Concerns the painting of architecture, interiors, and figures. (Earlier installments not identified. ERA files in American libraries are generally incomplete.)

594. Whistler, Rex. "Designs for the Theatre." THE MASQUE, no. 2 (1947): 5–20; no. 4 (1947): [3–31]; no. 7 (1948): 3–30. Illus., part color.

    Illustrations of Whistler's designs, with introductions by Cecil Beaton, Laurence Whistler, and James Laver. Reprinted in a single volume in 1950 by Batsford, London.

595. _____. "Problems of the Stage Designer." In FOOTNOTES TO THE THEATRE, edited by R.D. Charques, pp. 117–32. London: Peter Davies, 1938.

    Discusses the difficulty of coordinating the elements of a production, and of working with directors who insist on too much light and inappropriate designs.

596. _____. THE WORK OF REX WHISTLER. Compiled by Laurence Whistler and Ronald Fuller. London: Batsford, 1960. 146 p. Illus.,

part color. Biblio.

"Designs for the Theatre and Cinema," pp. 56-70 and plates 91-112.

597. Williams, Peter. "Creating Creation: Students of Slade School, London University, Design Milhaud's LA CREATION DU MONDE." DANCE AND DANCES 11 (May 1960): 16-21. Illus.

598. _____. "An Experiment in Ballet Design." DANCE AND DANCERS 10 (April 1959): 15-17; (May 1959): 14-17. Illus.

Discusses design projects for a Stravinsky ballet by students at the Slade School in London.

599. Windham, Donald, ed. "Gordon Craig and the Dance." DANCE IN-DEX 2 (August 1943): 97-116. Illus.

Essays and notes by Craig (mostly reprinted) on the Russian Ballet, the Javanese Ballet, and other dance subjects, as well as reproductions of his studies of Isadora Duncan.

600. Wood, T. Martin. "Norman Wilkinson's Decoration of 'A Midsummer Night's Dream' at the Savoy Theatre." INTERNATIONAL STUDIO 52 (June 1914): 301-7. Illus.

Perceptive commentary on a landmark of the New Stagecraft in England. Good illustrations.

601. Woodruff, Graham. "Terence Gray and Theatre Design." THEATRE RESEARCH / RECHERCHES THEATRALES 11 (1971): 114-32. Illus.

Describes Gray's architectural plans and stage settings at the Cambridge Festival Theatre, 1926-33. Shows the influence of Norman-Bel Geddes.

602. Woods, S. John, ed. JOHN PIPER: PAINTINGS, DRAWINGS & THEATRE DESIGNS, 1932-1954. New York: C. Valentin, 1955. 160 p. Prof. illus., part color. Biblio.

Biographical sketch and commentary by the editor, pp. 7-18, plus more than 250 illustrations.

Chapter 9

FRANCE

A. GENERAL HISTORIES

603. Bapst, Germain. ESSAI SUR L'HISTOIRE DU THEATRE: LA MISE EN SCENE, LE DECOR, LE COSTUME, L'ARCHITECTURE, L'ECIAIRAGE, L'HYGIENE. Paris: Lahure, 1893. 693 p. Illus.

Text in French. A well-documented history of theatrical production in France from the Middle Ages to the nineteenth century, with occasional reference to other European countries. Includes bio-bibliographical notes on scene painters and machinists in France from the Renaissance to the nineteenth century and a tabulation of productions at the Paris Opera, 1809-91, noting the designers of costumes and scenery.

604. Decugis, Nicole, and Reymond, Suzanne. LE DECOR DE THEATRE EN FRANCE DU MOYEN AGE A 1925. Paris: Compagnie Francaise des Arts Graphiques, 1953. 197 p. Prof. illus. Biblio.

Text in French. The best general history of French stage design. More than 300 excellent illustrations.

B. RENAISSANCE AND BAROQUE

SEE ALSO items 761, 762.

605. Beijer, Agne. "XVI-XVIII Century Theatrical Designs at the National Museum." GAZETTE DES BEAUX ARTS, s. 6, 28 (October 1945): 213-36. Illus.

Concerns designs at the National Museum, Stockholm, a collection especially rich in pre-eighteenth-century French material, which is the focus of this article.

606. Deierkauf-Holsboer, S. Wilma. L'HISTOIRE DE LA MISE EN SCENE DANS LE THEATRE FRANCAIS A PARIS DE 1600 A 1673. Paris:

A. Nizet, 1960. 167 p. Illus.

Text in French. Supplements her earlier study (see item 607). Chapter 3, pp. 39-80, concerns scenery, particularly that of Laurent Mahelot and Giacomo Torelli.

607. _____. L'HISTOIRE DE LA MISE EN SCENE DANS LE THEATRE FRANÇAIS DE 1600 A 1657. Paris: Librairie E. Droz, 1933. 336 p. Illus. Biblio.

Text in French. An important study of the seventeenth-century French theatre, including chapters on scenery and machinery.

608. England, Sylvia L. "An Unrecognized Document in the History of French Renaissance Staging." LIBRARY, s. 4, 16 (1935): 232-35. Illus.

Comments on an illustrated manuscript account of a pastoral play by Louis Papon performed in Montbrison in 1588.

609. Fletcher, Ifan Kyrle. "Stage Designers--VIII: Giacomo Torelli." BALLET 9 (February 1950): 28-37. Illus.

A sketch of this Italian designer's career, especially his work at the French court, 1645-60.

610. Hawley, James, and Jackson, Allan S[tuart]. "Scene-Changing at the Palais Royal (1770-1781)." OSU THEATRE COLLECTION BULLETIN 8 (1961): 9-23. Illus.

An analysis based on engravings published in the supplement to Diderot's ENCYCLOPEDIA.

611. Hippely, Edward Charles. "French Baroque Theatre Technology: The Second Palais Royal Theatre, 1770." Ph.D. dissertation, University of Denver, 1972. 284 p.

Analyzes illustrations in Diderot's ENCYCLOPEDIA, explaining technical details of scenery, machinery, and rigging. Includes glossaries of French and English terms relating to theatre technology.

612. Langlois, Walter Gordon, Jr. "The Evolution of Scenic Spectacles in France (1600-1673): National and Italian Origins of the Machine Play." Ph.D. dissertation, Yale University, 1955. 373 p.

613. Lawrence, W[illiam]. J[ohn]. "Louis XIV's Scene Painters." In his THE ELIZABETHAN PLAYHOUSE AND OTHER STUDIES, SECOND SERIES, pp. 203-12. Stratford-upon-Avon: Shakespeare Head Press, 1913.

Concerns Gaspare and Carlo Vigarani.

614. Lawrenson, T.E. THE FRENCH STAGE IN THE XVIIth CENTURY. Manchester, England: University of Manchester Press, 1957. 235 p. Illus. Biblio.

A scholarly study of the development of Italianate perspective stage design in France, set against the background of the neo-Vitruvianism of the Italian Renaissance and the nonclassical stage of the Middle Ages. Extensive bibliography.

615. Mahelot, Laurent, et al. LE MEMOIRE DE MAHELOT, LAURENT, ET D'AUTRES DECORATEURS DE L'HOTEL DE BOURGOGNE ET DE LA COMEDIE FRANCAISE AU XVIIe SIECLE. Edited by Henry Carrington Lancaster. Paris: E. Champion, 1920. 158 p. Illus.

Text in French. The only edition of the MEMOIRE, a unique manuscript including Mahelot's sketches of scenery at the Hotel de Bourgogne in the 1630s.

616. Niemeyer, G. Charles. "The Renaissance and Baroque Theatre in France: The Playhouses and the 'Mise en Scene' (1500-1700)." Ph.D. dissertation, Yale University, 1942. 436 p.

617. States, Bert Olen, Jr. "Jean Nicolas Servandoni: His Scenography and His Influence." Ph.D. dissertation, Yale University, 1960.

618. _____. "Servandoni's Successors at the French Opera: Boucher, Boquet, Algieri, Girault." THEATRE SURVEY 3 (1962): 41-58.

Examines mid-eighteenth-century productions designed by Francois Boucher, Louis-Rene Boquet, Pietro Algieri, and Louis-Alexandre Girault.

619. Stuart, Donald Clive. "Stage Decoration and the Unity of Place in France in the Seventeenth Century." MODERN PHILOLOGY 10 (1913): 393-406.

Describes the endurance of the polyscenic, medieval-style stage and notes that scene changes were not uncommon in the late seventeenth century.

C. NINETEENTH CENTURY

620. Allevy, Marie Antoinette. LA MISE EN SCENE EN FRANCE DANS LA PREMIERE MOITIE DU DIX-NEUVIEME SIECLE. Paris: Librairie E. Droz, 1938. xi, 245 p. Illus. Biblio.

Text in French. An important study of French scenic techniques in the first half of the nineteenth century. Examines the work of L.J.M. Daguerre, P.L.C. Ciceri, and other scene

painters of the period. Glossary of technical terms and an
excellent bibliography.

621. Brockett, Oscar G. "Pixerecourt and Unified Production." EDUCA-
      TIONAL THEATRE JOURNAL 11 (1959): 181-87.

      Pixerecourt attempted to integrate ensemble acting, local
      color, historically accurate sets and costumes, and spectacular
      effects into a coherent whole.

622. Carlson, Marvin. "Hernani's Revolt from the Tradition of French Stage
      Composition." THEATRE SURVEY 13 (1972): 1-27. Illus.

      A valuable study of early nineteenth-century French staging
      practices, based on a close examination of promptbooks. Dis-
      cusses box sets, furniture, and set pieces, placing them in the
      context of changing ideas about movement and stage composi-
      tion. In an article in EDUCATIONAL THEATRE JOURNAL 23
      (1971): 363-78, the author extends the study to the 1880s.

623.   . "A Theatre Inventory of the First Empire." THEATRE SURVEY
      11 (1970): 36-49. Illus.

      Translated transcription of an inventory of scenery, machinery,
      and furnishings at the theatre in Montpellier, France, 1806,
      with illustrations and commentary.

624. Goldwater, Robert. "Symbolist Art and Theater: Vuillard, Bonnard,
      Maurice Denis." MAGAZINE OF ART 39 (December 1946): 366-70.
      Illus.

      A brief, undocumented survey of the theatre work of these
      and other symbolist artists in the 1890s, particularly as they
      were associated with Lugne-Poe at the Theatre de l'Oeuvre.

625. Gradenwitz, Alfred. "A Glimpse of a Scenic Painter's Studio." SCIEN-
      TIFIC AMERICAN 107 (26 October 1912): 348-49, 355. Illus.

      Well-illustrated description of scene-painting techniques at the
      Jambon-Bailly Studio in Paris.

626. Guest, Ivor. "Stage Designers--VI: Pierre Ciceri." BALLET 8 (July
      1949): 20-28. Illus.

      An informative survey of Ciceri's career, with a list of his
      productions at the Paris Opera and excellent illustrations.

626a. "The Horse Race on the Stage." SCIENTIFIC AMERICAN 64 (25 April
      1891): 263-64. Illus.

      Live horses running on treadmills in PARIS PORT DE MER at
      the Theatre des Varietes, Paris.

627. Moynet, Georges. LA MACHINERIE THEATRALE: TRUCS ET DECORS. Paris: Librairie Illustree, 1893. 408 p. Illus.

Text in French. A valuable documentation of theatrical technology, mainly in France, in the late nineteenth century. Describes scene-changing devices, mechanical effects, lighting equipment, scene-painting techniques, etc. Good illustrations.

628. Moynet, J[ules?]. L'ENVERS DU THEATRE. 2d ed. Paris: Hachette et Cie., 1874. 292 p. Illus.

Text in French. A popular description of scenery, special effects, scene-changing devices, stage machinery, and lighting in the French theatre. Informative illustrations.

629. Paul, Charles Robert. "An Annotated Translation: THEATRICAL MACHINERY, STAGE SCENERY AND DEVICES by George [sic] Moynet." Ph.D. dissertation, University of Southern California, 1970. 516 p.

An English edition of item 627. Also includes a summary of information on European stage technology from other sources, including J. Moynet's L'ENVERS DU THEATRE (item 628).

630. Phillabaum, Corliss. "A Box Set for Moliere's DON JUAN." OSU THEATRE COLLECTION BULLETIN 7 (1960): 7-14. Illus.

Examines a promptbook for a French production of 1847 in which both wing-and-drop and enclosed sets were used.

631. Pougin, Arthur. DICTIONNAIRE HISTORIQUE ET PITTORESQUE DU THEATRE. Paris: Firmin-Didot, 1885. 790 p. Prof. illus., part color.

Text in French. Well-illustrated articles on such topics as "Decor," "Lumiere Electrique," "Machinerie Theatrale," "Truc," etc. Refers mainly to nineteenth-century French practices.

632. Rubin, William. "Shadows, Pantomimes and the Art of the FIN DE SIECLE." MAGAZINE OF ART 46 (March 1953): 114-22. Illus.

Includes discussion of the influential shadow plays produced by Henri Riviere and others at the Paris cabaret called the Chat Noir, opened in 1881.

633. "Scene Painting." BUILDER 20 (1862): 476.

Brief article describing the work of a Paris optician, Foucault, in attempting to develop a "panorama" (similar to the modern cyclorama) to replace side wings and drops.

634. Sechan, Charles. SOUVENIRS D'UN HOMME DE THEATRE, 1831-1855. Edited by Adolphe Badin. Paris: Calmann Levy, 1883. 338 p.

Text in French. A memoir by one of the great scene painters of the Romantic period in France.

D. TWENTIETH CENTURY

SEE ALSO item 122.

635. Allen, Patricia. "Decor for the Ballet." AMERICAN DANCER 10 (July 1937): 16, 44. Illus.

Brief article, based on an interview, concerning Constantine Terechkovich's designs for ballet.

636. "Andre Francois." DANCE AND DANCERS 15 (June 1964): 28-30. Illus.

An interview in which Francois, a Rumanian-born designer active in France, discusses his work for ballet.

637. Axsom, Richard Hayden. "PARADE: Cubism as Theatre." 2 vols. Ph.D. dissertation, University of Michigan, 1974. 378 p.

A discussion of the famous Paris production of 1917, emphasizing Picasso's decor and Cocteau's scenario, and showing how cubism was transferred from the canvas to the stage.

638. Ayrton, Michael. "Andre Derain as a Designer for the Ballet." In BALLET ANNUAL 1949, pp. 72-79. London: A. & C. Black, 1949. Illus.

639. Barthes, Roland. ERTE (ROMAIN DE TIRTOFF). Translated by William Weaver. Parma, Italy: Franco Maria Ricci, 1972. 179 p. Mounted color illus.

Commentary by Barthes, pp. 18-68; excerpt from Erte's memoirs, pp. 71-154; and a chronology of his life and work, identifying the productions he designed.

640. Beaumont, Cyril W. "Christian Berard." STUDIO 158 (1959): 75-80. Illus., part color.

A biographical sketch, enhanced by personal recollections, which considers Berard's work for ballet, film, and theatre.

641. Bielenberg, John Edward. "Scene Design at the Comedie Francaise, 1901-1920." Ph.D. dissertation, Ohio State University, 1970. 285 p.

642. _____. "Scenic Options at the Comedie Francaise, 1901-1920." THEATRE STUDIES 18 (1971-72): 34-45. Illus.

An analysis of scenic practices, noting the extensive use of stock pieces. Illustrated with production photographs and designs from the archives of the Comedie Francaise.

643. Boll, Andre. "Wakhevitch as Stage Designer." WORLD THEATRE 1, no. 3 (1951): 41-50. Illus.

Sketch of the theatrical career of Russian-born designer Georges Wakhevitch, active mainly in France.

644. Buckle, Richard. "Stage Designers—IX: Andre Beaurepaire." BALLET 10 (July-August 1950): 19-26. Illus.

Portfolio of illustrations, with brief commentary.

645. _____, ed. "Christian Berard, Stage Designer." BALLET AND OPERA 7 (April 1949): 20-32. Illus.

Sketch of his career and tributes by Buckle, Cecil Beaton, Oliver Messel, and others.

646. Carco, Francis. VERTES. Translated by Rosamond Frost. New York: Athenaeum Publishers, 1946. 169 p. Illus., part color.

Brief consideration of his stage designs.

647. Cassandre, A.M. DECOR DE DON JUAN. Geneva: Rene Kister, 1957. 112 p. 16 color pls.

Text in French, German, and English. Reproductions of Cassandre's designs for a production of Mozart's DON JUAN at the International Music Festival, Aix-en-Provence, 1956, and an essay in which he discusses the designs.

648. Cogniat, Raymond. "Carzou." GRAPHIS 11 (1955): 506-11. Illus., part color.

Text in French, German, and English. Includes reproductions of seven stage designs by this French artist.

649. _____. LES DECORATEURS DE THEATRE. Paris: Librairie theatrale, 1955. 222 p. Illus.

Text in French. A review of French stage design in the first half of the twentieth century, with about 180 excellent illustrations and an alphabetical list of designers and their work.

650. Cooper, Douglas. PICASSO THEATRE. New York: Harry N. Abrams, 1968. 360 p. Prof. illus., part color. Biblio.

The definitive work on Picasso's stage designs; also examines the role of the theatre in his art. Well documented and beautifully illustrated (447 plates and numerous illustrations in the text).

651. Corathiel, Elisabethe H.C. "George Wakhevitch." THEATRE WORLD 49 (November 1953): 16-17, 37. Illus.

652. _____. "Mariano Andreu." THEATRE WORLD 56 (May 1960): 18-21. Illus.

653. DREAMS IN THE THEATRE: DESIGNS OF SIMON LISSIM. New York: New York Public Library and Readex Books, 1975. 40 p. Paperbound. Prof. illus. Biblio.

Catalog of a recent exhibition. Includes essays on Lissim's work by Mahroni S. Young and Thor Wood.

654. Genauer, Emily. "Berard." THEATRE ARTS 35 (June 1951): 31-33, 101. Illus.

Sketch of the career of Christian Berard.

655. Hastings, Baird. CHRISTIAN BERARD: PAINTER, DECORATOR, DE-SIGNER. Boston: Institute of Contemporary Art, 1950. 62 p. Illus. Biblio.

Catalog of a traveling exhibition of Berard's work. Biographical sketch and commentary by Hastings, pp. 11-52.

656. _____. "The Designer." DANCE MAGAZINE 25 (May 1951): 24-28, 38, 40, 42. Illus.

A survey of French ballet decor, 1945-51.

657. _____. "Pageant in Paint and Silk." DANCE MAGAZINE 21 (October 1947): 21-23. Illus.

A review and appreciation of Christian Berard's work for the stage and ballet.

658. Hoctin, Luce. "French Stage Design." GRAPHIS 13 (May-June 1957): 250-59. Illus.

Text in German, French, and English. Brief commentary on twentieth-century French design and twenty-nine illustrations of stage designs from the 1950s.

659. "Joan Junyer." DANCE INDEX 6 (July 1947): 147-76. Illus.

A collection of articles, excerpts, and illustrations by and about this Spanish-born artist and stage designer, active mainly in France as a designer for ballet.

660. "Kieff." STUDIO 92 (15 October 1926): 296-99. Illus.

Brief commentary on Simon Lissim's stage designs and five illustrations.

661. Laver, James. "Twenty Years of French Theatrical Design." STUDIO 150 (August 1955): 40-45. Illus.

French design, 1935-55.

662. Lerminier, Georges. "From Stage Design to the Organization of Scenic Space." WORLD THEATRE 10 (1961): 251-61. Illus.

Remarks on new approaches to scenic design in France in the 1960s, discussing particularly the work of Rene Allio and Andre Acquart, with illustrations of the work of eight other designers as well.

663. Lieberman, William S. "Picasso and the Ballet." DANCE INDEX 5 (November-December 1946): 261-308. Illus. Biblio.

Entire issue devoted to Picasso's designs for the ballet, 1917-24. Largely reprinted in DANCE MAGAZINE 31 (September 1957): 24-37.

664. Lissim, Simon. SIMON LISSIM: FOURTEEN PLATES. New York: J. Hendrickson, 1949. 54 p. Illus., part color. Biblio.

Limited edition (280 copies). Only one of the plates is a stage design, but Lissim's theatrical career is discussed in George Freedley's introduction, pp. 7-16.

665. _____. "You and the Stage." DESIGN 56 (November-December 1954): 87-88. Illus.

Hints about the practice of stage design, with remarks on his own methods.

666. Lister, Raymond. "The Art of Simon Lissim." APOLLO 60 (November 1954): 125. Illus.

Brief biographical sketch and appreciation.

667. Loney, Glenn [M.]. "Dual Control." OPERA NEWS 34 (27 December 1969): 25-27. Illus.

Brief biographical sketch of designer Jean-Pierre Ponnelle.

668. MacArthur, Roderick. "Georges Braque and the Tartuffe Tradition." THEATRE ARTS 34 (April 1950): 36-38. Illus.

Based on an interview with Braque about his designs for a Paris production of Moliere's TARTUFFE.

669. "A New Version of the Revolving Stage Idea." SCIENTIFIC AMERICAN 128 (April 1923): 224-25. Illus.

A revolving stage with attached gridiron at the Grand Theatre, Lyons, France. Full-page schematic illustration.

670. Parmelin, Helene. CINQ PEINTRES ET LE THEATRE: DECORS ET COSTUMES DE LEGER, COUTAUD, GISCHIA, LABISSE, PIGNON. Paris: Cercle d'Art, 1956. 153 p. Prof. Illus., part color. Biblio.

Text in French. Illustrations of designs by Fernand Leger, Lucien Coutaud, Leon Gischia, Felix Labisse, and Edouard Pignon.

671. Pemberton, John. "An English Designer Looks at French Decor." SOUVENIRS DE BALLET, no. 1 (1949): 93-95. Illus.

Remarks on Christian Berard and others.

672. Polieri, Jacques. "New Production and Scenography." WORLD THE-ATRE 15 (1966): 10-17. Illus.

Describes his experiments in "polyvisual cinematographic projections and three-dimensional utilization of space" (a kind of multimedia approach to theatre).

673. Sacks, Lois. "Fernand Leger and the Ballets Suedois." APOLLO, n.s. 91 (June 1970): 463-68. Illus., part color.

Concerns Leger's designs for the ballets SKATING RINK and LA CREATION DU MONDE.

674. Spencer, Charles. ERTE. New York: C.N. Potter; distributed by Crown Publishers, 1970. 198 p. Prof. illus., part color. Biblio.

A handsomely illustrated biography of this Russian-born designer (real name Romain de Tirtoff), active mainly in France.

675. Spiers, A.G.H. "Modern Stage-Setting." NATION 105 (27 December 1917): 726-28.

Comments on the scenery at the Theatre du Vieux Colombier, directed by Jacques Copeau.

676. Tirtoff, Romain de [Erte]. THINGS I REMEMBER. New York: Quadrangle / New York Times Book Co., 1975. 208 p. Illus., part color.

677. Vasselon, Colette. "The Enchanted World of J.-D. Malcles." GRAPHIS 4 (1948): 50-57. Illus.

Text in French, German, and English. Includes illustrations of five stage designs, with brief commentary.

678.   "Vertes."   DANCE MAGAZINE 20 (September 1946):   19-21.   Illus.

Brief commentary and four illustrations of designs by Marcel Vertes.

Chapter 10

GERMANY AND AUSTRIA

A. RENAISSANCE AND BAROQUE

SEE ALSO item 351.

679. Burnim, Kalman A. "The Theatrical Career of Giuseppe Galli-Bibiena."
THEATRE SURVEY 6 (1965): 32-53. Illus.

An excellent, well-illustrated article on this baroque scene
designer and architect who worked mainly at the Hapsburg
court in Vienna. Discusses his major productions and cate-
gorizes his designs by type of locale.

680. [Draghi, Antonio]. IL FUCCO ETERNO. DAS VESTALISCHE EWIGE
FEUR. [The eternal fire]. 1674. Reprint. New York: Benjamin
Blom, 1970. 71 p. Illus.

Facsimile reprint of this libretto (in German) illustrated by
Ludovico Burnacini, who designed the original production in
Vienna. Ten-page introduction, "The Burnacini Style in High
Baroque Theatre," by Robert A. Griffin.

681. Frenzel, Herbert A. "The Introduction of the Perspective Stage into
the German Court and Castle Theatres." THEATRE RESEARCH / RE-
CHERCHES THEATRALES 3 (1961): 88-100.

A close examination of the earliest uses of perspective scenery
in Germany (mid-seventeenth-century), particularly as it was
associated with opera productions. A valuable study.

682. Griffin, Robert Arthur. HIGH BAROQUE CULTURE AND THEATRE IN
VIENNA. New York: Humanities Press, 1972. 175 p. Illus. Biblio.

Investigates the nature of theatrical performances in Vienna,
c. 1650-1710, particularly IL POMO D'ORO (1668), designed
by Ludovico Burnacini.

683. Jordan, Gilbert J. "Theatre Plans in Harsdoerffer's FRAUENZIMMER-GESPRAECHSPIELE." JOURNAL OF ENGLISH AND GERMANIC PHILOLOGY 42 (1943): 475-91. Illus.

Discusses the sections of Georg Philipp Harsdoerffer's FRAUEN-ZIMMER-GESPRAECHSPIELE (1643-57) that deal with theatrical scenery, machinery, and lighting; reproduces thirteen of Harsdoerffer's theatrical illustrations. A little-known source of data on the early German stage.

684. Kozelka, Edwin Paul. "Spectacles of the House of Savoy during the Seventeenth Century." Ph.D. dissertation, Yale University, 1970. 327 p.

Traces "the change from Renaissance pageantry to Baroque ostentation, and from intimate Court ballets to impersonal operatic performances" (DISSERTATION ABSTRACTS 31, no. 8, pt. A, p. 4320).

685. MONUMENTA SCENICA: THE ART OF THE THEATRE. NEW SERIES, I: GIUSEPPE GALLI-BIBIENA. Berkeley, Calif.: Samuel J. Hume, 1954. [9] p. 24 p. mounted pls., 28 pls. in all, 2 in color.

Limited edition (300 copies), published for the Society of Friends of the Austrian National Library. Five-page introduction by Joseph Gregor concerning Giuseppe Galli-Bibiena's style and some problems of attribution.

686. Nagler, A[lois]. M. "The Furttenbach Theatre in Ulm." THEATRE ANNUAL 11 (1953): 45-65. Illus.

A survey of Josef Furttenbach's career and a detailed examination of the periaktoi-equipped theatre he built in Ulm in 1641.

687. Sarlos, Robert K. "Two Outdoor Opera Productions of Giuseppe Galli Bibiena." THEATRE SURVEY 5 (1964): 27-42. Illus., diags.

ANGELICA, VINCITRICE DI ALCINA, at the Viennese imperial summer residence, 1716, and COSTANZA E FORTEZZA in Prague, 1723.

688. Seligman, Janet. "Stage Designers--I: Francesco Santurini." BALLET 5 (May 1948): 17-24. Illus.

Sketch of this Italian designer's career, focusing on his activities in Munich.

689. Southern, Richard. "Stage Designers--III: Lodovico [sic] Burnacini." BALLET 6 (November 1948): 28-35. Illus.

Illustrates and comments on Burnacini's scenery for IL FUOCO ETERNO, produced in Vienna in 1674.

690. States, Bert O. "Servandoni at Wuerttemberg." THEATRE SURVEY 5 1964): 87-98.

Describes Jean Nicolas Servandoni's work at the court theatre in Wuerttemberg, 1763-64, drawing largely on an account published by the court librarian, Joseph Uriot, in 1764.

B. NINETEENTH CENTURY

SEE ALSO items 725, 746.

691. Apthorp, William F. "Wagner and Scenic Art." SCRIBNER'S 2 (November 1887): 515-31. Illus.

Informative description of scenery, machinery, and lighting in the productions at Bayreuth in the 1870s and 1880s. Ten engraved illustrations after designs by Josef Hoffmann, the Brueckner brothers, and Paul Joukovsky.

692. Hoermann, Helmuth. "Ludwig Tieck, Theatrical Reformer." QUARTERLY JOURNAL OF SPEECH 31 (1945): 453-59.

A handy summary of the work of this far-sighted German critic and director who proposed an architectural, conventionalized setting for Shakespeare's plays long before it became common. The author adds a note on Karl Immermann, who was influenced by Tieck.

693. Hoffmann, Ernst T.A. "E.T.A. Hoffmann's 'The Perfect Stage Manager.'" Translated by Francis J. Nock. EDUCATIONAL THEATRE JOURNAL 2 (1950): 337-42.

An essay first published in 1814, reflecting Hoffmann's experiences as a conductor and technician at the opera house in Bamberg. Includes many details about scenery and special effects.

694. Lautenschlaeger, Carl. "Theatrical Engineering Past and Present." SCIENTIFIC AMERICAN SUPPLEMENT 60 (15, 22 July 1905): 24686-87, 24701-3.

Translation of an address delivered in Munich in January 1905. Recollections of scenery and machinery in his youth in Germany; the improvements made by Josef Muehldorfer in Mannheim and Karl Brandt in Darmstadt and Munich; the Asphaleia stage at Budapest; and his own work in applying electric motors to stage machinery and revolving stages.

695. Petzet, Detta, and Petzet, Michael. DIE RICHARD WAGNER-BUEHNE

KOENIG LUDWIGS II. Munich: Prestel-Verlag, 1970. 840 p. Prof. illus., part color.

Text in German. A comprehensive iconographic and historical study of the productions of Wagner's operas (FLYING DUTCH-MAN to PARSIFAL) in which he himself was involved. More than 800 illustrations, some in beautifully printed color, including many original designs for scenery and costumes, models of scenery, photographs of scenery onstage, and topographical and architectural sources of the designs. The most detailed study of its kind yet published.

696.   Schinkel, Karl Friedrich. SAMMLUNG VON THEATER-DEKORATIONEN. Berlin: Ernst & Kron, 1874. 32 pls.

Thirty-two engraved designs by Schinkel, mainly for opera, including some striking designs for Mozart's THE MAGIC FLUTE. No text.

697.   Schoene, Guenter. "Karl Lautenschlaeger: Reformer of Stage Scenery." In INNOVATIONS IN STAGE AND THEATRE DESIGN (see item 57), pp. 60-77. Illus.

Surveys the career of this German stage technician (1843-1906) who developed the first complete electrical lighting system in Germany, designed the Munich "Shakespeare-stage," and introduced the revolving stage to Europe. Excellent illustrations.

698.   Seligman, Janet. "Stage Designers--X: Theodor Jachimowicz." BALLET 11 (June 1951): 24-30. Illus.

Brief biography of a stage designer active in Vienna in the mid-nineteenth century. Illustrations of models of his scenery.

699.   Woodrow, Ernest A.E. "Theatres. [Part] XXII." BUILDING NEWS 64 (23 June 1893): 830-31. Illus.

Part of a series on theatre architecture. This part describes the stage machinery of the Vienna Burgtheater.

C. TWENTIETH CENTURY

SEE ALSO items 39, 143, 166, 178.

700.   Amundsen, Gerhard. "Benno von Arent." GEBRAUCHSGRAPHIK (INTERNATIONAL ADVERTISING ART) 12 (March 1935): 2-11. Illus., part color.

English and German text. Brief commentary and twenty-eight illustrations, including numerous designs for stage and film.

701. _____. "Der Buehnenbildner Ernst Schuette (The Scene Painter Ernst Schuette)." GEBRAUCHSGRAPHIK (INTERNATIONAL ADVERTISING ART) 13 (January 1936): 2-9. Illus., part color.

English and German text. Biographical sketch and commentary. Eighteen illustrations.

702. _____. "Paul Haferung." GEBRAUCHSGRAPHIK (INTERNATIONAL ADVERTISING ART) 16 (June 1939): 2-8. Illus., part color.

English and German text. Brief commentary and nineteen illustrations of Haferung's designs for ballet and opera.

703. _____. "Prof. Leo Pasetti." GEBRAUCHSGRAPHIK (INTERNATIONAL ADVERTISING ART) 10 (February 1933): 10-17. Illus., part color.

English and German text. Brief biographical notes and commentary on the work of this stage designer, plus eighteen illustrations.

704. "Behind the Wings in the Hoftheater in Dresden." SCIENTIFIC AMERICAN SUPPLEMENT 53 (1 February 1902): 21812-15. Illus.

Standard behind-the-scenes look at stage effects: waves, wind, moonlight, etc. Good illustrations.

705. Bie, Oscar. "Germany's New Scenecraft." INTERNATIONAL STUDIO 75 (August 1922): 425-29. Illus.

Comments on the New Stagecraft in Germany, with illustrations of designs by P. Aravantinos, Emil Pirchan, and Ernst Stern.

706. Brown, Frank Chouteau. "The 'Intimate' Theatre and Modern Stage-Setting in Germany." ARCHITECTURAL REVIEW, n.s. 2 (November 1913): 269-72. Illus.

Brief text and illustrations of scenery by Alfred Roller, Emil Orlik, and Fritz Schumacher.

707. BUEHNENBILDARBEIT IN DER DEUTSCHEN DEMOKRATISCHEN REPUBLIK (STAGE DESIGN IN THE GERMAN DEMOCRATIC REPUBLIC). Berlin: GDR Section of the International Organisation of Scenographers and Theatre Technicians (OSITT), 1971. 64 p. Paperbound. 57 illus., part color.

Text in German, with unillustrated English text in booklet (37 p.) inserted loose. Text by Karl von Appen, Heinrich Kilger, Andreas Reinhardt, and Reinhart Zimmermann. Essays on various aspects of stage design in East Germany.

708. Carter, Huntly. THE THEATRE OF MAX REINHARDT. New York:

Mitchell Kennerley, 1914. 332 p. Illus.

A detailed study of Reinhardt's early career and his contributions to the theatre.

709. Corathiel, Elisabethe H.C. "The Creative Artist in the Theatre." THEATRE WORLD 50 (January 1954)-51 (November 1955).

Part of a series of brief, illustrated profiles of stage designers, including the following German artists: Heinz Gallee (December 1954), Helmut Juergens (January 1954), Robert Kautsky (November 1955), and Wieland Wagner (February 1955).

710. Daniels, Robert D. "Designer at Large." OPERA NEWS 26 (17 March 1962): 13. Illus., port.

Brief sketch of the career of Ita Maximowna, Russian-born designer active mainly in Germany.

711. deShong, Andrew Walter III. "The Theatrical Designs of George Grosz." 2 vols. Ph.D. dissertation, Yale University, 1970.

Examines eleven productions designed by Grosz, including some collaborations with Brecht and Piscator. Includes a catalog of designs.

712. Dietrich, Margret. "Twentieth-Century Innovations in Stage Design, Stage Machinery, and Theatre Architecture in Austria." In INNOVATIONS IN STAGE AND THEATRE DESIGN (see item 57), pp. 95-125. Illus.

Discusses Alfred Roller's scenic innovations, Oskar Strnad's "ring theatre," Remigius Geyling's projection devices, and the stage work of Oskar Kokoschka and Fritz Wotruba. Excellent illustrations.

713. Dombrow, Sinclair. "Post-Expressionism: The Search for Productive Unity." THEATRE ARTS 8 (1924): 26-37. Illus.

German experiments in unifying action and scenery. Illustrated with designs by Friedrich Kiesler, P.G. Guderian, Robert Neppach, Walter Reimann, and Paul Ott.

714. Fuchs, Georg. REVOLUTION IN THE THEATRE: CONCLUSIONS CONCERNING THE MUNICH ARTISTS' THEATRE. Condensed, adapted, and translated by Constance Connor Kuhn. Ithaca, N.Y.: Cornell University Press, 1959. 250 p. Illus. Bibliographical notes.

First published in German in 1909. A record of the first season of the Artists' Theatre and an exposition of Fuchs's philosophy of production style. Discusses the "relief stage"

and simplified scenery (particularly the scenery of Fritz Erler).
An important document in the development of the New Stagecraft.

715. Georg, Hans. "Wilhelm Reinking, Hamburg." GEBRAUCHSGRAPHIK
(INTERNATIONAL ADVERTISING ART) 15 (December 1938): 39–48.
Illus.

English and German text. Brief commentary and twenty-five
illustrations of Reinking's stage designs, mainly for opera.

716. Gropius, Walter, ed. THE THEATER OF THE BAUHAUS. Translated by
Arthur S. Wensinger. Middletown, Conn.: Wesleyan University Press,
1961. 109 p. Illus.

An introduction by Gropius and essays (largely theoretical) by
Oskar Schlemmer, Laszlo Moholy-Nagy, and Farkus Molnar.
Numerous production photographs and designs relating to the
extraordinary Bauhaus productions of the 20s, in which Schlemmer created "moving architecture."

717. Hirschfeld, Kurt. "The Stage Designer Teo Otto." WORLD THEATRE
2, no. 4 (1953): 35–42. Illus.

Discussion of Otto's methods, illustrated with production photographs and scenic models.

718. Hoelscher, Eberhard. "Der Buehnenbildner Gerd Richter (The Scene
Painter Gerd Richter)." GEBRAUCHSGRAPHIK (INTERNATIONAL AD-
VERTISING ART) 15 (June 1938): 24–30. Illus.

English and German text. Very brief commentary and nineteen illustrations of designs for opera and ballet.

719. Innes, C.D. ERWIN PISCATOR'S POLITICAL THEATRE. Cambridge:
Cambridge University Press, 1972. 248 p. Illus. Biblio.

Describes Piscator's technological innovations in production
style.

720. Jenkins, Speight. "Look: Wolfram Skalicki." OPERA NEWS 33
(7 September 1968): 16. Port.

Mainly about Skalicki's current activity designing Wagner's
RING in San Francisco, with a brief sketch of his early
career.

721. Johnson, Harriett. "Light Touch." OPERA NEWS 29 (6 March 1965):
6. Illus., port.

Sketch of the career of Austrian designer Guenther Schneider-
Siemssen, based on an interview.

722. Keim, Walter. "Der Buehnenbildner Max Bignens (The Stage-Designer Max Bignens)." GEBRAUCHSGRAPHIK (INTERNATIONAL ADVERTISING ART) 32 (July 1961): 10-17. Illus., part color.

    English, French, and German text. Brief commentary and nine illustrations.

723. Kerz, Leo. "Brecht and Piscator." EDUCATIONAL THEATRE JOURNAL 20 (October 1968): 363-69. Illus.

    An appreciation of Piscator's contributions, by the designer who collaborated with him on Hochhuth's THE DEPUTY, 1963.

724. Knudsen, Hans. "Der Buehnenmaler Cesar Klein (Caesar Klein, Scenic Artist)." GEBRAUCHSGRAPHIK (INTERNATIONAL ADVERTISING ART) 3 (November 1926): 5-22. Illus., part color.

    English and German text. Commentary and twenty-six illustrations.

725. Kranich, Friedrich. BUEHNENTECHNIK DER GEGENWART. 2 vols. Munich and Berlin: R. Oldenbourg, 1929-33. Prof. illus., part color. Biblio.

    Text in German. A detailed study of late-nineteenth- and twentieth-century stage technology in Germany. Lavishly illustrated with charts, diagrams, designs, and photographs of scenery, machinery, special effects, and lighting equipment.

726. Leeper, Janet. "Peter Behrens and the Theatre." ARCHITECTURAL REVIEW 144 (August 1968): 138-39. Illus.

    Brief survey of the theatrical work of this innovative German architect and designer.

727. Melchinger, Siegfried. "Neher and Brecht." Edited by Erika Munk, translated by Martin Nicolaus. DRAMA REVIEW 12 (Winter 1968): 134-45. Illus.

    Illustrates and comments on Caspar Neher's designs for Brecht's plays, 1922-59, mostly created in collaboration with the author. Excerpted and translated from CASPAR NEHER, ed. Siegfried Melchinger and Gottfried von Einem (Hannover: Friedrich, 1966).

728. Mueller, Andre. "Der Buehnenbildner Horst Sagert (The Scenic Artist Horst Sagert)." GEBRAUCHSGRAPHIK (INTERNATIONAL ADVERTISING ART) 38 (March 1967): 2-9. Illus., part color.

    English, French, and German text. Brief commentary and twelve illustrations.

729. Muller, Ingevelde. "Theatre Design in Germany." WORLD THEATRE 3, no. 3 (1954): 38-48. Illus.

A brief but well-illustrated survey of recent German design.

730. Ould, Hermon. "Expressionism--Or What You Will." ENGLISH REVIEW 33 (1921): 310-13. Illus., pp. 299-300.

Brief discussion of recent German productions, particularly the famous production of RICHARD III directed by Leopold Jessner and designed by Emil Pirchan.

731. Pirchan, Emil. "New Stage Settings in Germany." STUDIO 101 (March 1931): 216-18. Illus.

Brief commentary and reproductions of four sets by the author.

732. Preetorius, Emil. "Zum Problem der Wagner-Szene (The Problem of Staging Wagner's Opera)." GEBRAUCHSGRAPHIK (INTERNATIONAL ADVERTISING ART) 12 (November 1935): 2-13. Illus., part color.

English and German text. Illustrated with nineteen designs for Wagner's operas, by the author.

733. Pridmore, J.E.O. "The Mechanical Development of the Modern German Stage." ARCHITECTURAL REVIEW, n.s. 2 (November 1913): 263-68. Illus.

Lautenschlaeger's revolving stage, rolling platforms, Asphaleia system, Fortuny system of lighting, and cycloramas.

734. Reinking, Wilhelm. "Stage Setting Since 1945." WORLD THEATRE 9 (1960): 249-58. Illus.

Stage design in West Germany, noting the special conditions after the war and how they influenced German artists.

735. Rood, Arnold, and Loney, Glenn [M.]. "Gordon Craig's Ghost Walks at Bayreuth." THEATRE DESIGN & TECHNOLOGY, no. 29 (May 1972): 4-18. Illus.

Discusses the belated influence of Craig and Appia in the Bayreuth productions designed by Wieland and Wolfgang Wagner. Eighteen illustrations.

736. Rothe, Hans. "Five Stage Designers of West Germany." THEATRE ANNUAL 12 (1954): 62-76. Illus.

Commentary on the postwar situation in German theatres, and brief biographies of Max Fritzsche, Paul Haferung, Franz Mertz, Willi Schmidt, and Rudolf Schulz.

737. Sayler, Oliver M., ed. MAX REINHARDT AND HIS THEATRE. Translated by Mariele S. Gudernatsch et al. New York: Brentano's, 1924. 404 p. Prof. illus., part color.

Includes a chapter on "Reinhardt and the Scenic Artist," pp. 131–43, with essays by Alfred Roller, Max Osborne, and E.J. Dent; and a chapter on "Reinhardt and the Formal Stage," by Kenneth Macgowan. Illustrated throughout with stage designs.

738. Schatzky, Brigitte E. "Stage Setting in Naturalist Drama." GERMAN LIFE & LETTERS 8 (1955): 161–70.

Generally literary, concerning the playwright's demands for carefully realized environments onstage.

739. Scheffauer, Herman George. THE NEW VISION IN THE GERMAN ARTS. New York: B.W. Huebsch, 1924. xi, 274 p. Illus.

A study of German expressionism, with two chapters on Shakespeare productions by Leopold Jessner and Emil Pirchan, pp. 208–227.

740. Schoene, Guenter. "The Munich Kuenstlertheater and Its First Season." APOLLO, n.s. 94 (November 1971): 396–401. Illus., one in color.

Discusses and illustrates the work of three designers: Fritz Erler, Julius Diez, and Adolf Hengeler.

741. Schreiber, Leopold. "Caspar Neher." GEBRAUCHSGRAPHIK (INTERNATIONAL ADVERTISING ART) 11 (March 1934): 2–11. Illus., part color.

English and German text. Commentary plus twelve illustrations.

742. _____. "Rochus Gliese." GEBRAUCHSGRAPHIK (INTERNATIONAL ADVERTISING ART) 10 (November 1933): 2–9. Illus., part color.

English and German text. Brief biographical notes on this German designer, plus fourteen illustrations.

743. _____. "Traugott Mueller." GEBRAUCHSGRAPHIK (INTERNATIONAL ADVERTISING ART) 11 (October 1934): 18–27. Illus., part color.

English and German text. Commentary on the work of this German designer, plus nineteen illustrations.

744. Simonson, Lee. "Down to the Cellar." THEATRE ARTS 6 (1922): 119–38. Illus.

A review of recent productions in Germany, with emphasis on stage design and machinery. Ten illustrations, including designs by Ludwig Sievert and Rudolf Bamberger.

745. Singer, Hans W. "Modern Stage Mounting in Germany." INTERNA-
TIONAL STUDIO 30 (January 1907): 244-47; 32 (September 1907):
219-24. Illus.

Part 1 promotes suggestiveness in place of literalism in stage design; part 2 concerns Emil Orlik's designs for A WINTER'S TALE at the Deutsches Theater, Berlin.

746. Skelton, Geoffrey. WAGNER AT BAYREUTH. New York: George Braziller, 1965. 239 p. Illus., part color. Biblio.

A survey of Wagnerian opera production at Bayreuth from the first productions under Wagner's direction in 1876 to the in- novations of Wieland Wagner in the 1950s and 1960s.

747. _____. WIELAND WAGNER: THE POSITIVE SCEPTIC. New York: St. Martin's Press, 1971. 222 p. Illus. Biblio.

A biography of Richard Wagner's grandson, who, as director and stage designer, revolutionized the style of opera produc- tion at Bayreuth.

748. Smith, Patrick J. "A Man Engaged." OPERA NEWS 29 (13 March 1965): 14-15. Illus., port.

Biographical sketch of German designer Rudolf Heinrich, with notes on his theories and methods.

749. Stephenson, Nathaniel Wright. "Reinhardt's Discovery." DRAMA 3 (May 1913): 225-33.

Analysis of the scenery and costumes by Ernst Stern for Rein- hardt's SUMURUN, suggesting that "he transforms Japanese prints into stage settings."

750. Stern, Ernst [Ernest]. MY LIFE, MY STAGE. Translated by Edward Fitzgerald. London: Gollancz, 1951. 302 p. Illus.

Like many other autobiographies by scene designers, this is a disappointing book, rather rambling and anecdotal and short on technical details. Still, there is useful material on Max Reinhardt's productions. Illustrated only with line drawings by the author.

751. Swoope, Charles. "Kandinsky and Kokoschka: Two Episodes in the Genesis of Total Theatre." YALE / THEATRE 3 (Fall 1970): 10-18. Illus.

Kandinsky in Munich and Kokoschka in Vienna experimented with the "fusion of dialogue, design and movement into total theatre."

752. Washburn-Freund, Frank E. "Max Reinhardt's Evolution." INTERNATIONAL STUDIO 78 (January 1924): 342-50. Illus., part color.

Useful survey of Reinhardt's varied styles of production, with numerous colored illustrations of designs.

753. _____. "The Stage and the Arts in Germany." In "THE STAGE" YEAR BOOK 1909, pp. 112-19. London: Carson & Comerford, 1909. Illus.

Discusses new scenery and theatre architecture in Germany, including Karl Hagemann's "Ideal Stage," Max Reinhardt's productions, Jocza Savits's Shakespeare stage, and the Munich Kuenstlertheater.

754. _____. "The Theatrical Year in Germany." In "THE STAGE" YEAR BOOK 1910, pp. 58-69. London: Carson & Comeford, 1910. Illus.

Includes twenty-eight illustrations of scenery and designs, mainly in the style of the New Stagecraft. Among the designers are Karl Hagemann, Julius V. Klein, Max Martersteig, and Alfred Roller. The 1914 YEAR BOOK, pp. 81-96, includes an equal number of illustrations (designs by Appia, Kurt Kempin, Ludwig Sievert, and G. Wunderwald; photographs of productions at Jaques-Dalcroze's school at Hellerau). Other issues of the YEAR BOOK from the pre-World War I period include some useful illustrations, as well.

Chapter 11

ITALY

A. GENERAL HISTORIES

SEE ALSO items 24, 51, 58, 81.

755. Ferrari, Giulio. LA SCENOGRAFIA: CENNI STORICI DALL'EVO
CLASSICO AI NOSTRI GIORNI [Stage design: its history from classical
times to our day]. Milan: U. Hoepli, 1902. 350 p. Illus., part
color.

A general history of stage design, most useful for its information on Italian designers. Lists hundreds of scene painters
active in various periods, with birth and death dates or dates
of their activities.

756. Monteverdi, Mario. LA SCALA: 400 YEARS OF STAGE DESIGN
FROM THE MUSEO TEATRALE ALLA SCALA, MILAN. N.p.: International Exhibitions Foundation, 1971. 91 p. Paperbound. Illus.

Catalog of a traveling exhibition. Includes an essay by Monteverdi on Italian stage design from the eighteenth to the early
twentieth century.

B. RENAISSANCE AND BAROQUE

SEE ALSO items 75, 95, 609, 613, 1159.

757. Beaumont, Maria Alice. "Stage Sets by the Bibienas in the Museu
Nacional de Arte Antiga, Lisbon." APOLLO, n.s. 97 (April 1973):
408-15. Illus. Biblio.

Discusses Giovanni Carlo Bibiena's career at the Portuguese
court during the second half of the eighteenth century; reproduces eleven designs by him and members of his family.

758.   Beijer, Agne.   "An Early 16th-Century Scenic Design in the National
       Museum, Stockholm, and Its Historical Background." THEATRE RE-
       SEARCH / RECHERCHES THEATRALES 4 (1962): 85-155. Illus.

       In effect, a brief history of the origins and early development
       of Italian perspective scenery, discussing the work of Girolamo
       Genga, Pellegrino da Udine, Baldassare Peruzzi, and other
       pioneers of the new art. A work of broad and impressive
       scholarship, carefully documented and well illustrated.

759.   Bielenberg, John E[dward]. "A Three-Dimensional Study of Two Scene
       Designs by Filippo Juvarra." OSU THEATRE COLLECTION BULLETIN
       11 (1964): 6-20. Illus.

       Attempts to reconstruct two of Juvarra's designs, an angle
       perspective and a curved vista scene.

760.   Bjurstrom, Per. FEAST AND THEATRE IN QUEEN CHRISTINA'S ROME.
       Stockholm: Nationalmuseum, 1966. 154 p. Illus., part color. Biblio.

       Chapter 5, "Christina and the Theatre," pp. 88-112, discusses
       certain mid-seventeenth-century stage designs associated with
       her Roman sojourns.

761.   _____. GIACOMO TORELLI AND BAROQUE STAGE DESIGN. Stock-
       holm: Almqvist & Wiksell, 1962. 271 p. Illus. Biblio.

       An authoritative study of the "Great Wizard," including de-
       tailed discussion of his productions in Venice and Paris in the
       mid-seventeenth century. Excellent bibliography.

762.   _____. "Notes on Giacomo Torelli." THEATRE RESEARCH / RECHER-
       CHES THEATRALES 3 (1961): 16-23.

       Summarizes Torelli's career and discusses his work in Venice
       and Paris, noting that his scene changes, enjoyed as "indepen-
       dent aesthetic moments" in Venice, changed their function
       and failed in Paris.

763.   Blumenthal, Arthur R. "A Newly-Identified Drawing of Brunelleschi's
       Stage Machinery." MARSYAS 13 (1966-67): 20-31. Illus.

       Discusses previous attempts to reconstruct Brunelleschi's "Para-
       dise machine" in the Church of San Felice in Piazza, Florence,
       and offers his own reconstruction, based on two drawings (one
       identified here for the first time).

764.   Burnim, Kalman A. "LA SCENA PER ANGOLO--Magic by the Bibi-
       enas?" THEATRE SURVEY 2 (1961): 67-76. Illus.

       Suggests that Ferdinando Galli-Bibiena used angle perspective as early as 1698-99 and attempts to explain how such scenes were executed on the stage.

765.   Collier, William. "Rediscovered Theatre Drawings by Antonio Bibiena." APOLLO, n.s. 86 (August 1967): 108-11. Illus.

Concerns certain drawings at the Royal Institute of British Architects; the author attributes them to Antonio Galli-Bibiena.

766.   Craig, Edward Anthony [Edward Carrick]. "Theatre Machines in Italy, 1400-1800." ARCHITECTURAL REVIEW 70 (July-August 1931): 9-14; 34-36. Pls.

Includes excellent illustrations of scenery and machinery and an informative text.

767.   Craig, Edward Gordon. "Filippo Juvarra: A Celebrated Italian Architect." ARCHITECTURAL REVIEW 60 (1926): 171-74, 226-30. Illus.

Eccentric treatment of Juvarra's career, with good illustrations.

768.   _____ [John Semar]. "Some Architectural Designs of Padre Pozzo (1649-1709)." MASK 7 (July 1914): 39-51. Illus.

Brief commentary and excerpts from the 1707 London edition of Pozzo's RULES AND EXAMPLES OF PERSPECTIVE (see 790).

769.   Dumont, Gabriel Pierre Martin. PARALLELE DE PLANS DES PLUS BELLES SALLES DE SPECTACLES D'ITALIE ET DE FRANCE. New York: Benjamin Blom, 1968. Unpaged [81 p.]; mainly pls.

Text, captions, and illustration keys in French. This new edition brings together all the plates published in various late eighteenth-century editions. Mainly of architectural interest, but it includes detailed drawings of the scenic machinery at three Italian theatres.

770.   Eckert, William Dean. "The Renaissance Stage in Italy: A Study of the Evolution of the Perspective Scene." Ph.D. dissertation, University of Iowa, 1961. 407 p.

Suggests that Donato Bramante, in Milan, was "the first to introduce the fully developed perspective setting to the Italian stage" (DISSERTATION ABSTRACTS 22, no. 5, p. 1745).

771.   Eddelman, William Smiley III. "Landscape on the Seventeenth and Eighteenth Century Italian Stage." Ph.D. dissertation, Stanford University, 1972. 326 p.

Examines changing styles of landscape scene painting and relates them to developments in easel painting. Appendices concern angle perspective and staging techniques.

772. Fahrner, Robert, and Kleb, William. "The Theatrical Activity of Gian-lorenzo Bernini." EDUCATIONAL THEATRE JOURNAL 25 (March 1973): 5-14. Illus.

> Survey of Bernini's work as stage designer, machinist, director, and performer, especially under the patronage of Pope Urban VIII, c. 1624-44.

773. Galliari, Gaspare. NUMERO XXIV INVENZIONI TEATRALI [Twenty-four theatrical designs]. 1814. Reprint. New York: Benjamin Blom, 1970. 10 p. 24 pls.

> Brief sketch of Galliari's career by Denise Addis (in English), plus the twenty-four designs.

774. Galli da Bibiena, Ferdinando. L'ARCHITETTURA CIVILE. 1711. Re-print. New York: Benjamin Blom, 1971. 169 p. Illus. Biblio.

> New introduction (in English) by Diane Kelder; text in Italian.

775. Galli da Bibiena, Giuseppe. ARCHITECTURAL AND PERSPECTIVE DE-SIGNS DEDICATED TO HIS MAJESTY CHARLES VI. 1740. Reprint. New York: Dover Publications, 1964. 6 p. 53 pls.

> Two-page introduction by A. Hyatt Mayor.

776. K[eith]., W[illiam]. G[rant]. "Notes on the History of Scenic Decora-tion." BUILDER 107 (1914): 46, 152-54, 312; 108 (1915): 331-33. Illus.

> A brief history of Italian Renaissance stage design from Peruzzi to Serlio.

777. Krautheimer, Richard. "The Tragic and Comic Scene of the Renaissance: The Baltimore and Urbino Panels." GAZETTE DES BEAUX ARTS, s. 6, 33 (1948): 327-46. Illus.

> Attempts to prove that two panels usually dated c. 1470 and attributed to Luciano Laurana are the first representations of the Renaissance tragic and comic scenes. An important study.

778. Larson, Orville K. "Bishop Abraham of Souzdal's Description of SACRE RAPPRESENTAZIONI." EDUCATIONAL THEATRE JOURNAL 9 (1957): 208-13.

> Translation of an account of spectacular church productions in Florence in 1439, with commentary.

779. _____. "Italian Stage Machinery, 1500-1700." Ph.D. dissertation, University of Illinois (Urbana-Champaign), 1956. 311 p.

780. _____. "Nicola Sabbattini's Description of Stage Machinery from PRACTICA DI FABRICAR SCENE E MACHINE NE'TEATRI: An Explanation and Commentary." PLAYERS 39 (October 1962): 13-20; 39 (November 1962): 47-53, 64. Illus.

Includes reproductions of some original drawings attributed to Sabbattini, as well as reproductions from the PRACTICA.

781. _____. "Spectacle in the Florentine INTERMEZZI." DRAMA SURVEY 2 (1962-63): 344-52. Pls.

Examines intermezzi performed in 1565, 1585, and 1589, with scenery and machinery by Giorgio Vasari and Bernardo Buontalenti.

782. _____. "Vasari's Descriptions of Stage Machinery." EDUCATIONAL THEATRE JOURNAL 9 (1957): 287-99. Illus.

An explanation of Vasari's sometimes obscure account of Filippo Brunelleschi's "Paradise machine" for a church performance in Florence, together with a new reconstruction in a drawing by James Watrous. Appended are the author's translations of Vasari's descriptions.

783. Lavin, Irving. "The Campidoglio and Sixteenth-Century Stage Design." MARSYAS SUPPLEMENT 2 (1965): 114-18. Illus.

Identifies two types of sixteenth-century stage designs and discusses their relation to Michelangelo's architectural design for the Campidoglio in Rome.

784. McClure, Theron Reading. "A Reconstruction of Theatrical and Musical Practice in the Production of Italian Opera in the Eighteenth Century." Ph.D. dissertation, Ohio State University, 1956. 202 p.

785. Mayor, A[lpheus]. Hyatt. THE BIBIENA FAMILY. New York: H. Bittner, 1945. 37 p. 53 Illus.

Sketch of the careers, milieu, and methods of this family of stage designers, followed by a list of their works and a selection of their designs, with attributions.

786. _____. "Carpentry and Candlelight in the Theater." METROPOLITAN MUSEUM BULLETIN, n.s. 1 (February 1943): 198-203. Illus.

An informal survey of Italian scenery, machinery, lighting, and theatre architecture during the Renaissance and Baroque periods.

787. Mohler, Frank C. II. "An Analysis of the Plans for the Theatre in the Seminary of the Collegio Romano." OSU THEATRE COLLECTION BUL-

LETIN 16 (1969): 39-53. Illus.

Analyzes four illustrations of a Roman theatre published in
G.P.M. Dumont's PARALLELE (c. 1770).

788.   Nagler, A[lois] M. "Periaktoi at the Medici Court?" THEATRE AN-
NUAL 14 (1956): 28-36. Illus.

Discusses Vasari's scenery for a Florentine festival production,
Francesco d'Amba's LA COFANARIA, 1565; Baldassare Lanci's
use of periaktoi in a later production, 1569; and Bernardo
Buontalenti's scenery for productions in 1585 and 1589.

789.   _____. THEATRE FESTIVALS OF THE MEDICI: 1539-1637. Translated
by George Hickenlooper. New Haven, Conn.: Yale University Press,
1964. 210 p. 136 Illus.

Detailed reconstructions of the theatrical entertainments presented in Florence by the Grand Dukes of Tuscany. Among
the designers were Giorgio Vasari, Baldassare Lanci, Bernardo
Buontalenti, and Giulio and Alfonso Parigi.

790.   Pozzo, Andrea. RULES AND EXAMPLES OF PERSPECTIVE. 1707. Reprint. New York: Benjamin Blom, 1971. Unpaged. Illus.

Reprint of a 1707 English translation of this treatise on perspective first published in Italian in 1693-1700. Includes a
discussion of perspective for stage designers.

791.   Rutledge, Barbara Louise Saenger. "The Theatrical Art of the Italian
Renaissance: Interchangeable Conventions in Painting and Theatre in
the Late Fifteenth and Early Sixteenth Centuries." Ph.D. dissertation,
University of Michigan, 1973. 281 p.

792.   Sabatini, Mary Hieber. "The Problem of Setting in Early Humanist
Comedy in Italy: A Study in Fifteenth-Century Goliardic Theatre."
Ph.D. dissertation, Columbia University, 1973. 170 p.

Drawing on evidence from early-fifteenth-century illuminated
manuscripts of the plays of Terence and other sources, the
author reconstructs the type of "skeletal" structures used to
stage the comedies, and shows how an awareness of the setting
increases appreciation of the plays.

793.   Serlio, Sebastiano. THE BOOK OF ARCHITECTURE. 1611. Reprint.
New York: Benjamin Blom, 1969. Unpaged. Illus. Biblio.

First published in 1545-47. An extremely important source of
information on Italian Renaissance scenery and machinery.
This edition is a facsimile of a 1611 English translation, with
a new introduction and bibliography.

794. Smith, Winifred. "Giovan Battista Andreini as a Theatrical Innovator."
MODERN LANGUAGE REVIEW 17 (1922): 31-41.

Discusses Andreini's innovations in scenery, costume, and effects, developed for his own plays in the 1620s and 1630s.

795. Southern, Richard. "The Staging of Eighteenth-Century Designs for
Scenery." JOURNAL OF THE ROYAL INSTITUTE OF BRITISH ARCHI-
TECTS, s. 3, 42 (1935): 1021-37. Illus.

Reproduces a very interesting scene design by Angelo Carboni,
1758, and analyzes it in detail. Demonstrates that an elaborate baroque set with central perspective and flanking angle
perspectives was painted on cut-out wings and flats, not a
series of cut cloths. Also examines three designs by Filippo
Juvarra and one by Giuseppe Bibiena, showing how wings on
"chariots" were placed all across the stage to create angle
perspectives. An ingenious and important study.

796. Speaight, George. "The Puppet Theatre of Cardinal Ottoboni." THE-
ATRE RESEARCH / RECHERCHES THEATRALES 1 (June 1958): 5-10.
Illus.

Offers persuasive evidence that the theatre designed by Filippo
Juvarra for Cardinal Ottoboni (c. 1708) was a puppet theatre.
Three of Juvarra's designs for this theatre are reproduced.

797. Steinetz, Kate T. "A Reconstruction of Leonardo Da Vinci's Revolving
Stage." ART QUARTERLY 12 (1949): 325-38. Illus.

Concerns a mountain setting possibly built for the performance
of Bellincioni's PARADISE in Milan, 1490. (A model of this
setting, prepared with Steinetz's assistance, is reproduced in
LE LIEU THEATRAL A LA RENAISSANCE [item 95], opposite
p. 35.)

798. Stout, R. Elliott. "Filippo Juvarra: An Introduction." OSU THEATRE
COLLECTION BULLETIN 11 (1964): 3-5.

Sketch of Juvarra's theatrical career, serving as a preface to
this entire issue devoted to articles on his activities as a scene
designer and theatre architect.

799. Tew, Thomas Charles. "A Reconstruction of the Settings for Three
Operas Designed by Filippo Juvarra in Rome, 1710-1712." Ph.D.
dissertation, Louisiana State University and Agricultural and Mechanical
College, 1973. 268 p.

Sets for COSTANTINO PIO, IL GIOVANE, and IL CIRO.

800. Viale Ferrero, Mercedes. FILIPPO JUVARRA: SCENOGRAFO E ARCHI-

TETTO TEATRALE [Filippo Juvarra: scenographer and theatre architect]. New York and London: Benjamin Blom, 1970. 391 p. Prof. illus., part color. Biblio.

Text in Italian. A splendid study of Juvarra's career as a stage designer and theatre architect.

801. _____. LA SCENOGRAFIA DEL '700 E I FRATELLI GALLIARI [Eighteenth-century stage design and the Galliari brothers]. Turin: Fratelli Pozzo, 1963. 283 p. Prof. illus., part color. Biblio.

Text in Italian. A scholarly survey of the careers of the Galliari family of stage designers: Bernardino, Fabrizio, Giovanni Antonio, Giovannino, Giuseppino, and Gaspare, and some of their colleagues, active in Turin and Milan. Excellent illustrations.

802. Weil, Mark S. "The Devotion of the Forty Hours and Roman Baroque Illusions." JOURNAL OF THE WARBURG AND COURTAULD INSTITUTE 37 (1974): 218-48. Illus. Biblio.

Examines the illusionistic altar decorations used in the church ceremony called the Devotion of the Forty Hours in seventeenth-century Rome. Closely related to stage designs, these decorations were executed by such artists as Bernini.

803. West, William Russell. "The Artistic Approach of Filippo Juvarra, Late-Baroque Scene Designer." Ph.D. dissertation, Ohio State University, 1962. 199 p.

804. _____. "Some Notes Concerning Staging at the Ottoboni Theatre Through an Analysis of IL TEODOSIA." OSU THEATRE COLLECTION BULLETIN 11 (1964): 21-34. Illus.

Attributes certain Juvarra designs at the Victoria and Albert Museum to a production of IL TEODOSIA in Rome in 1711; discusses the arrangement of scenic elements in this production.

C. NINETEENTH AND TWENTIETH CENTURIES

805. Adami, Giuseppe. UN SECOLO DI SCENOGRAFIA ALLA SCALA [A century of stage design at La Scala]. Milan: Emilio Bestetti, 1945. 33 p. 296 p. illus., part color.

Historical sketch (in Italian) and numerous valuable illustrations. Almost all the designers represented are Italian.

806. Basoli, Antonio. COLLEZIONE DI VARIE SCENE TEATRALI [A collection of various stage designs]. 1821. Reprint. New York: Benjamin

Blom, 1969. 100 pls. 4 p. index in Italian.

807. Corathiel, Elisabethe H.C. "Franco Zeffirelli." THEATRE WORLD 55 (April 1959): 9-12. Illus.

Concerns his designs for LUCIA DI LAMMERMOOR at Covent Garden.

808. _____. "Renzo Mongiardino." THEATRE WORLD 60 (August 1964): 28-29, 32. Illus.

An interview about his recent designs for TOSCA at Covent Garden.

809. Elvins, Peter. "A Lucky Man." OPERA NEWS 33 (7 December 1968): 8-13. Illus.

Concerns Nicola Benois, chief designer at La Scala for more than thirty years.

810. FIFTY YEARS OF OPERA AND BALLET IN ITALY. Edited by Carmine Siniscalco and Herman G. Weinberg. Rome: Carlo Bestetti, 1956. 54 p. 160 illus., part color.

Excellent selection of stage designs and production photographs.

811. Frette, Guido, ed. STAGE DESIGN. Translated by Blanche Michelesi Palmer. Milan: G.G. Goerlich, [1955]. 224 p. Prof. illus.

Brief essays by the editor and by Nicola Benois, Pino Casarini, Emanuele Luzzati, Mario Vellani Marchi, Guido Marussig, Gianni Vagnetti, and Piero Zuffi, plus 184 pages of illustrations, mainly for twentieth-century Italian productions.

812. Kirby, Michael. FUTURIST PERFORMANCE. New York: E.P. Dutton & Co., 1971. 351 p. Illus. Biblio.

"Futurist Scenography," pp. 71-90, with particular attention to the work of Enrico Prampolini, whose manifestos on scenography are translated in the appendix.

813. MacLeod, Joseph. "Guido Salvini." THEATRE RESEARCH / RECHERCHES THEATRALES 7 (1966): 110-16.

A short biography and tribute to Salvini (1893-1965), an Italian scene designer and director who worked with Pirandello and Reinhardt, presented plays at the Teatro Olimpico in Vicenza, and directed open-air spectacles in various Italian cities.

814. Matz, Mary Jane. "Enlightener." OPERA NEWS 34 (22 November

1969): 20-21. Illus.

Interview with designer Pier Luigi Pizzi.

815. Merkling, Frank. "Quaglio & Son." OPERA NEWS 36 (18 December 1971): 8-11. Illus.

Reproductions of seven designs by Simon, Giuseppe, and Angelo II Quaglio, with a brief sketch of this family of scene painters.

816. Pacuvio, Giulio. "Stage Design in Italy." WORLD THEATRE 5 (Autumn 1956): 269-80. Illus.

Critical sketch of twentieth-century Italian design, focusing on the years after 1945. Fourteen illustrations.

817. "Painter Onstage." SHOW 2 (March 1962): 76-81. Illus., part color.

Brief commentary and ten illustrations of Beni Montresor's stage designs.

818. Povoledo, Elena. "Stage Design in Italy." WORLD THEATRE 11 (1962): 139-54. Illus.

Review of twentieth-century Italian stage design, with stress on developments after World War II. Eighteen illustrations. A similar article by the same author appears in ITALIAN THE-ATRE REVIEW 12 (1963). 51-62.

819. Radice, Raul. "Some Aspects of Italian Design since the War." In INNOVATIONS IN STAGE AND THEATRE DESIGN (see item 57), pp. 153-57.

Contrasts opera design (especially at La Scala) with design for drama.

820. Rizzo, Francis. "Sorcerer's Apprenticeship." OPERA NEWS 35 (13 February 1971): 7-10. Ports.

Interview with Franco Zeffirelli, including informative auto-biographical comments.

821. "The Singularity of Gino Severini." APOLLO, n.s. 97 (May 1973): 448-61. Illus.

Brief discussion of Severini's stage designs.

822. Stevenson, Florence. "Gentleman of Verona: Beni Montresor." OPERA

NEWS 28 (8 February 1964): 26. Illus.

Brief sketch of his career, with notes on his designs for THE LAST SAVAGE at the Metropolitan Opera, New York.

823. _____. "Man from Milan." OPERA NEWS 29 (17 October 1964): 14-15. Port.

Brief biographical article on opera designer Attilio Colonnello.

824. Weaver, William. "Franco Zeffirelli." HIGH FIDELITY 14 (March 1964): 30, 34.

Survey of his career, based on an interview.

Chapter 12

RUSSIA AND THE SOVIET UNION

A. GENERAL HISTORIES

825.   THE BAKHRUSHIN STATE CENTRAL THEATRE MUSEUM (GOSUDARSTVEN-
NYI TSENTRAL'NYI TEATRAL'NYI MUZEI IMENI A.A. BAKHRUSHINA).
Moscow: Izobrazitelnoye Iskustvo Publishing House, 1971. 184 p.
(largely illustrations, part color).

> Text in Russian and English. A survey of the collections of
> one of the richest theatre museums in Russia. Brief introduc-
> tion by N. Yasulovich, translated by V. Friedman, plus 162
> illustrations (mostly of stage designs).

B. TWENTIETH CENTURY

SEE ALSO item 5.

826.   Akimov, Nikolai. "The Designer in the Theatre." THEATRE ARTS 20
(1936): 700-717. Illus.

> The author, a Russian stage designer, describes his methods.
> Illustrated with his own designs and those of Jacob Schtoffer,
> Moses Levin, Peter Williams, Ilya Shlepianov, Isaac Rabino-
> vitch, and one Knoblock.

827.   Alexandre, Arsene. THE DECORATIVE ART OF LEON BAKST. Translated by Harry Melvill. 1913. Reprint. New York: Dover Publications, 1972. x, 52 p. 77 pls., part color.

> Includes an appreciation by Alexandre and notes on the ballets
> by Jean Cocteau.

828.   ARTIST OF THE THEATRE: ALEXANDRA EXTER. New York: New
York Public Library and Readex Books, 1974. 40 p. Paperbound.
Illus. Biblio.

Exhibition catalog. Includes essays by Simon Lissim ("Alexandra Exter as I Knew Her"), Donald Oenslager, Andrei B. Nakov, and Nikita D. Lobanov.

829. Bakshy, Alexander. THE PATH OF THE MODERN RUSSIAN STAGE. London: Palmer & Hayward, 1916. 266 p.

Some discussion of the scenery of Meyerhold's productions, and of Gordon Craig.

830. Bakst, Leon. THE DESIGNS OF LEON BAKST FOR "THE SLEEPING PRINCESS." New York: Charles Scribner's Sons, 1923. 18 p. 54 color pls.

Preface by Andre Levinson sketches the background of the ballet and discusses Bakst's designs.

831. BAKST. New York: Brentano's, 1927. 127 p. Illus., part color.

Limited edition. Half-title: "Inedited Works of Bakst." Essays on Bakst's life and works by Louis Reau, Denis Roche, Valerian Svietlov, and Andre Tessier.

832. Bazanov, Vadim. "The Principles of the Preparation of Scenographers in the Leningrad Theatrical Institute." INTERSCAENA 4 (Winter 1970): 24-30. Illus.

833. Beaumont, Cyril W. "Mstislav Dobujinski: Some Recent Designs for Ballet." STUDIO 138 (July 1949): 20-23. Illus., one in color.

Designs for American Ballet Theatre and Ballet International.

834. Benois, Alexandre. "The Decor and Costume." In FOOTNOTES TO THE BALLET, edited by Doris Abrahams [Caryl Brahms], pp. 177-211. London: Lovat Dickson, 1936. Illus.

Benois first defines the place of decor in classical ballet, then discusses his own designs and the work of other artists.

835. _____. MEMOIRS. Translated by Moura Budberg. 2 vols. London: Chatto and Windus, 1960-64. Illus.

836. _____. REMINISCENCES OF THE RUSSIAN BALLET. Translated by Mary Britnieva. London: Putnam, 1941. 428 p. Illus.

837. Birnbaum, Harry. "Bakst and the Russian Ballet." HARPER'S WEEKLY 58 (29 November 1913): 13-15. Illus.

An early notice of Bakst in an American periodical.

838. Bragdon, Claude. "A Mighty Hunter (Nicholas Roerich)." In his
MERELY PLAYERS, pp. 127–34. New York: Alfred A. Knopf, 1929.
Illus.

Sketch of Roerich's career, with personal recollections.

839. Carter, Huntly. THE NEW SPIRIT IN THE RUSSIAN THEATRE, 1917–28.
New York: Brentano's, 1929. 370 p. Illus.

Includes discussion of the experiments of Meyerhold and Tairov.

840. Compton, Susan P. "Alexandra Exter and the Dynamic Stage." ART
IN AMERICA 62 (September–October 1974): 100–102. Illus., part
color.

Commentary on Exter's designs for Alexander Tairov's productions.

841. Corathiel, Elisabethe H.C. "Mstislav Dobujinsky." THEATRE WORLD
53 (April 1957): 18–20. Illus.

842. Cournand, Gilberte. "PETROUCHKA, Farewell." DANCE MAGAZINE
36 (April 1962): 44–45. Illus.

Brief biographical sketch of Alexandre Benois, with reminiscences.

843. Eisenstein, Sergei Y. EISENSTEIN: TEATRALNIE RISUNKI [Eisenstein:
theatrical sketches]. Moscow: Sovetskogo Kinoiskustva, 1970.

A portfolio of thirty mounted, colored reproductions of stage
designs by Eisenstein, 1917–44. An accompanying twelve-
page brochure in Russian, English, and French catalogs the
designs and includes an essay, "Eisenstein, Scene-Painter,"
by Sergei Yutkevich.

844. Elder, Eldon. "The Soviet Scene." OPERA NEWS 30 (7 May 1966):
8–13. Illus.

Observations by an American designer on current stage design
in the U.S.S.R., especially designs for operatic productions.

845. Fueloep-Miller, Rene, and Gregor, Joseph. THE RUSSIAN THEATRE:
ITS CHARACTER AND HISTORY. Philadelphia: J.B. Lippincott Co.,
[1930]. 136 p. 405 illus., part color.

Brief history of the Russian theatre and ballet and their "philo-
sophical" background (particularly during the Revolutionary
period), plus a large number of illustrations of productions,
scene designs, and performers, mainly twentieth-century.

846.   Gontcharova, Natalia. "The Creation of 'Les Noces.'" BALLET 8
        (September 1949): 23-26. Illus.

        Explains her work on scenery and costumes for this Diaghilev
        production first presented in 1923.

847.   Gorelik, Mordecai. "Soviet Scene Design." NEW THEATRE AND
        FILM 4 (April 1937): 22-23, 45. Illus.

        Notes on designs by Isaac Rabinovitch, Vadim Ryndin, and
        others.

848.   Gray, Camilla. THE GREAT EXPERIMENT: RUSSIAN ART, 1863-1922.
        London: Thames & Hudson, 1962. 326 p. Prof. illus., part color.
        Biblio.

        Since many of the leaders of the modern movement in Russia
        were stage designers, this general history devotes a great deal
        of attention to the theatre, ballet, and opera, including the
        work of Bakst, Benois, Gontcharova, Korovin, Larionov,
        Roerich, and others of the Diaghilev circle. Well illustrated.

849.   Hastings, Baird. "The Contribution of Michel Larionow to Ballet Design."
        DANCE MAGAZINE 23 (November 1949): 12-13, 37. Illus.

        An informative commentary.

850.   Hill, Derek. "The Russian Theatre of the Thirties." APOLLO, n.s. 86
        (August 1967): 142-47. Illus.

        Discussion of the work of Vadim Ryndin, Alexander Tischler,
        Isaac Rabinovitch, and others, by a designer who studied
        stage design in Moscow in the 1930s.

851.   Houghton, Norris. "Nikolai Akimov: Portrait of a Designer." THE-
        ATRE ARTS 20 (1936): 349-53. Illus.

        Brief discussion of Akimov's work and illustrations of his de-
        signs.

852.   Howard, Deborah. "A Sumptuous Revival: Bakst's Designs for Diaghi-
        lev's SLEEPING PRINCESS." APOLLO, n.s. 91 (April 1970): 301-8.
        Illus., part color.

        An ingenious study which shows how Bakst freely adapted
        scene designs by the Bibienas and costume designs by Berain,
        Martin, and Boquet. An important article, pointing a new
        direction in Ballets Russes scholarship.

853.   Kaplanova, S., comp. BORIS MIKHAILOVICH KUSTODIEV. Leningrad:
        Aurora Art Publishers, 1971. 127 p. Illus., part color.

Text in English and Russian. Includes twelve designs for theatre.

854. Klimoff, Eugene. "Alexandre Benois and His Role in Russian Art."
APOLLO, n.s. 98 (December 1973): 460-69. Illus., part color.

Only partly about his theatre work, but illustrated with unusual examples of his scene designs from Russian museums and
private collections.

855. Komisarjevsky, Theodore. "From Naturalism to Stage Design." In
FOOTNOTES TO THE THEATRE, edited by R.D. Charques, pp. 77-101.
London: Peter Davies, 1938. Illus.

Begins with an excellent summary of scenic techniques in
Russia in the 1890s, then proceeds to review developments in
stage design in Europe and America to the mid-1930s.

856. Korolev, Ivan. "Contemporary Stage Decoration in the U.S.S.R."
DRAMA 20 (January 1930): 99-103. Illus.

Describes recent work in the constructivist style. Illustrations
of models and settings by Ivan Vakhonin, Alexei Rudnyev,
Alexander Fomin, Victor Kiseler, and the author.

857. Kovarsky, Vera. "M.V. Dobujinsky: Pictorial Poet of St. Petersburg."
RUSSIAN REVIEW 19 (January 1960): 24-37.

A biographical study, drawing on Dobujinsky's memoirs, published in a Russian journal.

858. Larionov, Michel. "Diaghilev and His First Collaborators." BALLET 8
(September 1949): 9-15. Illus.

A portrait of Diaghilev by one of his early collaborators.

859. Levinson, Andre. BAKST: THE STORY OF THE ARTIST'S LIFE. 1923.
Reprint. New York: Benjamin Blom, 1971. Illus.

A somewhat awkward translation of an impressionistic biography,
short on facts, long on praise, but with some occasionally useful firsthand accounts of Bakst's work.

860. Leyda, Jay. "Alexander Tishler: Creative Stage Design." THEATRE
ARTS 18 (1934): 842-48. Illus.

Discusses and illustrates Tishler's use of unusual materials
(basketry, fur, lace) in making scenery.

861. Lister, Raymond. THE MUSCOVITE PEACOCK: A STUDY OF THE
ART OF LEON BAKST. Mortlocks, Meldreth, England: Golden Head

Press, 1954. 52 p. 11 illus., part color. Biblio.

Limited edition (150 copies), but available in a University Microfilm xerographic copy. Includes a reminiscence of Bakst by Simon Lissim, pp. 11-14. Notes on the ballets, pp. 45-52. The bibliography and notes on the ballets were reprinted in THEATRE RESEARCH / RECHERCHES THEATRALES 8 (1967): 145-55.

862.   Lobanov, Nikita D. "Russian Painters and the Stage." TRANSACTIONS OF THE ASSOCIATION OF RUSSIAN-AMERICAN SCHOLARS IN U.S.A. 2 (1968): 133-210. Biblio.

A valuable survey of the work of twentieth-century Russian stage designers, especially those associated with Diaghilev. Many were active outside Russia. Alphabetical list of designers, each with a chronology including biographical notes and productions designed. Good bibliography.

863.   Loney, Glenn M. "Behind the Soviet Scenes: Lawrence and Lee Tour USSR." THEATRE DESIGN & TECHNOLOGY, no. 33 (May 1973): 13-17. Illus.

Report on stage technology in the Soviet Union in 1971, illustrated with recent Soviet designs.

864.   Marshall, Herbert. "Design in the Theatre." STUDIO 127 (February 1944): 47-52. Illus., part color.

Commentary on Soviet design in the 1930s and 1940s.

865.   Meyer, Annie Nathan. "The Art of Leon Bakst." ART AND PROGRESS 5 (March 1914): 161-65. Illus.

An early appreciation by an American art critic.

866.   Meyerhold, Vsevolod. MEYERHOLD ON THEATRE. Translated by Edward Braun. New York: Hill & Wang, 1969. 336 p. Illus. Biblio.

A selection of Meyerhold's publications and speeches on theatre and film. Well illustrated with production photographs.

867.   MSTISLAV V. DOBUJINSKY. New York and Paris: The Group of Friends of Mstislav V. Dobujinsky's Art, 1973. 62 p. Paperbound. Illus. Biblio.

A useful little booklet including a biographical sketch; a list of Dobujinsky's designs in art galleries, museums, and public collections; a list of his designs for theatre, opera, and ballet; and a bibliography.

868. Nakov, Andrei B. ALEXANDRA EXTER. Paris: Galerie Jean Chauve-
lin, 1972. 63 p. Paperbound. Illus., part color. Biblio.

Text in French. The most recent monograph on Exter, reflecting renewed interest in her work. Well illustrated, with a
good bibliography.

869. Palmer, Elizabeth Cheatham. "A Study of the Art of Sergei Soudeikine."
MUSICAL COURIER 103 (7 November 1931): 6-7. Illus.

An excellent study, more extensive than the two-page cita-
tion suggests.

870. Pojarskaia, Militza. "Soviet Stage Design in the 20th Century."
WORLD THEATRE 10 (1961): 223-50. Illus.

A useful survey of design from the Revolution to 1960, describing work in various styles (constructivism, naturalism, permanent sets) and mentioning numerous designers. Thirty-eight
illustrations.

871. Raffe, Walter G. "Design in the Russian Theatre." STUDIO 123
(January 1942): 16-19. Illus.

Commentary on contemporary Russian designers' opportunities
and methods.

872. Rainey, Ada. "Leon Bakst: Brilliant Russian Colorist." CENTURY 87
(March 1914): 682-92. Illus.

Mainly concerns Bakst's costume designs.

873. Roberts, Mary Fanton. "The New Russian Stage, a Blaze of Color."
CRAFTSMAN 29 (December 1915): 257-69, 322. Illus.

Concerns Leon Bakst's work for the Ballets Russes.

874. Roerich, Nicholas. "The Unity of Art." THEATRE ARTS 5 (1921):
294-99. Illus.

Brief statement of his theory and methods of stage design.

875. Sayler, Oliver M. "Ultra-Modern Art in Relation to the Theatre."
ARTS AND DECORATION 24 (December 1925): 51-53, 85. Illus.

Discusses the scenic approach of the Moscow Art Theatre
Musical Studio, directed by Vladimir Nemirovich-Danchenko.

876. Siordet, Gerald C. "Leon Bakst's Designs for Scenery and Costumes."
INTERNATIONAL STUDIO 51 (November 1913): 3-7 and frontispiece.
Illus., part color.

877. Sokolova, Natalia. 50 LET SOVETSKOGO ISKUSTVA HUDOJNIKY TEATRA [50 years of soviet art: artists of the theatre]. Moscow: Sovetskii Khudozhnik, 1969. 272 p. Illus., part color.

Text in Russian and English. Sketch of Russian stage design since the 1917 Revolution, by Natalia Sokolova, plus 357 illustrations, with an alphabetical index of designers represented. Each illustration is fully identified in English. Excerpts from the text were published in ART AND ARTISTS 6 (April 1971): 16-19, with illustrations.

878. Spencer, Charles. LEON BAKST. New York: St. Martin's Press, 1973. 248 p. Prof. illus., part color. Biblio.

A new biography that attempts to correct earlier conflicting and fanciful accounts of Bakst's life. Thoroughly documented and well illustrated.

879. Symons, James M. MEYERHOLD'S THEATRE OF THE GROTESQUE: THE POST-REVOLUTIONARY PRODUCTIONS, 1920-1932. Coral Gables, Fla: University of Miami Press, 1971. 231 p. Illus. Biblio.

Useful material on Russian stage design in the 20s and 30s.

880. Tchelitchew, Pavel F. "What the Metropolitan Opera Might Do: An Ideal for THE MAGIC FLUTE." ART NEWS 41 (15 March 1942): 8. Illus.

Reproduces Tchelitchew's project for the Queen of the Night in Mozart's MAGIC FLUTE and reports his comments on it.

881. Tugendhold, J[acob]. ALEXANDRA EXTER. Translated by Count Petrovsky-Petrovo-Solovovo. Berlin: "Sarja" Editions, 1922. 30 p. Illus., part color, 39 pls.

Sketch of her career and commentary (in English), plus illustrations.

882. Tyler, Parker. THE DIVINE COMEDY OF PAVEL TCHELITCHEW. New York: Fleet Press Corp., 1967. viii, 504 p. Illus. Biblio.

883. VADIM FYODOROVICH RYNDIN. Moscow: Sovetskii Khudozhnik, 1971. 200 p. Prof. illus., part color.

Text in Russian and English. A record of the work of this Russian stage designer, active since the 1930s and principal artist of the Bolshoi Theatre from 1953 to 1970. Ten-page introduction by Natalia Sokolova, translated by N.I. Shebeko.

884. Vagenas, Peter Thomas. "Constructivism in Scenic Design: An Historical and Critical Study of the Basis and Development of Constructivism."

Ph.D. dissertation, University of Denver, 1966. 249 p.

Focusing on Russian artists, the author examines the development of constructivism in painting and sculpture, then traces its application to the theatre.

885. Windham, Donald. "The Stage and Ballet Designs of Pavel Tchelitchew." DANCE INDEX 3 (January-February 1944): 4-30. Illus.

An excellent survey and analysis.

Chapter 13

SWITZERLAND: NINETEENTH AND TWENTIETH CENTURIES

886. Albright, H. Darkes. "Appia Fifty Years After." QUARTERLY JOUR-
NAL OF SPEECH 35 (1949): 182-89, 297-303.

In two parts: the first summarizes Appia's ideas about stage
production; the second considers his influence (or lack of it) on
modern theatre and opera.

887. Appia, Adolphe. "The Elements of a Work of Living Art." Translated
by Rosamond Gilder. THEATRE ARTS 16 (1932): 667-78.

Translation of the first chapter of L'OEUVRE D'ART VIVANT
[The work of living art] (Paris: Edition Atar, 1921).

888. _____. "The Future of Production." Translated by Ralph Roeder.
THEATRE ARTS 16 (1932): 649-66. Illus.

A previously unpublished lecture, first presented in 1921, concerning the problem of "the animation of Space by music,
through the actor, transformed by musical proportions."

889. _____. "Goethe's FAUST: Notes from A PROJECT FOR THE PRODUC-
TION." THEATRE ARTS 16 (1932): 683-86. Illus.

Translated excerpts from an illustrated scenario published in
German in 1929.

890. _____. "Living Art or Frozen Nature?" Translated by Marvin Carlson.
PLAYERS 38 (1962): 124-26.

Translation of an essay first published in Milan in 1923.
Stresses the moving performer as the source of design. Another
translation, by S.A. Rhodes, was published in THEATRE AN-
NUAL 2 (1943): 38-46.

891. _____. MUSIC AND THE ART OF THE THEATRE. Translated by
Robert W. Corrigan and Mary D. Dirks. Edited by Barnard [W.] Hewitt.
Coral Gables, Fla.: University of Miami Press, 1962. 238 p. Illus.

Appia's best-known work, in which, as Lee Simonson says in
the foreword to this edition, he "elucidated the basic aesthetic
principles of modern scenic design." Includes appendices on
the staging of Wagner's TRISTAN AND ISOLDE and THE RING
OF THE NIBELUNGEN, translated by Walther R. Volbach.

892. _____. "THE WORK OF LIVING ART" AND "MAN IS THE MEASURE
OF ALL THINGS." Translated by H. Darkes Albright and Barnard
Hewitt, respectively. Edited by Barnard [W.] Hewitt. Coral Gables, Fla.:
University of Miami Press, 1960. 150 p. Illus.

Preceded by a useful summary of Appia's life and theories by
H.D. Albright, these essays present Appia's mature view of
theatre art, promoting stage setting that provides a "rhythmic
space" for the actor.

893. Beck, Gordon. "Adolphe Appia: His Life and Work." PLAYERS 38
(1962): 118-21. Illus., port.

A concise, well-documented summary.

894. Brodsky, Nina. "Light-Play." STUDIO 117 (February 1939): 68-69.
Illus.

Brief discussion of her designs for projected scenery; illustrations of her productions in Switzerland.

895. Kaucher, Dorothy. "Adolphe Appia's Theories of Production." QUAR-
TERLY JOURNAL OF SPEECH 14 (1928): 411-22.

A commentary on Appia's MUSIC AND THE ART OF THE THE-
ATRE.

896. Kernodle, George R. "Wagner, Appia, and the Idea of Musical Design."
EDUCATIONAL THEATRE JOURNAL 6 (1954): 223-30.

Discusses Wagner's romantic search for "deeper feeling and the
underlying myth," leading to "a deeper musical pattern underlying the entire play." Then explains how Appia's "plastic"
settings and changing light expressed that underlying pattern.
Suggests that this Wagner-Appia concept is basic to modern
drama and modern opera.

897. Leeper, Janet. "Appia." ARCHITECTURAL REVIEW 143 (February 1968):
113-18. Illus.

Excellent short summary of Appia's career and his contributions
to stage design and lighting. Includes considerable discussion
of Gordon Craig.

898. Matz, Mary Jane. "Let There Be Light." OPERA NEWS 35 (3 April

1971): 8-11. Illus.

Biographical sketch of Adolphe Appia and a summary of his theories about lighting and stage design.

899. Mercier, Jean. "Adolphe Appia: The Re-Birth of Dramatic Art." THE-ATRE ARTS 16 (1932): 615-30.

Biographical sketch and summary of his theory and influence, stressing the "social and ethical aesthetic" in his work.

900. Moderwell, Hiram K. "Impressionistic Settings for Modern Opera." HARVARD MUSICAL REVIEW 4 (October 1915): 1-3. Illus.

An early and farsighted appreciation of Appia's work, contrasting his designs with other examples of the New Stagecraft.

901. Rogers, Clark M. "Appia's Theory of Acting: Eurhythmics for the Stage." EDUCATIONAL THEATRE JOURNAL 19 (1967): 467-72.

902. Simonson, Lee. "Appia's Contribution to the Modern Stage." THEATRE ARTS 16 (1932): 631-44. Illus.

An advance publication of the chapter on Appia in Simonson's THE STAGE IS SET (see item 84), in which he analyzes Appia's theory of stage design and lighting.

903. Stadler, Edmund [Edmond]. "Jaques-Dalcroze et Adolphe Appia." In EMILE JAQUES-DALCROZE: L'HOMME, LE COMPOSITEUR, LE CRE-ATEUR DE LA RYTHMIQUE, pp. 413-59. Neuchatel, Switzerland: Editions de la Baconniere, 1965. Illus. Biblio.

Text in French. Authoritative study of an important collaboration. Transcribes many letters exchanged between Appia and Jaques-Dalcroze.

904. _____. "The Morax Brothers and the Theatre du Jorat." In INNOVA-TIONS IN STAGE AND THEATRE DESIGN (see item 57), pp. 78-94. Illus.

Rene and Jean Morax at the Theatre du Jorat in Mezieres, Switzerland (opened 1908), produced plays in a style that anticipated the New Stagecraft.

905. _____, comp. ADOLPHE APPIA. London: Victoria and Albert Museum, 1970. 26 p. 24 illus.

Exhibition catalog. Includes a useful survey of Appia's career, pp. 9-26.

906. Van Wyck, Jessica Davis. "Designing HAMLET with Appia." THEATRE

ARTS 9 (1925): 17-31. Illus.

Quotes letters from Appia, with whom the author collaborated in 1922-23.

907. "The Vision of Adolphe Appia." APOLLO, n.s. 93 (January 1971): 2-7. Illus.

A commentary on Appia's contributions.

908. Volbach, Walther R. ADOLPHE APPIA, PROPHET OF THE MODERN THEATRE: A PROFILE. Middletown, Conn.: Wesleyan University Press, 1968. 260 p. Illus. Biblio.

The best study in English of Appia's life and work, with an extensive bibliography.

909. _____. "Appia's Productions and Contemporary Reaction." EDUCA-TIONAL THEATRE JOURNAL 13 (1961): 1-10.

910. _____. "The Beginnings of a Genius." PLAYERS 38 (1962): 122-23.

Brief but informative description of Appia's youth.

911. _____. "A Profile of Adolphe Appia." EDUCATIONAL THEATRE JOURNAL 15 (1963): 7-14.

A portrait of Appia the man--his personality, habits, and attitudes--based on unpublished material and interviews.

Chapter 14

UNITED STATES

A. GENERAL HISTORIES

912. Austin, Mary. "Primitive Stage Setting." THEATRE ARTS 12 (January 1928): 49-59. Illus.

Altar, wall decorations, and symbolic set pieces form "settings" for Pueblo Indian ritual drama. Illustrated with paintings of backgrounds used in temples.

913. Gillette, Arnold S. "American Scenography: 1716-1969." In THE AMERICAN THEATRE: A SUM OF ITS PARTS, pp. 180-96. New York: Samuel French, 1971.

One of very few publications that attempt a historical survey of American stage design. Sketchy and generalized.

914. Hamar, Clifford E. "Scenery on the Early American Stage." THEATRE ANNUAL 7 (1948-49): 84-103. Illus.

Traces the development of scenery in the United States from 1716 to 1830. A useful survey of a subject still waiting to be researched in depth.

915. Joyce, Robert S[uddards]. "The Armbruster Scenic Studio." OSU THE- ATRE COLLECTION BULLETIN 12 (1965): 6-19. Illus.

A brief history of this Columbus, Ohio, studio for the period 1875 to 1958. A description of the Armbruster Collection of scenery and archives acquired by the Ohio State University Theatre Research Institute. Valuable illustrations of designs, models, and scenery onstage.

916. _____. "A History of the Armbruster Scenic Studio of Columbus, Ohio." Ph.D. dissertation, Ohio State University, 1970. 236 p.

917. Lawrence, W[illiam]. J[ohn]. "Early American Scene Painters." NEW

YORK DRAMATIC MIRROR, 13 January 1917, p. 7.

A brief but unusual study of American scene painters and their techniques in the eighteenth and nineteenth centuries.

918.   Lerche, Frank Martin. "The Growth and Development of Scenic Design for the Professional Musical Comedy Stage in New York from 1866 to 1920." Ph.D. dissertation, New York University, 1969. 490 p.

Examines one hundred productions, tracing changes from painted illusionism (1866-99) to built-up illusionism (1900-1909) to the New Stagecraft (1910-20, stressing the work of Joseph Urban).

919.   Lounsbury, Warren C. THEATRE BACKSTAGE FROM A TO Z. Seattle: University of Washington Press, 1967. 200 p. Illus. Biblio.

Includes a twenty-page introductory sketch of the history of scenery and lighting in the American theatre.

920.   Swanson, Wesley. "Wings and Backdrops: The Story of American Stage Scenery from the Beginnings to 1875." DRAMA 18 (October 1927-January 1928): 5-7, 30, 41-42, 63-64, 78-80, 107-110. Illus.

One of the first attempts at a general history of early American stage design. Undocumented, outdated, incomplete.

B. EIGHTEENTH CENTURY

SEE ALSO items 963, 966.

921.   Alden, John. "A Season in Federal Street: J.B. Williamson and the Boston Theatre, 1796-1797." PROCEEDINGS OF THE AMERICAN ANTIQUARIAN SOCIETY 65 (1955): 9-74.

A detailed examination of the repertoire, personnel, and expenses under Williamson's management. Includes a transcription of an inventory of scenery, machinery, and lighting equipment in the theatre, pp. 44-52.

922.   Duerr, Edwin. "Charles Ciceri and the Background of American Scene Design." THEATRE ARTS 16 (1932): 983-90.

Notes on eighteenth-century American scenery and scene painters, particularly Antony Audin and Charles Ciceri.

923.   Stoddard, Richard. "The Haymarket Theatre, Boston." EDUCATIONAL THEATRE JOURNAL 27 (March 1975): 63-69. Illus.

Transcribes an inventory of scenery at the Haymarket in the years 1796-1800.

924. _____. "Stock Scenery in 1798." THEATRE SURVEY 13 (1972): 102-3.

> Transcription of a list of stock scenery intended for the Federal Street Theatre, Boston.

C. NINETEENTH CENTURY

SEE ALSO items 413, 427, 439, 1218.

925. Adler, Dankmar. "The Chicago Auditorium." ARCHITECTURAL RECORD 1 (April-June 1892): 415-34. Illus.

> See pp. 424-28 for an account of the Asphaleia-type stage and stage machinery at this theatre.

926. American Society of Scenic Painters. CONSTITUTION AND BY-LAWS OF THE AMERICAN SOCIETY OF SCENIC PAINTERS. New York: 1892. 8 p. Paperbound.

> Includes a list of thirty-eight charter members.

927. Arnold, Richard L[ee]. "The Great Chariot Race: Scenic Effects at the Turn of the Century." THEATRE DESIGN & TECHNOLOGY, no. 23 (December 1970): 12-15. Illus.

> Brief description of Claude L. Hagen's machinery for the chariot race in BEN HUR, 1899. Good illustrations.

928. Arrington, Joseph Earl. "Lewis and Bartholomew's Mechanical Panorama of the Battle of Bunker Hill." OLD-TIME NEW ENGLAND 52 (Fall 1961, Winter 1962): 50-58, 81-89. Illus.

> Describes a panorama painted by Minard Lewis and Truman C. Bartholomew in 1838 and exhibited for some twenty years.

929. "Art on the Stage." NEW-YORK DAILY TRIBUNE, 27 December 1880, p. 5.

> An informative, detailed description of the preparation of scenery in New York theatres.

930. Barrow, Jack W. "The Town Hall Theatre at Put-in-Bay, Ohio." OSU THEATRE COLLECTION BULLETIN 8 (1961): 24-34. Illus.

> A description and photographic record of the old scenery and stage machinery preserved in this late nineteenth-century playhouse.

931. Bunce, Oliver Bell. "Behind, Below, and Above the Scenes." APPLETON'S JOURNAL 3 (1870): 589-94. Illus.

An important record of the scenery and hydraulic stage machinery at Booth's Theatre in New York (opened in 1869). Informative illustrations. Also published anonymously as a pamphlet, with the title BOOTH'S THEATRE: BEHIND THE SCENES (New York: Hinton, 1870).

932. Cohen, Robert. "Hamlet as Edwin Booth." THEATRE SURVEY 10 (1969): 53–74. Illus.

A reconstruction of Booth's production in 1870, at his own theatre in New York. Charles Witham's scenery is described in detail. Illustrations include detailed ground plans.

933. Cole, Wendell. "The Nineteenth Century Stage at Piper's Opera House." THEATRE NOTEBOOK 15 (1960–61): 52–55.

Describes in detail the stage and "grooves" for scenery preserved in this opera house, built in 1883–84 in Virginia City, Nevada.

934. Day, Susan Stockbridge. "Productions at Niblo's Garden Theatre, 1862–1868, during the Management of William Wheatley." Ph.D. dissertation, University of Oregon, 1972. 362 p.

Considers, among other productions, Wheatley's spectacles THE BLACK CROOK and THE WHITE FAWN.

935. Fox, John A. "American Dramatic Theatres, [part] VII." AMERICAN ARCHITECT AND BUILDING NEWS 6 (6 September 1879): 74–75.

An architect's description of stage construction, traps, fly floor, gridiron, and scenery in a typical American theatre.

936. Guthrie, David Gordon. "The Innovations of Steele MacKaye in Scenic Design and Stage Practice as Contributions to the American Theatre." Ph.D. dissertation, New York University, 1974. 403 p.

Discusses thirty-three inventions for improving stage mechanism, lighting, and audience comfort and safety.

937. Hannon, Daniel Leroy. "The MacKaye Spectatorium: A Reconstruction and Analysis of a Theatrical Spectacle Planned for the World's Columbian Exposition of 1893, with a History of the Producing Organizations." Ph.D. dissertation, Tulane University, 1970. 341 p.

938. Harvey, E.T. RECOLLECTIONS OF A SCENE PAINTER. Cincinnati: E.T. Harvey, 1916. 64 p.

Anecdotes about scene painters Thomas B. Glessing and William T. Porter, with some notes on early techniques.

939.   DELETED

940.   Jackson, Allan S[tuart].   "A Theatre from the Past."   PLAYERS 43
        (December–January 1968):   43–47.   Illus.

> Illustrates old scenery, machinery, and switchboard in the
> Assembly Hall, New York State Hospital at Binghamton, built
> 1897.

941.   Kobbe, Gustav.   "Behind the Scenes of an Opera-House."   SCRIBNER'S
        4 (October 1888):   435–54.   Illus.

> Scenery, machinery, and special effects at the Metropolitan
> Opera House, New York, especially in productions of Wagner's
> operas.   Excellent illustrations, including a plan of the traps
> and bridges in the stage, a scene plot, and a gas plot.

942.   Ledger Job Printing Office, Philadelphia.   SPECIMENS OF SHOW
        PRINTING.   Circa 1870.   Reprint.   Hollywood: Cherokee Books in
        association with Lee Freeson Theatre Books, n.d. [1965?].   [14] p.
        284 pls.

> Reprint of a catalog of miniature (sample) theatrical posters.
> Most depict scenes from melodramas, pantomimes, and similar
> popular entertainments.   Many show scenery and special effects.
> Cover title: EARLY AMERICAN THEATRICAL POSTERS.

943.   Leverton, Garrett H.   PRODUCTION OF LATER NINETEENTH CENTURY
        DRAMA: A BASIS FOR TEACHING.   New York: Teachers College,
        Columbia University, Bureau of Publications, 1936.   130 p.   Illus.
        Biblio.

> Describes the typical stage, scenery, special effects, and other
> aspects of the late nineteenth-century American theatre, as a
> basis for revivals of period plays.

944.   Lewis, Virginia E.   RUSSELL SMITH, ROMANTIC REALIST.   Pittsburgh:
        University of Pittsburgh Press, 1956.   367 p.   Illus.   Biblio.

> In a sense, this is the only book-length study yet published
> of a nineteenth-century American scene painter.   But Smith
> (1812–96) was as much an easel painter as a scene painter,
> and the stress here is on the former.   Still, the author pro-
> vides much useful information, largely from unpublished sources,
> on Smith's theatre work.   Nine theatrical illustrations, mainly
> designs for drop curtains.

United States

945. McCullough, Jack W. "Edward Kilyani and American Tableaux Vivants."
THEATRE SURVEY 16 (May 1975): 25-41.

> Brief history of theatrical tableaux vivants, followed by a more
> detailed discussion of Kilyani, a producer of these spectacles
> during the 1890s. He developed a system of tableaux on
> moving platforms, the "Glyptorama."

946. McDermott, John Francis. THE LOST PANORAMAS OF THE MISSISSIPPI.
Chicago: University of Chicago Press, 1958. 228 p. Illus. Biblio.

> Sketch of the early history of the panorama followed by sepa-
> rate chapters on panoramas painted by John Banvard, John Row-
> son Smith, Samuel Stockwell, Henry Lewis, and Leon Pomarede,
> plus appendices on several minor panoramas. Excellent bibli-
> ography and illustrations.

947. MacKaye, Percy. EPOCH: THE LIFE OF STEELE MACKAYE. 2 vols.
New York: Boni & Liveright, 1927. Illus. Biblio.

> An elaborate biography by MacKaye's son, including extensive
> discussion of MacKaye's technical inventions (elevator stage,
> Spectatorium, "cloud-creator," light curtain and other lighting
> effects, sliding stage, and so on).

948. Manson, George J. "The Making of the Theatre. II. The Scenery."
NEW YORK DRAMATIC MIRROR, 27 June 1896, p. 14.

> A broad view of scene painting in America, with remarks on
> the scene painter's sources and techniques, lighting, changes
> in scenic fashions, drop curtains, and working conditions.

949. Marker, Lise-Lone. DAVID BELASCO: NATURALISM IN THE AMERI-
CAN THEATRE. Princeton, N.J.: Princeton University Press, 1975.
262 p. Illus. Biblio.

> Examines Belasco's naturalistic settings and his carefully planned
> stage lighting. Based on the author's Ph.D. dissertation, "The
> Scenic Art of David Belasco: A Reappraisal," Yale University,
> 1968.

950. Marsh, John L. "Captain E.C. Williams and the Panoramic School of
Acting." EDUCATIONAL THEATRE JOURNAL 23 (1971): 289-97.

> Describes Captain Williams's exhibitions of a "South Sea Whal-
> ing Voyage" panorama in New York and New England, 1858-
> 66.

951. Marshall, Thomas F. "Charles W. Witham: Scenic Artist to the Nineteenth-Century American Stage." In ANATOMY OF AN ILLUSION
(see item 102), pp. 26-30, 78-79. Illus.

Sketch of the career of this important American scene painter (one of Edwin Booth's collaborators), with six reproductions of his surviving designs.

952. Marston, Richard. "Art in the Theatre: The Decline of Scenic Art in America." MAGAZINE OF ART 17 (1894): 163–68. Illus.

A significant article, attacking scenery "factories" that compete unfairly with individual artists, produce inferior work, and suppress creativity. Illustrated with photographs of scenic models by the author.

953. Oliver, George B. "The Changing Pattern of Spectacle on the New York Stage (1850–1890)." Parts 1–3. Ph.D. dissertation, Pennsylvania State University, 1956. 351 p.

954. Parry, Lee. "Landscape Theater in America." ART IN AMERICA 59 (November–December 1971): 52–61. Illus., part color.

Concerns panoramas in America in the first half of the nineteenth century, including the work of John Vanderlyn and John Banvard. Excellent illustrations.

955. Reed, Ronald Michael. "The Nature of the Scenic Practices in Augustin Daly's New York Productions, 1869–1899." Ph.D. dissertation, University of Oregon, 1968. 360 p.

956. Ritter, John P. "Scene-Painting as a Fine Art." COSMOPOLITAN 8 (November 1889): 43–49. Illus.

Informative article about American scene-painting techniques, with remarks on the career of Henry E. Hoyt, scene painter at the Metropolitan Opera House, and reproductions of four of Hoyt's designs.

957. Robinson, C.D. "Painting a Yosemite Panorama." OVERLAND, s. 2, 22 (September 1893): 243–56. Illus.

Describes and illustrates the technique of panorama painting.

958. "Scene Painting." NEW-YORK DAILY TRIBUNE, 21 April 1895, p. 25.

An interview with Henry E. Hoyt, scenic artist at the Metropolitan Opera House, New York. Sketch of his career and description of his methods.

959. Shank, Theodore J. "Shakespeare and Nineteenth-Century Realism." THEATRE SURVEY 4 (1963): 59–75. Illus.

A valuable survey of romantic realism and antiquarianism in

American Shakespeare production, well illustrated with twenty-one prints and photographs, mostly from productions at Booth's and Daly's theatres.

960.　Shattuck, Charles H.　"Edwin Booth's Hamlet:　A New Promptbook."　HARVARD LIBRARY BULLETIN 15 (January 1967):　20–48.　Illus.

Describes a souvenir promptbook including ten stage designs attributed to Charles Witham.　See also the author's THE HAMLET OF EDWIN BOOTH (Urbana:　University of Illinois Press, 1969).

961.　"Stage Effects in BEN HUR."　SCIENTIFIC AMERICAN 83 (25 August 1900):　113, 119.　Illus.

Well-illustrated explanation of the machinery of the chariot race and other scenes in BEN HUR at the Broadway Theatre, New York.

962.　"Stage Scenes Reversed."　NEW YORK TIMES, 11 November 1883, p. 5.

An informative backstage report on setting and changing scenes, placing props, and arranging the lights in an unidentified New York theatre.

963.　Stoddard, Richard.　"The Architecture and Technology of Boston Theatres, 1794-1854."　Ph.D. dissertation, Yale University, 1971.　315 p.

964.　_____.　"Notes on John Joseph Holland, with a Design for the Baltimore Theatre, 1802."　THEATRE SURVEY 12 (1971):　58–66.　Illus.

Identifies and reproduces for the first time the oldest surviving American scene design that has yet come to light; provides a biographical sketch and a portrait of the designer.

965.　Wilson, M[ardis]. Glen, Jr.　"Theatrical Significance of Specimen Book Designs."　OSU THEATRE COLLECTION BULLETIN 4 (Spring 1957):　13–32.　Illus.

Examines "specimen books" of poster designs, c. 1875, as sources of information on American scenic practices.　(Cf. item 942.)

966.　Wolcott, John R[utherford].　"A Case Study of American Production:　English Source and American Practice."　OSU THEATRE COLLECTION BULLETIN 15 (1968):　9–19.　Illus.

Concerns American use of scenery and scenic models sent from England in the eighteenth and early nineteenth centuries, particularly material sent by John Worroll, a New England scene painter, to Henry Warren, a Philadelphia scene painter, in 1816.

967. _____. "English Influences on American Staging Practice: A Case Study of the Chestnut Street Theatre, Philadelphia, 1794-1820." Ph.D. dissertation, Ohio State University, 1967.

968. Woodrow, Ernest A.E. "Theatres. [Part] XVIII." BUILDING NEWS 64 (10 March 1893): 330-31. Illus.

Part of a series of articles on theatre construction. Describes the Asphaleia-type stage at the Auditorium Theatre, Chicago.

D. TWENTIETH CENTURY

SEE ALSO item 949.

969. "Adding Art to Music for Comedy's Sake." VOGUE 47 (1 February 1916): 50-51, 112. Illus., color.

Illustrates and comments on stage designs by Robert McQuinn.

970. Amberg, George. "Design for Theatre." THEATRE ARTS 32 (April 1948): 40-41. Illus.

Brief sketch of recent American design, noting that much of it is dull and unimaginative.

971. _____. "RIGOLETTO." INTERIORS 111 (December 1951): 106-13. Illus., part color.

Concerns Eugene Berman's designs for the Metropolitan Opera, New York.

972. "The American Ballet Theatre, 1940-1960." DANCE PERSPECTIVES, no. 6 (1960). Illus.

Entire issue comprises a chronology of this company's activities, 1940-60, with an index of designers and their productions.

973. Anderson, John, and Fueloep-Miller, Rene. THE AMERICAN THEATRE AND THE MOTION PICTURE IN AMERICA. New York: Dial Press, 1938. 430 p. Prof. illus., part color.

The American theatre section includes 124 pages of illustrations, mainly production photographs and stage designs.

974. "Arch Lauterer--Poet in the Theatre. IMPULSE 1959. Illus. Biblio.

Whole issue (64 p.) devoted to Lauterer. Lists of his productions, illustrations of his theatre and dance designs, tributes, and essays by him.

975. Ardoin, John. "Set to Go." OPERA NEWS 31 (18 March 1967): 6-7. Illus.

Sketch of the career and current activities of Peter Wolf, scenic studio operator in Dallas, Texas.

976. Armistead, Horace. "Designing for Ballet." In SCENE DESIGN FOR STAGE AND SCREEN (see item 1161), pp. 208-13.

Identifies the music as the source of design.

977. Arnold, Richard L[ee]. "Animated Scenery." EDUCATIONAL THEATRE JOURNAL 16 (1964): 249-52.

Special effects such as sandstorms, volcanoes, chariot races, etc., c. 1900-1910.

978. _____. "The Changing Concepts of Realism in Scenery on the New York Stage, 1900 to 1915." Ph.D. dissertation, Northwestern University, 1962. 230 p.

979. Aronson, Boris. "Designing SWEET BYE AND BYE." THEATRE ARTS 30 (1946): 573-75. Illus.

Describes the conception of his design for this futuristic play and reproduces seven of his sketches.

980. "The Artist in the American Theatre: Illustrated by the Work of American Stage Craftsmen." TOUCHSTONE 5 (April 1919): 40-50, 77-79. Illus.

Good summary of the principles and progress of the New Stagecraft in America.

981. Atkinson, Brooks. "Six Vital Stage Sets." NEW YORK TIMES MAGAZINE, 11 April 1954, pp. 24-25. Illus.

Brief text and six photographs of "the most vital stage designing among current theatre works."

982. Atkinson, Frank H. SCENE PAINTING AND BULLETIN ART. Chicago: Drake Publishers, 1916. 249 p. Illus.

The section on scene painting, pp. 143-204, includes data on equipment, colors, painting techniques, and arrangement of scenery on the stage.

983. Baker, George Pierce. "HAMLET on an Elizabethan Stage." JAHRBUCH
DER DEUTSCHEN SHAKESPEARE-GESELLSCHAFT 41 (1905): 296-301.
Illus.

Describes the reconstruction of the Elizabethan Fortune Theatre
built in Sanders Theatre at Harvard University for a production
in 1904.

984. Barnes, Djuna. "His World's a Stage." THEATRE GUILD MAGAZINE
8 (June 1931): 25-29. Illus.

An early survey of Jo Mielziner's career, based on an interview.

985. _____. "'I've Always Suffered from Sirens.'" THEATRE GUILD MAGA-
ZINE 8 (March 1931): 23-25. Illus.

Survey of the career of designer Raymond Sovey, based on an
interview.

986. _____. "Mordecai Gorelik." THEATRE GUILD MAGAZINE 8 (February 1931): 42-45. Illus.

987. Barton, Mike Alan. "Aline Bernstein: A History and Evaluation."
Ph.D. dissertation, Indiana University, 1971. 336 p.

A study of her career as a designer.

988. Bay, Howard. "Design for the Musical Stage." THEATRE ARTS 29
(November 1945): 650-55. Illus.

A sketch of developments in scenic design for musicals, from
Joseph Urban's loveliness to Albert Johnson's slick revue style
and the nostalgic period pieces of the 1940s. Bay discusses
this subject again in THEATRE ARTS 43 (April 1959): 56-59.

989. _____. "Settings." THEATRE ARTS 37 (February 1953): 66-69. Illus.

A personal view of trends in stage design since the 1920s,
noting with dismay a recent trend towards unnecessary lavish-
ness and artistic exhibitionism. A shortened version of this
article appears, without illustrations, in SCENE DESIGN FOR
STAGE AND SCREEN (see item 1161), pp. 292-98.

990. Beiswanger, George. "Opera for the Eye" Richard Rychtarik at the
Metropolitan." THEATRE ARTS 27 (1943): 57-62. Illus.

Brief discussion of the problems of opera design, plus a biographical sketch of Rychtarik and two illustrations of his designs for opera.

991. Belasco, David. "Stage Art, New and Old." SATURDAY EVENING

POST 192 (20 March 1920): 22-23, 66, 69-70. Illus.

Reminiscence about stage lighting in the late nineteenth century (mainly referring to his own productions); hostile remarks on the New Stagecraft ("mystic bosh").

992. Berman, Eugene. "Hail 'Don Giovanni,' Farewell Theatre." SATURDAY REVIEW 40 (26 October 1957): 45, 47, 63-65. Illus.

Describes his difficulties in designing Mozart's opera for an American production; declares that it will be his last work for the stage. Reprinted, without illustrations, in SCENE DESIGN FOR STAGE AND SCREEN (see item 1161), pp. 320-28.

993. _____. "Notes on Designing OTELLO." SHOW 3 (March 1963): 26-28. Illus., color.

994. _____. "Scene Design and Theatre." In SCENE DESIGN FOR STAGE AND SCREEN (see item 1161), pp. 300-319.

Revised translation of an article first published in PROSPETTIVE, no. 12 (1956). This is Berman's artistic "credo," identifying sources of influence on him, laying down criteria for success in stage design, and criticizing the limitations on the designer in America.

995. Bernstein, Aline. "'In Production.'" ATLANTIC 166 (September 1940): 323-32.

A step-by-step explanation of how the author goes about designing scenery and costumes.

996. Berry, R.D. "Stage Equipment and Lighting." ARCHITECTURAL FORUM 52 (April 1930): 605-8. Illus.

New equipment at the Chicago Civic Opera House.

997. Billings, Alan Gailey. "Design in the Works Progress Administration's Federal Theatre Project (1935 to 1939)." Ph.D. dissertation, University of Illinois (Urbana-Champaign), 1967. 184 p.

Examines productions in New York, San Francisco, Los Angeles, Chicago, and Atlanta. Identifies three styles: realism, simplified realism (in the manner of Howard Bay), and Hallie Flanagan's "no scenery" style, dependent on lighting.

998. Bishop, John Peale. "The Youngest among the Moderns: James Reynolds as an Artist in Settings and Costumes." THEATRE ARTS 5 (1921): 69-79. Illus.

Describes his work for revues. Twelve illustrations.

999. Black, Eugene Robert. "Robert Edmond Jones: Poetic Artist of the New Stagecraft." Ph.D. dissertation, University of Wisconsin, 1955. 361 p.

1000. Blackall, Clarence H. "The American Theater--IX: The Stage." BRICKBUILDER 17 (August 1908): 163-66; 17 (September 1908): 185-86, 211-13. Illus.

Informative discussion of stage construction and machinery, by a veteran theatre architect.

1001. Bliven, Bruce. "Norman-Bel Geddes: His Art and Ideas." THEATRE ARTS 3 (1919): 179-91. Illus.

Biographical sketch and assessment of Geddes's achievement, with emphasis on his work for Aline Barnsdall in California.

1002. Bogusch, George [Edwin]. "An American in Paris: Norman Bel Geddes Produces JEANNE D'ARC." THEATRE DESIGN & TECHNOLOGY, no. 18 (October 1969): 4-11. Illus.

A detailed account, largely based on unpublished sources, of Geddes's 1925 Paris production.

1003. _____. "Unity in the New Stagecraft: A Study of Productions Designed and Directed by Norman Bel Geddes." Ph.D. dissertation, Indiana University, 1968. 506 p.

1004. Bolin, John Seelye. "Samuel Hume: Artist and Exponent of American Art Theatre." Ph.D. dissertation, University of Michigan, 1970. 237 p.

A study of the director, designer, and educator who promoted the use of permanent sets in the style of Gordon Craig's designs; directed the Detroit Arts and Crafts Theatre from 1916 to 1918; and encouraged the New Stagecraft in America.

1005. Bower, Homer Thomas. "San Francisco Opera Company Scene Design, 1932-1955." Ph.D. dissertation, Stanford University, 1963. 327 p.

Examines the impact of the New Stagecraft on this company's designs for opera.

1006. Bowers, Faubion. "Opera Primer III: Who Paints the Scenery?" OPERA NEWS 33 (8 February 1969): 26-29. Illus.

Description of the scenery-making facilities of the Metropolitan Opera House and of the work of chief artist Vladimir Odinokov and his staff.

1007. Bragdon, Claude. "Art and Arithmetic." THEATRE ARTS 8 (1924): 505-12. Illus.

Explains Bragdon's system of deriving new ornamental motifs from geometrical arrangements called "magic squares." The illustrations include a stage design in which Bragdon applies the idea.

1008. _____. "'The Hamlet Problem' from the Standpoint of the Artist in the Theatre." ARCHITECTURAL RECORD 59 (January 1926): 1-6. Illus.

Discusses his designs for Walter Hampden's production.

1009. _____. MORE LIVES THAN ONE. New York: Alfred A. Knopf, 1938. 368 p. Illus.

An autobiography. For reminiscences about his work as a stage designer, see part 3, "My Theatrical Life," pp. 185-241.

1010. _____. "Producing Shakespeare, as Illustrated by Walter Hampden's Production of OTHELLO." ARCHITECTURAL RECORD 57 (March 1925): 266-75. Illus.

The author discusses his conception and design of the scenery.

1011. _____. "The Scenery for Walter Hampden's HAMLET." THEATRE ARTS 3 (1919): 192-95. Illus.

Brief text by the author, who designed this production, plus four illustrations.

1012. _____. "The Technique of Theatrical Production." ARCHITECTURAL RECORD 66 (August 1929): 109-22. Illus.

Discusses his designs for Walter Hampden's production of THE LIGHT OF ASIA. Excellent illustrations.

1013. _____. "A Theatre Transformed." ARCHITECTURAL RECORD 55 (April 1924): 388-97. Illus.

Excellent description of Norman-Bel Geddes's cathedral setting for THE MIRACLE at the Century Theatre, New York. Illustrated with scale drawings and photographs.

1014. _____. "Walter Hampden's Production of CYRANO DE BERGERAC." ARCHITECTURAL RECORD 54 (December 1923): 553-64. Illus.

Well-illustrated account of Bragdon's scenery for this production.

1015. Brasmer, William. "Early Scene Design of Mordecai Gorelik." OSU THEATRE COLLECTION BULLETIN 12 (1965): 44-52. Illus.

Concerns Gorelik's designs for productions in the 1920s and 1930s, especially those for plays with a social "message."

1016. Bricker, Herschel L., ed. OUR THEATRE TODAY. New York: Samuel French, 1936. 454 p. Illus.

A collection of essays including "Scenic Art" and "Technical Methods" by Cleon Throckmorton, and two essays on lighting by Stanley R. McCandless and Louis Ehrhardt. Illustrated with lighting plots, ground plans, and production photographs.

1017. Brown, Frank Chouteau. "The Bel Geddes' 'Hamlet, a Melodrama.'" DRAMA 20 (December 1929): 73-74. Illus.

Concerns Geddes's unit set for a production at the Lakewood Theatre, Skowhegan, Maine.

1018. _____. "Modern Stage Settings, Shakespearian and Otherwise." HARVARD ENGINEERING JOURNAL 5 (January 1907): 158-74; 6 (April 1907): 16-34; (June 1907): 11-30. Illus.

A series of articles (the third part entitled "The Preparation and Handling of a Shakespearian Production") describing the practical requirements of constructing and changing built-up realistic settings, with particular reference to the author's scenery for MUCH ADO ABOUT NOTHING at the Castle Square Theatre, Boston. Informative photographs.

1019. _____. "A New Series of Stage Settings for Shakespeare's 'Romeo and Juliet.'" ARCHITECTURAL RECORD 18 (September 1905): 175-91. Illus.

Discusses his scenery for a production at the Castle Square Theatre, Boston: his aims, his sources, and the limitations imposed on him.

1020. Brown, John Mason. "Enter the Scenic Artist." In his UPSTAGE: THE AMERICAN THEATRE IN PERFORMANCE, pp. 136-73. New York: W.W. Norton & Co., [1930].

A review of the New Stagecraft in America, stressing the work of Robert Edmond Jones, Norman-Bel Geddes, and Lee Simonson.

1021. _____. "Robert Edmond Jones: 1887-1954." SATURDAY REVIEW 38 (1 January 1955): 60-62. Illus.

Recollections and a tribute.

1022. Buchau, Stephanie von. "Darling of San Francisco." OPERA NEWS 35 (20 March 1971): 12-13. Port.

Interview with opera designer Robert Edward Darling.

1023. Burlingame, Lloyd. "Will Steven Armstrong: An Appreciation." YALE / THEATRE 3 (Fall 1970): 33-37. Illus.

1024. Burlyuk [Burliuk], David D. VAN ROSEN, 1926: A STUDY OF HIS LIFE AND ART, TOGETHER WITH AN ESSAY ON STYLE. New York: E. & J. Weiss, [1926]. 62 p. Illus.

Text in English and Russian. A sketch of designer Robert Van Rosen's career, together with some theoretical observations and illustrations of his work (particularly for the Yiddish Art Theatre).

1025. Burris-Meyer, Harold. "Building Number 10." THEATRE ARTS 16 (1932): 934-37. Illus.

Description of the projected Radio City Music Hall and its technical equipment.

1026. Burris-Meyer, Harold, and Cole, Edward C. SCENERY FOR THE THEATRE. Boston: Little, Brown & Co., 1938. 486 p. Illus. Biblio.

A popular textbook published in a revised edition in 1971 (see item 1397). This first edition may be of some historical interest.

1027. Caparn, Anne. "Stream-Line in the Theatre." ARTS AND DECORATION 44 (March 1936): 16-18, 43. Illus.

An interview with designer Jo Mielziner.

1028. Carr, Michael Carrmichael. "The Scenic Art of J. Blanding Sloan." THEATRE ARTS 2 (1917-18): 155-63. Illus.

An appreciation, illustrated with five of Sloan's designs for the Player's Workshop, Chicago.

1029. Carter, Randolph. THE WORLD OF FLO ZIEGFELD. New York and Washington, D.C.: Praeger Publishers, 1974. 176 p. Prof. illus., part color.

At times, this seems to be a book about Joseph Urban, who designed many of the sets for the Ziegfeld Follies. Includes the best selection of Urban's designs yet published.

1030. Cheney, Sheldon. "The American Artist and the Stage." INTERNATIONAL STUDIO 74 (1921): cl-clvii. Illus.

A review of the achievements of the New Stagecraft in America, illustrated with four designs by Ernest De Weerth.

1031. _____. "Hermann Rosse's Stage Designs." THEATRE ARTS 5 (1921): 148-56. Illus.

> Biographical sketch and appreciation. Ten illustrations, including three stages designed for projected scenery.

1032. _____. "Sam Hume's Adaptable Settings." THEATRE ARTS 1 (1916-17): 119-27. Illus.

> Describes and illustrates Hume's work for the Arts and Crafts Playhouse, Detroit.

1033. [_____]. "The Stage Designs of A.A. Andries." THEATRE ARTS 1 (1916-17): 21-23, 42. Illus.

> Very brief sketch of his career and three illustrations of his designs.

1034. Clark, Peter. "Behind the Scenes." ARCHITECTURAL FORUM 57 (September 1932): 266-72. Illus.

> Survey of elevators, counterweight systems, and other stage equipment, by a well-known theatrical contractor.

1035. Clements, Colin C. "School of Scene Design." DRAMA 8 (February 1918): 135-38.

> Briefly describes training in stage design at the Carnegie Institute of Technology.

1036. Cleon Throckmorton, Inc. CATALOG OF THE THEATRE: SCENERY, LIGHTING, HARDWARE, PAINTING, COSTUME, MAKE UP. New York: n.d. [c. 1932]. 72 p. Illus.

> The first of a series of commercial catalogs issued by this theatrical supply company. A valuable document of American theatre practice in the 30s. Here, for example, Throckmorton offers interchangeable scenic units similar to Gordon Craig's screens; other units that will form a "typically Urbanesque exterior"; and detailed drawings of stage hardware and lighting equipment.

1037. Cole, Edward C. "Multum in Parvo." THEATRE ARTS 27 (July 1943): 447-49. Illus.

> Describes and illustrates a multipurpose set designed by Donald Oenslager for wartime service at the Yale University Theatre, to conserve materials.

1038. Cole, Wendell. "A Chronicle of Recent American Scene Design." EDUCATIONAL THEATRE JOURNAL 8 (1956): 283-94.

A review of design in the years 1945-55.

1039. _____. "Designing for an Open Stage." PLAYERS 41 (February 1965): 126-28, 132. Illus.

> Discusses open-stage designs in Stanford University productions.

1040. _____. "Notes for Technicians." EDUCATIONAL THEATRE JOURNAL 3 (1951): 349-51.

> Brief notes on the state of American scene design in the piv-
> otal year 1911, when Belasco-style naturalism was at its height
> and, at the same time, the first signs of the New Stagecraft
> were seen in New York.

1041. _____. "Scenery on the New York Stage, 1900-1920." Ph.D. dissertation, Stanford University, 1951.

1042. _____. "Training for Scene Design." PLAYERS 42 (Spring-Summer 1966): 98-99.

> A brief analysis of the current situation.

1043. CONTEMPORARY STAGE DESIGN U.S.A. Edited by Elizabeth B.
Burdick et al. [New York]: International Theatre Institute of the
United States, distributed by Wesleyan University Press, 1974. 163 p.
Illus., part color.

> Includes the following essays: Donald Oenslager, "U.S. Stage
> Design--Past and Present"; Howard Bay, "The Designer and the
> Broadway Scene"; Jerry N. Rojo, "Environmental Design";
> David Jenkins, "Designing for Resident Theatres"; Patricia
> Zipprodt, "Designing Costumes"; Boris Aronson, "Notes on
> Designing Musicals"; Ming Cho Lee, "Designing Opera";
> Rouben Ter-Arutunian, "Decor for Dance"; Charles Elson,
> "Training the Stage Designer"; and Eldon Elder, "The New
> International Designer." Eighty-eight pages of illustrations
> and brief biographies of the designers.

1044. Copeau, Jacques. "The New School of Stage Scenery." VANITY
FAIR 8 (June 1917): 36, 114. Illus.

> Warns against exaggeration and pretentiousness in the New
> Stagecraft, as in a production of Ossip Dymow's play NJU at
> the Bandbox Theatre, New York, with scenery by Joseph Urban.

1045. Corbin, John. "Sanity and Stage Settings." NEW YORK TIMES, 20
April 1919, sec. 4, p. 2.

> Describes recent productions with scenery by Norman-Bel

Geddes, Rollo Peters, Robert Edmond Jones, and Livingston Platt.

1046. _____. "Shakspere his own Stage-Manager." CENTURY 83 (December 1911): 260-70. Illus.

Describes Shakespeare productions at the New Theatre, New York, in which the conditions of the original performances served to guide the director. Among the designers were Maxfield Parrish and Jules Guerin.

1047. Craven, Thomas. "An American Theatre." THEATRE ARTS 10 (1926): 533-44. Illus.

Condemns the use of European modes of theatre architecture and stage design in American play production.

1048. Crepeau, George Paul. "Pictorial Composition in American Stage Design." Ph.D. dissertation, Cornell University, 1962. 247 p.

Analyzes designs by Robert Edmond Jones, Lee Simonson, Donald Oenslager, and Jo Mielziner.

1049. _____. "Robert Edmond Jones on the Creative Process: An Interview with a group of High School Students." EDUCATIONAL THEATRE JOURNAL 19 (1967): 124-33.

Transcription of an interview recorded in Columbus, Ohio, in 1947.

1050. Davids, Edith. "Modern Stage Effects." MUNSEY'S 25 (July 1901): 524-32. Illus.

Popular treatment of scene-painters' methods, with biographical data on a number of New York artists: Joseph A. Physioc, Homer F. Emens, Ernest M. Gros, and Ernest Albert.

1051. Davis, Jerry L. "A Howard Bay Design Potpourri." THEATRE DESIGN & TECHNOLOGY, no. 19 (December 1969): 21-24. Illus.

Brief discussion of Bay's methods, with eleven illustrations.

1052. _____. "Howard Bay, Scene Designer." Ph.D. dissertation, University of Kansas, 1968. 214 p.

Partly based on interviews.

1053. Davis, Washington. "Successful California Scenic Artists." OVERLAND MONTHLY 45 (February 1905): 171-74. Illus.

Sketches of the work of Edward S. Williams, Frank E. Cutler, and Steve I. Cutler. Brief remarks on "the only woman scenic artist in the world," Grace Wishaar.

1054. De Foe, Louis V. "A New Experiment with the Fairy Play." GREEN BOOK MAGAZINE 13 (February 1915): 267-78. Illus.

Discusses a recent production of Edward Sheldon's THE GARDEN OF PARADISE, with scenery by Joseph Urban.

1055. De Fornaro, Carlo. JOHN WENGER. New York: Joseph Lawren, 1925. 24 p. 49 pls. Colored frontispiece.

Text is mainly puffery, but it supplies a few biographical facts about this Russian-American designer.

1056. Delarue, Allison. "The Stage and Ballet Designs of Eugene Berman." DANCE INDEX 5 (January 1946): 4-23. Illus.

Brief biography and perceptive commentary.

1057. "The Designer Talks: Oliver Smith in Interview with Robert Waterhouse." PLAYS AND PLAYERS 18 (November 1970): 20-21. Illus.

1058. Dodge, Wendell Phillips. "New Theatre's New Stage." TECHNICAL WORLD 14 (February 1911): 697-99. Illus.

Description of the revolving stage at the New Theatre, New York.

1059. _____. "Staging a Popular Restaurant." THEATRE (New York) 16 (October 1912): 104, x-xi. Illus.

Describes and illustrates the famous Childs Restaurant scene in Belasco's production of THE GOVERNOR'S LADY.

1060. Dorr, Charles H. "The Stage Designs of Herman Rosse." THEATRE (New York) 34 (September 1921): 162-63. Illus.

Sketch of his career, with three illustrations and a portrait.

1061. Douty, John T. "Scenic Styles in the Modern American Theatre." Ph.D. dissertation, University of Denver, 1953. 241 p.

1062. Downing, Robert. "From the CAT-Bird Seat." THEATRE ANNUAL 14 (1956): 46-50.

Downing, stage manager for the original Broadway production of Williams's CAT ON A HOT TIN ROOF, describes Jo Mielziner's set and discusses Mielziner's close collaboration with the director, Elia Kazan.

1063. Dresen, James William. "The Theatrical Contributions of Norman Bel Geddes." Ph.D. dissertation, Northwestern University, 1968. 256 p.

1064. Eaton, Quaintance. "Ming Dynasty." OPERA NEWS 33 (12 October 1968): 15. Port.

Brief remarks on the career of designer Ming Cho Lee and commentary on his designs for FAUST at the New York City Opera.

1065. _____. "Opera Urbanized." OPERA NEWS 29 (27 February 1965): 26-30. Illus.

Popular treatment of Joseph Urban's career.

1066. Eaton, Walter Prichard. "The Lesson of a Failure." AMERICAN MAGAZINE 79 (April 1915): 42-45, 76-80. Illus.

Perceptive appreciation of Joseph Urban's scenery for Edward Sheldon's THE GARDEN OF PARADISE.

1067. _____. "The Question of Scenery." AMERICAN MAGAZINE 72 (July 1911): 374-84. Illus.

Condemns elaborate realistic sets and calls for simplified, symbolic scenery.

1068. Eckart, William, and Eckart, Jean. "Scenic Design and Lighting." Edited by John S. Wilson. THEATRE ARTS 44 (July 1960): 55-57, 67-68. Illus.

The Eckarts, a design team, discuss their methods.

1069. Eide, Joel Sylvester. "Scenic Design of the Central City Opera Company, 1946-1970." Ed.D. dissertation, University of Northern Colorado, 1972. 270 p.

Analyzes productions designed by Elemer Nagy, Donald Oenslager, Jean-Claude Rinfret, Robert O'Hearn, and Klaus Holm.

1070. Eisenberg, Lawrence. "Design for Keeping Scenic Standards High." THEATRE ARTS 38 (September 1954): 78-79, 96. Illus.

Describes the examinations required for admission to the scenic artists' union in New York.

1071. "The Elements on the Stage: Thunder, Lightning, Wind, Rain, and Fire." SCIENTIFIC AMERICAN 108 (26 April 1913): 373-74. Illus.

Special effects in THE DAUGHTER OF HEAVEN and other productions at the Century Theatre, New York.

1072. Eliot, Samuel A., Jr. "The New Art of the Theater." CENTURY 96 (May 1918): 46–60. Illus.

Excellent summary of the beginnings of the New Stagecraft in America and a discussion of the methods and prospects of American "little theatres."

1073. _____. "Le Theatre du Vieux Colombier." THEATRE ARTS 3 (January 1919): 25–30.

Reviews of Jacques Copeau's New York productions, including some remarks on scenery.

1074. Ellsworth, William W. "Behind the Scenes at BEN HUR." CRITIC 36 (March 1900): 245–49. Illus.

Informative backstage account of the scenery, lighting, and special effects in this famous production.

1075. EUGENE BERMAN. Edited by Julien Levy. New York and London: American Studio, n.d. xv p. text, 80 p. illus.

Includes illustrations of scenery and costumes for ballet, 1932–1946.

1076. Eustis, Morton. "Norman Bel Geddes at Work." THEATRE ARTS 24 (1940): 872–81. Illus.

Geddes at work on IT HAPPENS ON ICE at the Center Theatre, New York.

1077. _____. "Scene Designing as a Business." THEATRE ARTS 18 (1934): 499–507.

Concerns unionization, contracts, union entrance examinations, and salaries, generally with reference to the professional theatre in New York.

1078. "The Exhibition of American Stage Designs at the Bourgeois Galleries." THEATRE ARTS 3 (1919): 83–130. Illus.

Introductory essay by Kenneth Macgowan and brief statements by the designers: Maxwell Armfield, Michael C. Carr, Norman-Bel Geddes, C. Raymond Johnson, Robert Edmond Jones, Rollo Peters, Irving Pichel, Herman Rosse, J. Blanding Sloan, Joseph Urban, and John Wenger. Sixteen illustrations. An important source of information.

1079. Farwell, E.L. "The Latest Stage Realism." TECHNICAL WORLD 19 (June 1913): 512–19, 620. Illus.

Popular treatment of special effects such as train wrecks, starry skies, sandstorms, etc.

1080. Fatt, Amelia. "Designers for the Dance." DANCE MAGAZINE 41 (February 1967): 42-50; (March 1967): 50-55; (April 1967): 55-58. Illus.

A series of thumbnail biographies, brief commentaries, and excerpts from interviews with the following designers: Cecil Beaton, Eugene Berman, Salvador Dali, Raoul Pene du Bois, David Hays, Willa Kim, Robert O'Hearn, Jo Mielziner, Isamu Noguchi, Robert Rauschenberg, Oliver Smith, and Rouben Ter-Arutunian.

1081. "Feller's Scenic Studio." NEW YORKER 51 (2 June 1975): 29-32.

A conversation with Peter Feller, operator of a scenic studio in New York.

1082. Findlay, Robert R. "THE EMPEROR JONES: O'Neill as Scene Designer." PLAYERS 45 (October-November 1969): 21-24. Illus.

O'Neill had a "sound awareness of design principles" and of "the power of setting to underline dramatic action."

1083. Fitzroy, Dariel [Dariel Fitzkee]. PROFESSIONAL SCENERY CONSTRUCTION. Edited by Ellen M. Gall. San Francisco: Banner Play Bureau, 1930. 94 p. Illus.

Claims to divulge "for the first time, the real, true, trade-secrets of the professional scenery builder."

1084. "Ford's Theatre." NEW YORKER 42 (21 January 1967): 19-20.

Interview with American stage designer Sointu Syrjala, who took part in restoring the stage and period-style scenery of Ford's Theatre, Washington, D.C.

1085. "Four Yale Designers: A Portfolio." YALE / THEATRE 3 (Fall 1970): 19-25. Illus.

Designs by Santo Loquasto, Stewart Johnson, Peter Gould, and Paul Zalon.

1086. Fox, Frederick. "Some Differences between Scenery for Television, Opera, and Legitimate Theatre." In SCENE DESIGN FOR STAGE AND SCREEN (see item 1161), pp. 244-50.

By a designer who worked in all three media.

1087. Geddes, Norman-Bel. MIRACLE IN THE EVENING. Edited by William Kelley. Garden City, N.Y.: Doubleday & Co., 1960. 352 p.

A disappointing book, unillustrated and, where Geddes's stage designs are concerned, rather uninformative. Only THE MIRACLE gets detailed treatment, and even that leaves many unanswered questions about the designer's conception. The story stops in mid-career, omitting Geddes's later work as an industrial designer.

1088. _____. PROJECT FOR A THEATRICAL PRESENTATION OF THE DIVINE COMEDY OF DANTE ALIGHIERI. New York: Theatre Arts Books, 1924. 21 p. 40 illus.

Geddes's vast project, never realized, with his account of the hallucinations from which it grew. Illustrated with photographs of his models.

1089. Genauer, Emily. "Mielziner." THEATRE ARTS 35 (September 1951): 34-37, 86-87. Illus.

Sketch of Jo Mielziner's methods and achievements.

1090. _____. "More than Interior Decoration." THEATRE ARTS 42 (June 1958):* 19-21. Illus.

Survey of the career of Oliver Smith and discussion of his methods. In THEATRE ARTS 42 (October 1958): 9, 76, the editor quotes letters from Wolfgang Roth and Robert L.B. Tobin in reply to this article.

1091. Gerard, Rolf. "Some Notes on Designing for Opera." In SCENE DESIGN FOR STAGE AND SCREEN (see item 1161), pp. 200-206.

Identifies the music as the source of design.

1092. Gilder, Rosamond. "'Set by Stewart Chaney.'" THEATRE ARTS 29 (1945): 152-60. Illus.

Sketch of this American designer's career and methods.

1093. Glassgold, C. Adolph. "Art in the Theatre: Boris Aronson." ARTS (New York) 13 (January 1928): 46-47. Illus.

1094. Gomez, Simonetta. "Stage Designers--VII: Eugene Berman." BALLET 8 (December 1949): 25-32. Illus.

1095. Gorelik, Mordecai. "I Design for the Group Theatre." THEATRE ARTS 23 (1939): 180-86. Illus.

Describes his close collaboration with directors and actors in this New York company.

1096. _____. "In Search of Metaphor." PLAYERS 44 (August–September 1969): 258–63. Illus.

Discusses the method of finding a scenic metaphor on which to build a design. Examples from his own work.

1097. _____. "Life with Bobby." THEATRE ARTS 39 (April 1955): 30–32, 94–95; 39 (June 1955): 65, 89–91. Illus.

A personal view of Robert Edmond Jones, with informative recollections and comments on his work.

1098. _____. "Metaphorically Speaking." THEATRE ARTS 38 (November 1954): 78–80, 91. Illus.

Discusses his designs for Shaw's SAINT JOAN in terms of "scenic metaphors." Reprinted, without illustrations, in SCENE DESIGN FOR STAGE AND SCREEN (see item 1161), pp. 98–104.

1099. _____. "The Scenic Imagination." THEATRE ARTS 40 (April 1956): 70–72, 77–78, 83. Illus.

Describes his methods in teaching a course called "The Scenic Imagination," in which he stresses ideas rather than crafts.

1100. _____. "The Scenic Imagination: Still Evolving." PLAYERS 43 (October–November 1967): 22–27.

More discussion of the aesthetics of stage design, and how Gorelik goes about teaching them.

1101. _____. "The Scenic Imagination: Twenty Years After." PLAYERS 42 (December 1965): 62–66. Illus.

An updated description of his course in stage design (cf. items 1099 and 1100).

1102. _____. "The Setting and the Image." DRAMA SURVEY 2 (1962–63): 353–59.

Another article on the "scenic metaphor." See also items 1096, 1098–1101, and a similar article in TULANE DRAMA REVIEW 5 (March 1961): 85–94.

1103. _____. "Social vs. Irrational Theatre." PLAYERS 46 (June–July 1971): 208–10.

Contrasts the "social theatre" of the 1930s with the theatre of the New Left of the 1960s.

1104. Gorham, Mercy. "Grand Opera beyond the Curtain Line." THEATRE (New York) 21 (January 1915): 21-22, 41.

Interview with Edward Siedle, technical director of the Metropolitan Opera.

1105. Gottholdt, Ruth. "New Scenic Art of the Theatre." THEATRE (New York) 21 (May 1915): 248, 250.

Sketch of the career of Robert Edmond Jones, based on an interview. Jones recalls the productions at Hellerau directed by Jaques-Dalcroze.

1106. Gottlieb, Beatrice. "Settings by Alswang." THEATRE ARTS 35 (July 1951): 42-43, 81. Illus.

Profile of Ralph Alswang, based on an interview.

1107. Hagen, Claude L. "Theatrical Equipment of the Stage." ARCHITECTURE AND BUILDING 45 (November 1913): 457-61.

Describes the counterweight system he installed in the New Theatre, New York; provides some practical hints about stage construction.

1108. Hamilton, Clayton. "The 'New' Stagecraft Ceases to Be New and Is Immediate and Necessary." VOGUE 47 (15 February 1916): 62-63, 118, 120. Illus.

Comments on Robert Edmond Jones's scenery for Edith Ellis's THE DEVIL'S GARDEN.

1109. _____. "Scenic Settings in America." BOOKMAN (New York) 43 (March 1916): 20-29. Illus.

Comments on the New Stagecraft in America and on indifference to it from commercial theatre owners.

1110. _____. "Stage Pictures: The Visual Appeal of the Contemporary Drama." ART AND PROGRESS 2 (March 1911): 133-37. Illus.

Discusses recent improvements in American design.

1111. _____. "Stage Scenery as an Art." ART AND PROGRESS 1 (June 1910): 213-18. Illus.

Remarks on the function of stage design, with examples from

American productions. Illustrated with photographs of scenery
by Jules Guerin and E. Hamilton Bell.

1112. Hart, Jerome. "The Decor of the New Operas." INTERNATIONAL
STUDIO 83 (1926): 67-70. Illus.

Commentary on Joseph Urban's scenery for the Metropolitan
Opera House, New York.

1113. Hatch, Robert. "On Being Upstaged by Scenery." HORIZON 5 (September 1962): 110-12.

Analyzes current U.S. stage design, suggesting that it often
falls into two categories: pictures or playing spaces.

1114. Hellman, Geoffrey T. "Design for a Living." NEW YORKER 16 (8 February 1941)-17 (15, 22 February 1941). Illus., ports.

Three-part profile of Norman-Bel Geddes. Largely concerns
his nontheatrical activities, but includes informative anecdotes
about his work on THE ETERNAL ROAD.

1115. Hersh, Burton. "Boris Aronson." SHOW 2 (February 1962): 8.

Brief survey of his career, based on an interview.

1116. Hewes, Henry. "Scene Designers: Their Art and Their Impact." SAT-
URDAY REVIEW 27 (12 December 1964): 26-31. Illus.

Results of a survey of thirty American stage designers, asking
them to identify their favorites among their own designs and
those of other designers. For a similar, more recent survey,
see Gene Chesley, "Ten Years of American Scene Design: A
Project Report," THEATRE DESIGN & TECHNOLOGY, no. 39
(December 1974): 16-19, 37.

1117. Hewlett, J. Monroe. "Scenery and Stage Decoration." AMERICAN
ARCHITECT 112 (1917): 41-47. Illus.

Comments on an exhibition of American stage designs at the
Brooklyn Museum, with excellent illustrations (including a
model of one of the author's designs). A similar article by
the same author was published in BROOKLYN MUSEUM QUAR-
TERLY 4 (1917): 114-23.

1118. _____. "Scenery and Stage Decorations: Color--Light--'The New
Art.'" AMERICAN ARCHITECT 113 (1918): 425-30. Illus.

Remarks on the New Stagecraft in America, particularly the
work of Joseph Urban. Illustrated with eight designs by Urban
and three by Ernest Gros.

1119. Hicks, Lee Roy. "Robert Edmond Jones: Stage Director." Ph.D. dissertation, University of Colorado, 1969. 251 p.

1120. Hild, Stephen Glenn. "United States Patents Pertaining to Theatre, 1916-1945." Ph.D. dissertation, University of Missouri (Columbia), 1972. 440 p.

1121. Horner, Harry. "Designer in Action." THEATRE ARTS 25 (April 1941): 265-75. Illus.

> Describes the steps in his work as designer of LADY IN THE DARK. Illustrated with designs, production photographs, and plans. Reprinted, with fewer illustrations, in SCENE DESIGN FOR STAGE AND SCREEN (see item 1161), pp. 138-48.

1122. _____. "Designing a 'Magic Flute.'" THEATRE ARTS 40 (January 1956): 58-60, 90. Illus.

> Discusses his designs for a production of Mozart's opera at the Metropolitan Opera House, New York.

1123. Houghton, Norris. "Credits." THEATRE ARTS 30 (1946): 656-60. Illus.

> Briefly describes the methods of New York's scenic studios; makes some general comments on the progress of stage design in America.

1124. _____. "The Designer Sets the Stage." THEATRE ARTS 20 (October-December 1936): 776-88, 878-91, 966-75; 21 (February 1937): 113-25. Illus.

> An informative series on the methods of American designers: Norman-Bel Geddes, Vincente Minelli, Lee Simonson, Donald Oenslager, Robert Edmond Jones, Mordecai Gorelik, Jo Mielziner, and Aline Bernstein. Reprinted, without illustrations, in SCENE DESIGN FOR STAGE AND SCREEN (see item 1161), pp. 112-36.

1125. _____. "Tomorrow Arrives Today." THEATRE ARTS 30 (February 1946): 83-90.

> Brief profiles of up-and-coming theatre people, including an informative sketch of designer Oliver Smith, pp. 87-88.

1126. Howe, Samuel. "Stage Setting: Realistic and Impressionistic." INTERNATIONAL STUDIO 47 (October 1912): xlix-liv.

> Scenery by J. Monroe Hewlett for Maude Adams's production of CHANTECLER.

1127. Hume, Samuel J. "A Permanent Set for the School Stage." THEATRE AND SCHOOL 7 (October 1928): 14-19. Reprinted in THEATRE AND SCHOOL 11 (October 1932): 8-12.

> A set composed of pylons, flats, stairs, platforms, and screens, showing the influence of Gordon Craig (with whom the author studied).

1128. Hunter, Frederick J. "Norman Bel Geddes' Conception of Dante's DIVINE COMEDY." EDUCATIONAL THEATRE JOURNAL 18 (1966): 238-46. Illus.

> Drawing on the rich collection of Geddes material at the University of Texas, the author examines the designer's adaptation of Dante's great work to the stage.

1129. _____. "Norman Bel Geddes' Notes on Art in the Theatre." THEATRE SURVEY 3 (1962): 32-40.

> Transcription of notes made by Geddes in the 1920s, pertaining to aesthetics, design, and form in the theatre.

1130. _____. "Norman Bel Geddes, Renaissance Man of the American Theatre." In INNOVATIONS IN STAGE AND THEATRE DESIGN (see Item 57), pp. 15-28. Illus.

> Biographical sketch and discussion of his chief accomplishments as a stage designer, director, and industrial designer.

1131. _____. "Norman Bel Geddes: Theatre Artist." TEXAS QUARTERLY 5 (Winter 1962): 164-89. Illus.

> Similar to the preceding item. Thirteen pages of illustrations.

1132. Ilko, Donald Wilson. "Joseph Urban: The Relation of Stage Design and Architecture in His Work." Ph.D. dissertation, Case-Western Reserve University, 1969. 244 p.

1133. Isaacs, Hermine Rich. "Howard Bay." THEATRE ARTS 27 (1943): 349-58. Illus.

> Sketch of Bay's career, interpreting his work as typical of a new practicality in stage design (a reaction to the personality-cult of the New Stagecraft).

1134. _____. "Jo Mielziner." WORLD THEATRE 2, no. 2 (1952): 41-48. Illus.

1135. Jackson, Allan S[tuart]. "The Artistic Practices of the Armbruster Scenic Studio." OSU THEATRE COLLECTION BULLETIN 12 (1965): 20-27. Illus.

Identifies types of scenery, painting techniques, and artistic styles, based on examination of surviving scenery from this Columbus, Ohio, studio. The scenes were mostly painted in 1900-1930.

1136. "Jacques Copeau and His Theatre." THEATRE (New York) 26 (December 1917): 342. Illus.

Describes Copeau's permanent setting at the Garrick Theatre, New York.

1137. Jenkins, Speight. "A Boris Aronson Sketchbook." OPERA NEWS 35 (2 January 1971): 20-23. Illus.

Aronson discusses his designs for FIDELIO at the Metropolitan Opera House, New York.

1138. _____. "A Meeting of Minds." OPERA NEWS 35 (17 April 1971): 6-9. Port.

Describes a partnership formed by singer Regina Resnik and designer Arbit Blatas, to design and direct operas.

1139. Johnston, Alva. "Aider and Abettor." NEW YORKER 24 (23 October 1948): 37-51; (30 October 1948): 28-39. Illus., ports.

An informative profile of Jo Mielziner.

1140. Jones, Robert Edmond. DRAWINGS FOR THE THEATRE. New York: Theatre Arts Books, 1925. 16 p. 35 pls.

Limited edition (600 autographed copies). Brief introduction by Arthur Hopkins, brief foreword by Jones, and the plates.

1141. _____. "The Future Decorative Art of the Theatre." THEATRE (New York) 25 (May 1917): 266. Illus.

Jones hopes to integrate scenery with other theatrical elements by close collaboration between author, director, and designer. Reprinted, without illustrations, in SCENE DESIGN FOR STAGE AND SCREEN (see item 1161), pp. 10-14.

1142. _____. "Nijinsky and TIL EULENSPIEGL." DANCE INDEX 4 (April 1945): 44-54. Illus.

Vivid recollections of his collaboration with Nijinsky in 1916.

1143. Jossic, Yvonne Francoise. STAGE AND STAGE SETTINGS. Philadelphia: H.C. Perlberg, [1933]. Title page and 20 pls.

Each of the twenty plates has two to eight photographs of

scenery, models, and designs, some by prominent designers, others unidentified. Intended for classroom use.

1144. Kadlec, Anthony Lawrence. "A Descriptive Study of Scenic Styles in the Productions of Successful Serious American Drama on the New York Stage of the 1920's." Ph.D. dissertation, Michigan State University, 1969. 469 p.

1145. Katz, Albert Michael. "A Historical Study of Jacques Copeau and the Vieux-Colombier Company at the Garrick Theatre in New York City (1917-1919)." Ph.D. dissertation, University of Michigan, 1966. 433 p.

Includes discussion of the architectural setting built at the Garrick Theatre.

1146. Kerz, Leo. "Scenery or Stage Setting." In SCENE DESIGN FOR STAGE AND SCREEN (see item 1161), pp. 106-10.

Reprinted from the NEW YORK TIMES, 2 August 1954, pt. 2, p. 1. Contrasts unimaginative literalism with creative design.

1147. _____. "Scenic Design: RHINOCEROS." THEATRE ARTS 45 (July 1961): 20-21. Illus.

Brief statement of his aim in designing Ionesco's play.

1148. Kirstein, Lincoln. "The Craft of Horace Armistead." CHRYSALIS 10, nos. 1-2 (1957): 3-15. Illus.

An informative commentary, with a few biographical notes.

1149. Kitchen, Karl K. "Revolution in Stage Scenery." THEATRE (New York) 13 (April 1911): 113, viii. Illus.

Describes John W. Alexander's scenery (sometimes attributed to J. Monroe Hewlett, with whom Alexander collaborated) for Maude Adams's production of CHANTECLER.

1150. Krows, Arthur Edwin. EQUIPMENT FOR STAGE PRODUCTION. New York and London: D. Appleton and Co., 1928. x, 152 p. Illus. Biblio.

Largely out of date as a technical guide, but of some historical interest.

1151. _____. "Ernest Albert, Twenty Years After." NEW YORK DRAMATIC MIRROR, 19 November 1913, p. 3. Port.

Based on an interview with this successful American designer, who explains how he designs a show, builds the scenery, and lights the stage.

1152. _____. PLAY PRODUCTION IN AMERICA. New York: Henry Holt and Co., 1916. x, 414 p. Illus. Biblio.

> A complete view of the subject, thorough to a fault, with about 170 pages on scenery and lighting. Krows documents the current style of built-up realism and looks ahead to the New Stagecraft, commenting on Appia, Craig, Livingston Platt, and other exponents of the new style. Excellent illustrations.

1153. Kuemmerle, Clyde Victor, Jr. "An Investigation of Selected Contemporary American Scene Designers." Ph.D. dissertation, University of Minnesota, 1970. 349 p.

> Includes edited transcripts of two-hour interviews with Karl Eigsti, David Hays, Eugene Lee, Ming Cho Lee, Jo Mielziner, William Ritman, and Robin Wagner.

1154. Lansdale, Nelson. "To the Dawn of a Better Decor at the Opera." ART NEWS 41 (15 March 1942): 9-11, 33-34. Illus.

> Criticizes the scenery of the Metropolitan Opera and other opera companies in New York. Discusses the work of Richard Rychtarik, Joseph Urban, and others.

1155. Larson, Orville K. "Jo Mielziner and Arena Theatre Scene Design." PLAYERS 37 (January 1961): 80-82. Illus.

> Discusses Mielziner's ideas about simplifying scenery as expressed in an article published in 1939.

1156. _____. "Leo Kerz's Design for RICHARD III." PLAYERS 35 (February 1959): 100-101. Illus.

> An architectural setting for a 1948 Jose Ferrer production, never realized.

1157. _____. "A Note on the New Stagecraft in America." EDUCATIONAL THEATRE JOURNAL 13 (1961): 278-79.

> Concerns the first exhibition of the New Stagecraft in America, organized by Samuel J. Hume in Cambridge, Massachusetts, in 1914.

1158. _____. "Robert Edmond Jones' HENRY VIII." PLAYERS 37 (December 1960): 52-54. Illus.

> Concerns an unrealized production in 1944.

1158a. _____. "Rolf Gerard's Scene Design for Opera." PLAYERS 36 (March 1960): 130-32. Illus.

1159. _____. "Scrim Curtains: Mielziner and Ingegnieri." EDUCATIONAL THEATRE JOURNAL 14 (1962): 228-30.

Discusses Jo Mielziner's use of a moving scrim curtain to "dissolve" one scene into another. Shows that Angelo Ingegnieri suggested a similar device in 1598, for ghost effects.

1160. _____. "Settings and Costumes by Lee Simonson." THEATRE DESIGN & TECHNOLOGY, no. 32 (February 1973): 6-11. Illus.

Largely concerns Simonson's costume designs.

1161. _____, ed. SCENE DESIGN FOR STAGE AND SCREEN. East Lansing: Michigan State University Press, 1961. 352 p. 2 illus.

A handy collection of essays on the aesthetics and practice of stage design in the United States beginning with World War I. Includes reprinted articles and excerpts from books as well as some previously unpublished essays. Each selection is entered separately in the present guide. Larson's introduction provides an overview.

1162. Lauterer, Arch. "Some Notes on Stage Design." THEATRE ARTS 29 (October 1945): 596-98. Illus.

Designs and diagrams by the author, with notes on the relation of actors' movements to the scenery.

1163. Lee, Ming Cho. "An Interview with Ming Cho Lee." YALE / THEATRE 3 (Fall 1970): 26-31. Illus.

Lee discusses some of his recent work and some problems of the stage designer.

1164. Leitner, Margaret. "Gorelik's Metaphor in Design." PLAYERS 38 (January 1962): 129, 132.

1165. Lingg, Ann M. "Sounding the Depths: Harry Horner." OPERA NEWS 28 (25 January 1964): 33. Port.

Biographical sketch, with notes on his current activities.

1166. Louchheim, Aline. "From Script to Stage: Case History of a Set." In SCENE DESIGN FOR STAGE AND SCREEN (see item 1161), pp. 150-60.

Case history of Jo Mielziner's work as designer for POINT OF NO RETURN, 1951. Reprinted from NEW YORK TIMES MAGAZINE, 9 December 1951.

1167. Lowrey, Edward W. "The Staging of Grand Opera." NEW ENGLAND

MAGAZINE 50 (1913-14): 415-18, 423-27. Illus.

An appreciation of Joseph Urban's scenery for productions at the Boston Opera House (his first work in the United States). Good illustrations.

1168. McConnell, Frederic. "Using the Open Stage: A Ten-Year Experiment at the Cleveland Playhouse." THEATRE ANNUAL 17 (1960): 48-67. Illus.

Includes production photographs and discussion of scenery on the open stage.

1169. McDowell, John H., and Fruth, Mary Ann. "Scenery and Staging of UNCLE TOM'S CABIN." OSU THEATRE COLLECTION BULLETIN 10 (1963): 19-39. Illus.

Includes illustrations of surviving scenery used by the Harmount Company c. 1900-1930.

1170. Macgowan, Kenneth. "The Leonardo of Our Theatre." THEATRE ARTS 45 (January 1961): 63-65, 71. Illus.

An appreciation of the work of Norman-Bel Geddes.

1171. _____. "The Myth of Urban." THEATRE ARTS 1 (1916-17): 98-109. Illus.

Suggests that Joseph Urban has not had an opportunity to follow his real genius for expressive, "architectural" settings. Sketches his career and analyzes a number of his designs.

1172. _____. "The New Path of the Theatre." THEATRE ARTS 3 (1919): 84-90.

A review of the New Stagecraft, evaluating its progress in the United States. Reprinted in SCENE DESIGN FOR STAGE AND SCREEN (see item 1161), pp. 16-24.

1173. _____. "The New Stage-Craft in America." CENTURY 87 (January 1914): 416-21. Illus.

One of the earliest appreciations of Joseph Urban and the New Stagecraft in an American periodical of wide circulation. Reprinted in SCENE DESIGN FOR STAGE AND SCREEN (see item 1161), pp. 2-9.

1174. _____. "Robert Edmond Jones." THEATRE ARTS 9 (1925): 720-28. Illus.

Recollections of Jones at Harvard; a sketch of his career and an appreciation.

1175. Mahnken, Harry, and Mahnken, Janine. "Joseph Urban: An Appreciation." EDUCATIONAL THEATRE JOURNAL 15 (1963): 55-61.

Survey of his career as stage designer, decorator, and architect.

1176. Mann, Dorothea Lawrance. "The New Stagecraft: Illustrated by Josef Urban's Imaginative Setting of Shakespeare." CRAFTSMAN 30 (May 1916): 168-78. Illus.

Focuses on Urban's scenery for James K. Hackett's MACBETH. Excellent illustrations.

1177. Mannes, Marya. "Art Must Work for Its Living." THEATRE GUILD MAGAZINE 9 (October 1931): 30-35. Illus.

Survey of Lee Simonson's career and methods.

1178. _____. "Robert Edmond Jones." THEATRE GUILD MAGAZINE 8 (November 1930): 14-19, 62-63. Illus.

1179. Marks, Samuel M. "Settings by Joseph Urban: An Evaluation of His Stagecraft." Ph.D. dissertation, University of Wisconsin, 1955. 930 p.

1180. Meltzer, Charles Henry. "Stage Decoration as It Is and Used to Be." ARTS AND DECORATION 12 (April 1920): 408-9, 440-41. Illus.

Informative article on the theories and techniques of the New Stagecraft in America.

1181. Merkling, Frank. "Loving Care." OPERA NEWS 27 (5 January 1963): 15. Illus.

Profile of designer Robert O'Hearn.

1182. _____. "Prodigal Return." OPERA NEWS 27 (23 March 1963): 12-13. Illus., port.

Concerns Eugene Berman, with particular reference to his designs for Verdi's OTELLO at the Metropolitan Opera House, New York.

1183. "The Met's Amazing Stage." ARCHITECTURAL RECORD 140 (September 1966): 156-60. Illus.

Stage machinery at the new Metropolitan Opera House, Lincoln Center, New York.

1184. Middleton, Herman David. "The Use of the Design Elements in the Stage Designs of Robert Edmond Jones and Lee Simonson." Ph.D. dissertation, University of Florida, 1964. 217 p.

1185. Mielziner, Jo. "Death of a Painter." AMERICAN ARTIST 13 (November 1949): 32-37, 61-63. Illus., part color.

Discusses his early training, his transition from the easel to the stage, and his work on DEATH OF A SALESMAN. Reprinted, without illustrations, in SCENE DESIGN FOR STAGE AND SCREEN (see item 1161), pp. 162-70.

1186. _____. DESIGNING FOR THE THEATRE. New York: Bramhall House, 1965. x, 243 p. Prof. illus., part color.

A brief memoir, essays on designing a theatre and on the stylistic demands of some plays, and a fascinating forty-page record of his work on DEATH OF A SALESMAN, tracing his setting from conception to opening night. Plus a portfolio of designs, 1929-65, with notes by the author, and a list of his productions.

1187. _____. "Scenery in This Play?" In SCENE DESIGN FOR STAGE AND SCREEN (see item 1161), pp. 172-77.

Discusses his simplification of scenic elements in ABE LINCOLN IN ILLINOIS. Reprinted from the NEW YORK TIMES, 22 October 1939, pt. 10, p. 1.

1188. "Mielziner." NEW YORKER 42 (19 March 1966): 44-45.

Jo Mielziner discusses his methods.

1189. "Ming Cho Lee on Six of His Sets." THEATRE DESIGN & TECHNOLOGY, no. 24 (February 1971): 4-9. Illus.

1190. Moderwell, Hiram K. "The Art of Robert Edmond Jones." THEATRE ARTS 1 (1916-17): 50-61. Illus.

Informative discussion of Jones's early career--his work at Harvard, his European tour, and his success as a designer for Arthur Hopkins and the Ballets Russes.

1191. "Mordecai Gorelik--Robert Edmond Jones: Correspondence about NEW THEATRES FOR OLD." EDUCATIONAL THEATRE JOURNAL 20 (1968): 32-52.

Concerns Gorelik's request that Jones write a preface for Gorelik's book NEW THEATRES FOR OLD.

1192. Mumford, Claire Dana. "A New Master and the Audience." THEATRE ARTS 2 (1917-18): 66-78. Illus.

An appreciation of the stage designs of Rollo Peters.

1193. Mussey, Kendall K. "Costume and Scenic Design for Opera Comique."
BROOKLYN MUSEUM QUARTERLY 18 (January 1931): 29-33. Illus.

Describes the design methods of the Little Theatre Opera
Company, New York, and mentions a number of its designers
whose work was exhibited at the Brooklyn Museum.

1194. Nagy, Elemer. "An Influence in Design." INTERIOR DESIGN AND
DECORATION 14 (March 1940): 48-51. Illus.

Notes on an exhibition of American stage designs in New York.

1195. _____. "New Plastic Effects and the Revival of Perspective." PLAY-
ERS 18 (January 1942): 4, 6-7, 23. Illus.

Describes a reaction against simplification of scenery.

1196. "The New Stage of the Metropolitan Opera House." SCIENTIFIC
AMERICAN 90 (6 February 1904): 113, 117-18. Illus.

Description of stage machinery installed by Karl Lautenschlaeger
and Theodore G. Stein. Full-page schematic illustration.

1197. "A New Triumph in the Art of the Theatre." ARTS AND DECORATION
11 (June 1919): 80-81. Illus.

Robert Edmond Jones's sets for THE JEST at the Plymouth Theatre, New York.

1198. Noguchi, Isamu. A SCULPTOR'S WORLD. New York and Evanston:
Harper & Row Publishers, 1968. 259 p. Illus., part color.

Includes a section on stage designs (mainly for Martha Graham's
dance company), pp. 123-56.

1199. Nordvold, Robert O. "Showcase for the New Stagecraft: The Scenic
Designs of the Washington Square Players and the Theatre Guild."
Ph.D. dissertation, Indiana University, 1973. 554 p.

1200. "Norman Edwards." GEBRAUCHSGRAPHIK (INTERNATIONAL ADVER-
TISING ART) 9 (March 1932): 50-53. Illus.

English and German text. Very brief commentary and eleven
illustrations of the work of this American-born artist, including
seven stage designs.

1201. Oenslager, Donald M[itchell]. "Design in the Theatre Today." In
DONALD OENSLAGER: STATE DESIGNER AND TEACHER, pp. 7-12.
Detroit: Detroit Institute of Arts, [1956].

Part of an exhibition catalog. A wide-ranging essay on the future of stage design and the nature of its craftsmanship. Reprinted in SCENE DESIGN FOR STAGE AND SCREEN (see item 1161), pp. 92-96.

1202. _____ . "The Donald Oenslager Collection of Drawings for the Theatre." OSU THEATRE COLLECTION BULLETIN 2 (Autumn 1955): 3-5.

Brief description of the provenance of the collection, and some prominent examples.

1203. _____ . "Passing Scenes." THEATRE ARTS 33 (November 1949): 16-25, 93-94. Illus.

An informative and well-illustrated memoir.

1204. _____ . "A Project for THE RING." THEATRE ARTS 11 (January 1927): 35-48. Illus.

Remarks on the history of staging Wagner's RING OF THE NIBELUNGEN, an explanation of his own designs, and eight illustrations.

1205. _____ . "Robert Edmond Jones." YALE / THEATRE 3 (Fall 1970): 7-9. Illus.

Quotes and reproduces a letter Jones wrote to the author and John Mason Brown on their departure for Europe after graduating from Harvard. Oenslager calls it "Jones' vision of the theatre . . . the dream of his theatre of tomorrow."

1206. _____ . "Robert Edmond Jones: Artist of the Theatre." In INNOVATIONS IN STAGE AND THEATRE DESIGN (see item 57), pp. 1-14. Illus.

Sketches Jones's career, discusses his methods, and defines his contributions.

1207. _____ . "Stage Design: New Directions or Dead End?" THEATRE ARTS 40 (October 1956): 26-28, 91. Illus.

Notes on some current trends.

1208. O'Hearn, Robert. "How I See THE WOMAN WITHOUT A SHADOW." OPERA NEWS 31 (17 September 1966): 48-51. Illus., part color.

Commentary on his designs for a new production of the Strauss opera at the Metropolitan Opera House, New York.

1209. Packard, Frederick C., Jr. "Robert Edmond Jones, 1887-1954." CHRYSALIS 8, nos. 1-2 (1955): 4-12. Illus.

Excerpts from a recording of Jones's lectures, "Towards a New Theatre," 1952.

1210. "Painting Acres of Scenery for Opera." POPULAR MECHANICS 42 (November 1924): 744–46. Illus.

   Generalized account of scene-painting techniques for operatic productions. Good illustrations.

1211. Parker, Robert Allerton. "'Acting Scenery.'" ARTS AND DECORATION 17 (June 1922): 110–11, 156. Illus.

   Comments on modern scenery that contributes to mood and dramatic effect.

1212. Pendleton, Ralph, ed. THE THEATRE OF ROBERT EDMOND JONES. Middletown, Conn.: Wesleyan University Press, 1958. 209 p. 51 pls., port., and 16 other illus.

   Essays on various aspects of Jones's life and work, by Stark Young, Mary Hall Furber, Lee Simonson, Jo Mielziner, Donald Oenslager, Kenneth Macgowan, and John Mason Brown, plus an extensive chronology of his career by the editor.

1213. Peters, Rollo. "The Newest Art." THEATRE ARTS 2 (1917–18): 118–30. Illus.

   A critique of the ideals and practices of both the progressive and the commercial stage designer. Somewhat impressionistic.

1214. Philippi, Herbert. "Away from Scenic Realism." PLAYERS 30 (February 1954): 105–6.

   Promotes nonrealistic scenery even for naturalistic plays.

1215. Phillips, J.H. "Interior Settings of the Stage." ARCHITECTURAL REVIEW. n.s. 8 (February 1919): 33–44. Illus.

   Brief text and twenty-three illustrations, including four designs and a model by the American studio of Dodge & Castle.

1216. Pichel, Irving. "Stage Machinery and Lighting Equipment for Small Theatres and Community Buildings." THEATRE ARTS 4 (1920): 137–52.

1217. Platt, Livingston. "Decorating Shakespeare." THEATRE (New York) 23 (April 1916): 219–20. Illus.

   One of Platt's rare publications. Discusses his designs for Margaret Anglin's productions.

1218. Plugge, Domis Edward. HISTORY OF GREEK PLAY PRODUCTION IN AMERICAN COLLEGES AND UNIVERSITIES FROM 1881 TO 1936. New York: Teachers College, Columbia University, Bureau of Publications, 1938. xii, 175 p.

"Setting or Scenic Background," pp. 76–86.

1219. Pulos, Arthur J. "The Restless Genius of Norman Bel Geddes." ARCHI-
TECTURAL FORUM 133 (July–August 1970): 46–51. Illus.

Mainly concerns his nontheatrical work.

1220. Quarnstrom, I. Blaine. "Early Twentieth Century Staging of UNCLE
TOM'S CABIN." OSU THEATRE COLLECTION BULLETIN 15 (1968):
32–42. Illus.

Describes the scenery of productions by the Harmount Company
of Ohio. Illustrated with photographs of scenery actually used
by the company.

1221. Quinn, Germain. FIFTY YEARS BACKSTAGE, BEING THE LIFE STORY
OF A THEATRICAL STAGE MECHANIC. Minneapolis: Stage Publishing
Co., 1926. 204 p. Illus.

A disappointing book, mainly devoted to anecdotes about actors. It does, however, include some information on the early
years of the theatrical mechanics' union.

1222. "Radio City Music Hall: Last of the Moving Picture Palaces." THE-
ATRE CRAFTS 8 (October 1974): 6–13, 28–31. Illus.

Includes information on scenery, stage machinery, and lighting
equipment.

1223. Ranck, Edwin Carty. "An American Stage Wizard." THEATRE (New
York) 22 (August 1915): 83, 92–93. Port.

Sketch of the career of Livingston Platt, discussing his work
in Boston and for Margaret Anglin.

1224. Reed, Edward. "American Theatre Designers." MAGAZINE OF ART
33 (May, October, December 1940): 274–79, 314, 316, 576–80, 594–
95, 688–93, 707; 34 (May 1941): 254–59, 276–77. Illus.

A series of well-illustrated profiles of (in this order) Albert
Johnson, Howard Bay, Stewart Chaney, and Harry Horner.

1225. Reid, Kenneth. "Masters of Design: 2--Norman Bel Geddes." PENCIL
POINTS 18 (January 1937): 1–32. Illus.

Mainly concerns his nontheatrical work.

1226. Remisoff, Nikolai. "An Architectural Problem in Stage Setting." CALI-
FORNIA ARTS & ARCHITECTURE 54 (October 1938): 11–12. Illus.

Discusses his sets for a Max Reinhardt production of FAUST in
Hollywood.

1227. "Robert Edmond Jones, Designer for the Theater." AMERICAN ARTIST 22 (June–August 1958): 52–57, 85–87. Illus.

Brief commentary, excerpts from Jones's THE DRAMATIC IMAGI-NATION, and ten illustrations.

1228. Roberts, Mary Fanton. "An Essentially American Producer at Last--John Murray Anderson." TOUCHSTONE 8 (November 1920): 86-94, 149. Illus.

Discusses and illustrates stage designs by Robert Locher and James Reynolds.

1229. "The Role of the Costume in the New Stagecraft." VOGUE 45 (15 March 1915): 65, 106, 108. Illus.

Concerns both the costumes and scenery for Granville-Barker's production of THE MAN WHO MARRIED A DUMB WIFE, de-signed by Robert Edmond Jones.

1230. Rosse, Herman. "Artificiality and Reality in the Future Theatre." THE-ATRE ARTS 3 (1919): 95-97.

Foresees an actorless theatre of moving shapes and colors.

1231. _____. "The Circus Theatre." THEATRE ARTS 7 (1923): 228-43. Illus.

Discusses the European circus and its adaptation to drama and spectacle. Illustrated with eleven of Rosse's projects for circus-style staging with gauze scenery.

1232. _____. DESIGNS AND IMPRESSIONS. Chicago: Ralph Fletcher Seymour, 1920. Unpaged [32 leaves]. Illus., part color.

Brief introductory remarks on stage reform, twenty-four illustra-tions, and fourteen brief, prose "impressions" of places and people.

1233. _____. "The Stage Designer." THEATRE ARTS 8 (1924): 317-23. Illus.

Describes the designer's task.

1234. _____. "When New Theatre Arts Were New." CHAPTER ONE 2 (Summer 1964): 4-5, 9-10. Illus.

Notes on the early years of the New Stagecraft in America, stressing the unifying role of THEATRE ARTS MAGAZINE.

1235. Roth, Wolfgang. "Reflections of a Stage-Builder." THEATRE DESIGN

& TECHNOLOGY, no. 42 (Fall 1975): 18-22. Illus.

A statement of his principles and methods of design.

1236. Salzer, Beeb. "George Jenkins: A Pragmatic Designer." THEATRE DESIGN & TECHNOLOGY, no. 25 (May 1971): 10-15. Illus.

Biographical sketch and close examination of Jenkins's designs for THE MIRACLE WORKER.

1237. Sayler, Oliver M. "Robert Edmond Jones, Artist of the Theatre." NEW REPUBLIC 23 (23 June 1920): 122-24.

1238. _____. "Theater Delays Shortened." SCIENTIFIC AMERICAN 138 (March 1928): 248-49. Illus.

Describes Norman-Bel Geddes's jackknife stage, with flown units, for THE PATRIOT at the Majestic Theatre, New York.

1239. Sayler, Oliver M., et al. REVOLT IN THE ARTS. New York: Brentano's, 1930. 365 p.

Includes "The Wasted Gifts of the Scene Designer," by Herman Rosse, pp. 197-201; a brief article on design for the cinema, by Joseph Urban; and general commentary on stage design by Sayler.

1240. "Scenery and Furniture." HOUSE BEAUTIFUL 36 (November 1914): 180-84. Illus.

Designs by Frank Chouteau Brown for SHE STOOPS TO CONQUER at the Castle Square Theatre, Boston.

1241. "Scenery or No Scenery? A Symposium." THEATRE WORKSHOP 2 (April-June 1938): 5-21.

The participants included Howard Bay and Mordecai Gorelik.

1242. "Scenic Wonders of the Stage." POPULAR MECHANICS 49 (April 1928): 627-32. Illus.

Explanation of fire, water, and other special effects on stage, including several invented by Esten B. Beeler.

1243. Selden, Samuel, and Sellman, Hunton D. STAGE SCENERY AND LIGHTING: A HANDBOOK FOR NON-PROFESSIONALS. New York: F.S. Crofts & Co., 1930. 415 p. Illus. Biblio.

A popular textbook for many years, issued in several editions. This first edition may be of some historical interest.

1244. Seligmann, Kurt. "The Stage Image." In THE DANCE HAS MANY FACES, edited by Walter Sorrell, pp. 177–86. 2d ed. New York and London: Columbia University Press, 1966. Illus.

>   Commentary on scene and costume design for the dance, by a designer.

1245. "Setting by Donald Oenslager." THEATRE ANNUAL 9 (1951): 70–71. 8 pls.

>   Brief introduction and eight pages of illustrations relating to a production of WASHINGTON SQUARE: designs, ground plan, model, architectural details, and a photograph of the finished scenery onstage.

1246. Shannon, Betty. "Theatricalizing Commerce." THEATRE GUILD MAGAZINE 6 (February 1929): 15–19. Illus.

>   Notes on American stage designers who have also worked as commercial and industrial designers.

1247. Shipp, Horace. "The Art of Robert Edmond Jones." ENGLISH REVIEW 34 (1922): 355–57. Illus.

>   A perceptive appreciation of Jones's work.

1248. Simonson, Lee. "Apologizing for America." THEATRE ARTS 6 (1922): 226–30.

>   Replying to Sheldon Cheney's comments on the American designs in the International Theatre Exhibition in Amsterdam, Simonson defends American contributions to stage design, particularly to design in the realistic style. On pp. 231–32, Cheney responds.

1249. _____. "Basic Theater Planning." ARCHITECTURAL FORUM 57 (September 1932): 185–93. Illus.

>   A presentation directed to architects, including descriptions of types of scenery and scene-changing methods.

1250. _____. "A Lesson in Stagecraft." DRAMA 14 (January 1924): 133–35. Illus.

>   Seven photographs from the Theatre Guild production of Lenormand's THE FAILURES, with Simonson's comments on his designs.

1251. _____. "The Necessary Illusion." THEATRE ARTS 3 (1919): 91–92.

>   A brief theoretical statement.

1252. _____. "The Painter and the Stage." THEATRE ARTS (1917-18): 2-12. Illus.

> Discusses easel painters' contributions to stage design: "Every innovation in stage-craft we have witnessed in America is based upon the aesthetic discoveries of twenty years ago." Illustrated with designs by Simonson and followed by a biographical sketch of him, pp. 12-17, by Hiram K. Moderwell.

1253. _____. PART OF A LIFETIME: DRAWINGS AND DESIGNS, 1919-1940. New York: Duell, Sloan and Pearce, 1943. 119 p. 80 p., mainly illus., part color.

> An informative autobiography, admirably well written and illustrated with numerous production photographs and designs.

1254. _____. "Scenery and the Drama." ATLANTIC 143 (May 1929): 639-45.

> Explains that the various styles of the New Stagecraft are relative to the plays they serve to interpret.

1255. _____. "Scenic Design in the U.S.A." STUDIO 127 (June 1944): 196-200. Illus.

> A useful review of American design since 1915.

1256. _____. "Setting the Stage." In THE THEATRE GUILD: THE FIRST TEN YEARS, by Walter Prichard Eaton et al., pp. 184-206. New York: Brentano's, 1929. Illus.

> Discusses his early career, his methods, and the function of design in Guild productions.

1257. Simonson, Lee, and Graf, Herbert. "From a Wagnerian Rockpile." THEATRE ARTS 32 (January 1948): 39-46. Illus.

> Simonson briefly reviews the history of the staging of Wagner's RING OF THE NIBELUNGEN, then discusses his own approach for a Metropolitan Opera production. Graf, director of the production, adds some technical notes.

1258. Simonson, Lee, and Young, Stark. "Earth to Earth." NEW REPUBLIC 73 (16 November 1932): 19-20.

> Young replies to Simonson's reply to his criticism of the scenery for THE GOOD EARTH. Their interchange includes some interesting remarks on historical accuracy in scene design.

1259. "Six Stages in One." SCIENTIFIC AMERICAN 128 (March 1923): 154-55. Illus.

Multiple sets on sliding platforms, invented by Svend Gade
for JOHANNES KREISLER at the Apollo Theatre, New York.

1260. Smith, Oliver. "Musical Comedy Design for Stage and Screen." In
SCENE DESIGN FOR STAGE AND SCREEN (see item 1161), pp. 188-
99.

Describes the special demands made on the designer by musical
comedy in both media.

1261. Soria, Dorle J. "Artist Life." HIGH FIDELITY-MUSICAL AMERICA 23
(November 1973): MA6-MA8. Illus.

Survey of the career of American designer Peter Wexler, with
discussion of his designs for THE TROJANS at the Metropolitan
Opera, New York.

1262. Sowers, William Leigh. "Keeping Up with the New Stagecraft."
DRAMA 8 (November 1918): 515-23.

Discussion of recent work by Willy Pogany, Joseph Urban,
Robert Edmond Jones, Livingston Platt, Rollo Peters, Clifford
Pember, and others.

1263. _____. "The Progress of the New Stagecraft in America." DRAMA 7
(November 1917): 570-89.

Excellent summary of the progressive movement in America,
1911-17, with particular reference to the work of Livingston
Platt, Joseph Urban, and Robert Edmond Jones.

1264. Squire, Tom. "Stage Design, 1937-1938." THEATRE ARTS 22 (1938):
350-64. Illus.

A review of the season, including discussion of the fad for
"sceneryless" productions, begun by OUR TOWN. Nineteen
excellent illustrations.

1265. "Stage Design circa 1962: Will Steven Armstrong on TCHIN TCHIN."
INTERIORS 122 (October 1962): 138-41. Illus.

General comments on a trend towards minimal scenery, and
Armstrong's comments on his sets for TCHIN TCHIN.

1266. "Stage Scenery on the Building Block Principle." SCIENTIFIC AMERI-
CAN 130 (February 1924): 95. Illus.

Blocks and steps to form an Appia-like setting at Earl Carroll's
theatre in New York.

1267. Stage Society of New York. THE ART OF THE THEATRE: AN EXHIBI-
TION . . . . NOVEMBER, 1914. [New York]: 1914. 7 p. Illus.

Catalog of one of the earliest exhibitions of the New Stagecraft in America. Among the contributors were Samuel Hume,
Joseph Urban, and Livingston Platt.

1268. Stearns, H.E. "John Craig's Notable Undertaking." NEW YORK DRA-
MATIC MIRROR, 28 May 1913, pp. 4, 9. Illus.

Detailed description of Livingston Platt's scenery and lighting
at the Castle Square Theatre, Boston.

1269. Steell, Willis. "The Art of Joseph Urban." THEATRE (New York) 22
(September 1915): 124-25, 140. Illus.

Brief but early notice of Urban's work.

1270. Stevenson, Florence. "Behind the Scenes: 1. The Framework." OP-
ERA NEWS 26 (24 February 1962): 26-29. Illus.

Description of the scenery-construction shop at the old Metropolitan Opera House, New York.

1271. _____. "Behind the Scenes: 3. The Illusion." OPERA NEWS 26
(10 March 1962): 26-29. Illus.

Popular treatment of the property, lighting, makeup, and wig
departments at the Metropolitan Opera, New York.

1272. _____. "Space Man." OPERA NEWS 33 (21 September 1968): 14-16.
Illus.

Profile of designer Rouben Ter-Arutunian.

1273. Stowell, Don, Jr. "Unionization of the Stage Designer: Male and
Female." THEATRE DESIGN & TECHNOLOGY, no. 38 (October 1974):
7-9, 36-37. Illus.

Brief but informative historical sketch of the early years of
the scenic artists' union in New York, and its belated admit-
tance of female members.

1274. Stratton, Clarence. THEATRON. New York: Henry Holt and Co.,
1928. 319 p. Illus.

A record of Little Theatre productions in the United States,
including chapters on lighting, design, and multiple settings.
Illustrated with numerous production photographs.

1275. Sullivan, Catherine. "Gerard: Designer for the Theater." AMERICAN

ARTIST 18 (April 1954): 34–39. Illus.

Survey of the career of Rolf Gerard.

1276. Sweet, Harvey. "Eugene O'Neill and Robert Edmond Jones: Text into Scene." Ph.D. dissertation, University of Wisconsin, 1974. 264 p.

Concerns Jones's collaboration with O'Neill on productions of DESIRE UNDER THE ELMS, MOURNING BECOMES ELECTRA, and THE ICEMAN COMETH.

1277. Syrjala, Sointu. "Scenery Is for Seeing." In SCENE DESIGN FOR STAGE AND SCREEN (see item 1161), pp. 232–43.

Contrasts stage design with design for television and film.

1278. Taylor, Deems. "The Scenic Art of Joseph Urban: His Protean Work in the Theatre." ARCHITECTURE 69 (May 1934): 275–90. Illus.

Excellent survey, unusually well illustrated. This issue also includes a tribute by Otto Teegen, an article on Urban's philosophy of color by Teegen, and Ralph Walker's "Joseph Urban, the Man."

1279. Ter-Arutunian, Rouben. "In Search of Design." DANCE PERSPECTIVES 28 (Winter 1966): 6–48. Illus., part color.

The author, a Russian-born designer who since 1951 has been active mainly in the United States, discusses his extensive work for the dance. Excellent illustrations.

1280. THEATRICAL SCENE PAINTING. Omaha, Neb.: Appleton Publishing Co., [1916]. 181 p. Illus.

A scarce practical manual with instructions for painting landscapes, interiors, drop curtains, exotic sets, transparencies, and transformation scenes. Also has a chapter on mounting and installing scenery in smaller theatres.

1281. Tietjens, Eunice. "The Work of C. Raymond Johnson." THEATRE ARTS 4 (1920): 227–37. Illus.

Concerns Johnson's work at the Chicago Little Theatre, with stress on his lighting techniques.

1282. Tollini, Frederick Paul, S.J. "The Fine Art of Variation in the Scene Designs of Donald Mitchell Oenslager." Ph.D. dissertation, Yale University, 1971. 357 p.

Based on a first-hand acquaintance with the artist and his designs.

1283. Traube, Shepard. "Boris Aronson." THEATRE GUILD MAGAZINE 8 (January 1931): 26-30. Illus.

1283a. United Scenic Artists of America [Local 829]. PUT "THEATRE" IN YOUR WORLD'S FAIR THINKING. [New York: 1963]. 29 p. Paperbound. Illus.

> Promotes the talents of the union members in preparing World's Fair exhibitions. On pp. 12-29, a list of union members, with notes on their specialties--scene designer, costume designer, mural artist, etc.--and credits.

1284. _____. UNITED SCENIC ARTISTS 1940-1941 ALMANAC. [New York: c. 1940]. 64 p. Paperbound. Illus.

> Includes articles and notes by Norman-Bel Geddes, Lee Simonson, Donald Oenslager, Robert Edmond Jones, Aline Bernstein, Raoul Pene Du Bois, Robert W. Bergman, and other union members on various aspects of scene and costume design, makeup, motion picture art direction, mural painting, dioramas, and advertising displays. On pp. 57-63, a classified directory of union members.

1285. "Vincente Minelli: The Whole Show but the Actors." THEATRE ARTS 20 (1936): 37-46. Illus.

> Some biographical notes and a selection of his designs for the revue AT HOME ABROAD and for the Ziegfeld Follies.

1286. Von Wien, Florence. "Women Who Are Stage Designers." INDEPENDENT WOMAN 25 (May 1946): 134-36. Illus.

> Sketch of Aline Bernstein's career and brief notes on a dozen others.

1287. Wade, Robert J. "Neo-Perspectivism." PLAYERS 19 (November 1942): 6-8, 17. Illus.

> Describes a method of design based on stylized or distorted perspective. Illustrated by the author. (This is only one of Wade's many brief articles on stage design and technology in PLAYERS, 1937-45; often they were illustrated with his own designs.)

1288. Waldo, Paul Robert. "Production Concepts Exemplified in Selected Presentations Directed by Robert Edmond Jones." Ph.D. dissertation, University of Oregon, 1970. 585 p.

1289. Washburn-Freund, Frank E. "Joseph Urban, Scenic Artist." INTERNATIONAL STUDIO 76 (January 1923): 357-59. Illus.

Comments on the Viennese background of Urban's new style, and a sketch of his career in America.

1290. Weiss, David William. "Jo Mielziner's Contribution to the American Theatre." 2 vols. Ph.D. dissertation, Indiana University, 1965. 399 p.

1291. Wexler, Peter. "Of Time and Design." PLAYERS 44 (April–May 1969): 144–47. Illus.

Promotes close and early collaboration between designer, director, and actors in a given production.

1292. "'The Whip' and Its Mechanism." SCIENTIFIC AMERICAN 108 (25 January 1913): 89, 102. Illus.

Machinery for a train wreck in THE WHIP at the Manhattan Opera House, New York.

1293. Williams, Peter. "A Designer for Exotic Movement." DANCE AND DANCERS 3 (March 1952): 14–15. Illus.

Sketch of the career of John Pratt, designer for Katherine Dunham's dance company.

1294. Works, Bernhard Russell. "Norman Bel Geddes, Man of Ideas." Ph.D. dissertation, University of Wisconsin, 1966. 252 p.

Concerns the early period in Geddes's life, up to his production of THE MIRACLE, 1925.

1295. York, Zack L. "Lee Simonson, Artist-Craftsman of the Theatre." Ph.D. dissertation, University of Wisconsin, 1951. 217 p.

1296. Young, Roland. "Roland Young's Own International Exhibition." THEATRE ARTS 7 (1923): 153–57. Illus.

A portfolio of ten amusing caricatures of American stage designs and designers.

1297. Young, Stark. THE THEATER. New York: Doran, 1927. 182 p.

"Decor," pp. 139–56, discusses the function of scenery, with particular attention to the work of Robert Edmond Jones and Norman-Bel Geddes. Reprinted in SCENE DESIGN FOR STAGE AND SCREEN (see item 1161), pp. 252–60.

Chapter 15

OTHER COUNTRIES

1298. Akers-Douglas, Eric. "The Work of Gustave Olah." THEATRE ARTS 22 (1938): 380-83. Illus.

Olah was artistic director of the Royal Hungarian Opera House. Photographs of four productions he designed.

1299. Alarma Tastas, Salvador. ESCENOGRAFIA [Stage design]. Barcelona: Bayes, [1919]. 4 p. 32 mounted illus., part color.

Text in Spanish. Brief sketch of the career of this Spanish stage designer, plus illustrations of his work.

1300. Amberg, George. "Marc Chagall's Designs for ALEKO and THE FIRE-BIRD." DANCE INDEX 4 (November 1945): 185-204. Illus.

Mainly illustrations.

1301. Amundsen, Gerhard. "Der Buehnenmaler Ludolf Liberts (The Scene Painter Ludolf Liberts)." GEBRAUCHSGRAPHIK (INTERNATIONAL AD-VERTISING ART) 8 (March 1931): 12-17. Illus., part color.

Text in English and German. Brief commentary on the work of Liberts, scenic director of the National Theatre in Riga, Latvia, and ten illustrations.

1302. Ashbolt, Allan. "Stage Design in Australia." WORLD THEATRE 3, no. 4 (1954): 64-68. Illus.

Briefly discusses the work of William Constable, Loudon Saint-hill, and a few others.

1303. Association of Finnish Stage Designers. LAVASTUS / FINNISH STAGE DESIGN. Helsinki: Association of Finnish Stage Designers and Finnish Ministry of Education, 1962. Unpaged [32 p.]. Paperbound. Illus.

A collection of production photographs, 1959-62, with brief explanatory captions in Finnish and English.

1304. Beijer, Agne. COURT THEATRES OF DROTTNINGHOLM AND GRIP-
SHOLM. Translated by G.L. Froelich. Malmo: John Kroon, [1933].
122 pls.

A portfolio of plates illustrating these eighteenth-century Swedish theatres and their remarkably well-preserved scenery and
machinery. Explanatory text by Agne Beijer.

1305. _____. "The Drottningholm Theatre Museum." THEATRE ARTS 18
(1934): 193-205. Illus.

Describes the formation of the collection in the eighteenth
century and illustrates some of its treasures.

1306. Bergman, Goesta M. "Modernism in Stage Designing." AMERICAN
SCANDANAVIAN REVIEW 20 (1932): 204-11. Illus.

Discusses and illustrates the work of two Swedish designers of
the 1920s, Jon-And and Sandro Malmquist.

1307. _____. "Strindberg and the Intima Teatern." THEATRE RESEARCH /
RECHERCHES THEATRALES 9 (1967): 14-47. Illus.

Examines the productions at Strindberg's Intimate Theatre in
Stockholm, founded in 1907, with which he was closely associated until 1910. Illustrated with production photographs and
sketches of scenery by Strindberg.

1308. Blomquist, Allen Palmer. "The Scenic Designs of Isaac Gruenewald."
Ph.D. dissertation, University of Minnesota, 1967. 331 p.

Study of the theatre work of this Swedish artist, beginning
with his first stage designs in 1921.

1309. Borgen, Johan. "Scene Painting or Stage Design." WORLD THEATRE
12 (1963-64): 327-43. Illus.

A review of recent Norwegian work, mentioning a number of
designers and singling out Arne Walentin as an important source
of new ideas.

1310. Bortnovski, Paul. "Architecture, Scenography, and Theatre." ROMA-
NIAN REVIEW 20, no. 4 (1966): 100-104. Illus.

A Rumanian designer discusses the close relationship between
modern stage design and architecture, and their social purposes.

1311. Brady, Cyrus T., Jr. "Lively Theatre in Buenos Aires." THEATRE ARTS
23 (1939): 355-59. Illus.

Illustrated with scene designs by Laerte Baldini and Mario
Vanarelli.

1312. Burleigh, Frederick. "The Polish Theatre." THEATRE ARTS 16 (1932): 45-53. Illus.

A survey of the progressive movement in Polish theatre, illustrated with six photographs of productions designed by Wincent Drabik and Stanislaw Sliwinski.

1313. Chagall, Marc. "Marc Chagall: . . . Opinions on the Relation of Decor to Choreography." Translated by George Amberg. DANCE MAGAZINE 20 (May 1946): 26-27, 45. Illus.

Brief remarks on the need for close designer-choreographer collaboration; five illustrations of Chagall's designs for ALEKO and THE FIREBIRD.

1314. Corathiel, Elisabethe H.C. "The Irish Trend." THEATRE WORLD 57 (May 1961): 44-45, 56. Illus.

Mainly concerns Irish designer Joan Denise Moriarty.

1315. _____. "Rufino Tamayo." THEATRE WORLD 56 (December 1959): 17-18, 56. Illus.

Profile of a Mexican artist who designed John Cranko's ballet ANTIGONE.

1316. "Decorados teatrales [Stage designs]." REVISTA NACIONAL DE ARQUITECTURA 10 (September 1950): 415-24. Illus.

Brief commentary (in Spanish) and illustrations of designs by three Spanish artists: Salvador Dali, Emilio Burgos, and Victor Cortezo.

1317. Denes, Tibor. LE DECOR DE THEATRE EN HONGRIE: PASSE, PRESENT. Munich: Danubia, 1973. 72 p. 14 pls. Paperbound.

Text in French. Reviews the scant evidence about medieval and Renaissance performances; discusses the more fully documented Italianate performances of the Jesuits and the Esterhazys in the eighteenth century and the "Meiningerism" of the late nineteenth century; then discusses in some detail the reforms of Jeno Kemendy and his disciple Gusztav Olah and the work of Almos Jaschik, Laszlo Moholy-Nagy, and other twentieth-century designers.

1318. Dennis, Wendell. "Ubu in the New World." CANADIAN THEATRE REVIEW, no. 5 (Winter 1975): 129-35. Illus.

Designs by the author for a condensation of two Jarry plays produced at the Theatre du Nouveau Monde, Montreal.

1319. Dinova-Ruseva, Vera. "Bulgarian Scenography." INTERSCAENA-ACTA SCAENOGRAPHICA 4 (Spring 1974): 32-48; (Autumn 1974): 13-50; (Winter 1974): 1-36. Illus.

Informative history of Bulgarian stage design from the 1840s to the 1920s. Continued to the 1970s in later issues (not seen).

1320. Gascoigne, Bamber. "Shuffling the Schouwburg Scenes." THEATRE RESEARCH / RECHERCHES THEATRALES 9 (1968): 88-103. Illus.

Reproduces a series of etchings of the Schouwburg Theatre in Amsterdam, c. 1774 (a ground plan and six views of scenery), which, with their descriptive text, comprise "the most complete available illustrated account of the everyday scenic practice of an eighteenth-century theatre." The descriptive text is here transcribed in French.

1321. Gilliman, Florence. "A New Genius of Stage Production." ARTS AND DECORATION 19 (June 1923): 24-25, 56. Illus.

Sketch of the career of Swedish designer Isaac Gruenewald, with commentary and four illustrations.

1322. Gilmer, Albert H. "The Art Theatre of Riga." THEATRE ARTS 11 (1927): 132-40. Illus.

Description of the work of this Latvian theatre, illustrated with six constructivist designs by its scenic director, Jan Muncis.

1323. Hillestrom, Gustaf. "The Art of Stage Decoration, 1940-1955." WORLD THEATRE 4, no. 2 (1955): 27-42. Illus.

Stage design in Sweden, with remarks on designers Sven Erixson, Stellan Moerner, and others.

1324. Hont, Ferenc. "Traditions and Innovations in the Hungarian Theatre." In INNOVATIONS IN STAGE AND THEATRE DESIGN (see item 57), pp. 146-52.

A review of twentieth-century Hungarian theatre, mentioning a few stage designers.

1325. Hood, Hugh. "Murray Laufer and the Art of Scenic Design." ARTS-CANADA 29 (December 1972): 59-64. Illus.

Commentary on Laufer's designs for Canadian productions.

1326. Horanyi, Matyas. THE MAGNIFICENCE OF ESZTERHAZA. Translated by Andras Deak. London: Barrie & Rockliff, 1962. 260 p. Prof. illus., part color. Biblio.

A record of dramatic and musical festivals at the palaces of the Esterhazy princes in Hungary in the eighteenth and early nineteenth centuries. Most of the illustrations are designs for scenery and costumes.

1327. Hunningher, Benjamin. "A Baroque Architect among Painters and Poets." THEATRE RESEARCH / RECHERCHES THEATRALES 3 (1961): 23-31. Illus.

Discusses several aspects of Dutch theatre in the early seventeenth century, including the arrangement of the stage, scenery, and machinery at the Schouwburg Theatre (1617).

1328. Kerr, Mary. "A Designer's Portfolio." CANADIAN THEATRE REVIEW, no. 2 (Spring 1974): 34-39. Illus.

Designs by the author for Machiavelli's MANDRAGOLA at the Vancouver Playhouse, 1974.

1329. Kitamura, Kihachi. "Stage Decoration in Japan." WORLD THEATRE 3, no. 4 (1954): 11-22. Illus.

Considers both Kabuki-style and western-style design in recent Japanese productions.

1330. Krol-Kaczorowska, Barbara. "Les Decors et les decorateurs de l'opera en Pologne au XVIIIe siecle." THEATRE RESEARCH / RECHERCHES THEATRALES 13 (1973): 129-38. Illus.

Text in French. Identifies stage designers active in Poland in the eighteenth century: Giuseppe Galli-Bibiena, Jean-Jerome Servandoni, Carlo Quaglio, Jan Plersch, Antoni Smuglewicz, and others.

1331. Lassaigne, Jacques. MARC CHAGALL: DRAWINGS AND WATER COLORS FOR THE BALLET. New York: Tudor Publishing Co., [1969]. 155 p. Prof. illus., color.

Sketch of Chagall's career as a designer for ballet, together with illustrations and commentary on each of his ballet commissions.

1332. Laufer, Murray. "Designing at the Centre." CANADIAN THEATRE REVIEW, no. 3 (Summer 1974): 42-45. Illus.

Comments on his work as designer at the St. Lawrence Centre.

1333. LIETUVOS SCENOGRAFIJA (LITHUANIAN SCENOGRAPHY). Vilna, Lithuania: Vaga, 1968. 149 p. Illus.

Text apparently in Lithuanian and English. Cited in LIBRARY OF CONGRESS CATALOG--BOOKS: SUBJECTS, 1970, vol. 8. Not seen.

1334. Loney, Glenn [M.]. "The Design Techniques of Gabor Forray, National Opera, Budapest." THEATRE DESIGN & TECHNOLOGY, no. 38 (October 1974): 10-16. Illus.

Describes the methods and working conditions of the chief designer of the Hungarian National Opera.

1335. _____. "Two Hundred Candles--Simulated--for the Drottningholm." THEATRE DESIGN & TECHNOLOGY, no. 7 (December 1966): 3-11. Illus.

Description of the remarkably well-preserved Drottningholm Court Theatre in Sweden, opened in 1766, and its eighteenth-century scenery and machinery.

1336. Martinez Sierra, Gregorio, ed. UN TEATRO DE ARTE EN ESPANA, 1917-1925 [An art theatre in Spain, 1917-1925]. Madrid: [G. Martinez Sierra], 1926. 198 p. Prof. illus., part color.

Text in Spanish. A collection of essays on the productions of the Teatro de Eslava in Madrid, directed by Martinez Sierra, including an essay by Manuel Abril on three of the stage designers active there: Manuel Fontanals, Rafael Barradas, and Siegfried Buermann. Numerous illustrations of their work.

1337. Matkovic, Marijan. "Production and Scenic Expression." WORLD THEATRE 15 (1966): 379-83. Illus.

Brief remarks about recent Yugoslavian stage design; six illustrations.

1338. Noris, Stefan. "Rumanian Set and Costume Designs on Tour." RUMANIA TODAY, no. 6 (1963): 4 p. insert following p. 24. Illus., part color.

Brief commentary and eleven illustrations.

1339. "Opera and Stage Design." THEATRE ARTS 24 (1940): 579-82. Illus.

A portfolio of illustrations of stage designs by Swedish designers Carl Milles, Otte Skoeld, Knut Stroem, Alf Sjoeberg, and Thorolf Jansson.

1340. Palmstierna-Weiss, Gunilla. "Craft and the Theater." CRAFT HORIZONS 28 (May-June 1968): 24-30, 68-69. Illus.

A Swedish designer comments on her career and her methods.

1341. Popov, Vladimir. "Scenography and the Architecture of the Performance." ROMANIAN REVIEW 27, no. 1 (1973): 101-11. Illus.

A review of innovations and experiments in Rumanian stage
design since World War II, including the author's own designs.

1342. "Scenic Design, Brazilian Style." THEATRE ARTS 40 (November 1956):
75. Illus.

Reproductions of designs by Nilson Penna, Anizio Medeiros,
Pernambuco de Oliviera, and Paulo Beckar.

1343. SCENOGRAPHIA HUNGARICA (CONTEMPORARY STAGE AND COS-
TUME DESIGN IN HUNGARY). Edited by Joszef Boegel and Lajos
Janosa. Budapest: Corvina Press, 1973. 44 p. 131 illus., part
color.

Text and captions in Hungarian, English, and French. Brief
historical remarks on Hungarian design and biographical notes
on the designers, plus the illustrations.

1344. SCENOGRAFIA ROMANEASCA (STAGE DESIGN IN RUMANIA). [Bucha-
rest: Arta Grafica, 1965]. 32 p. 454 illus., part color.

Text and captions in Rumanian, English, and French. Introductory remarks on modern Rumanian stage design by Eugen
Schileru. The illustrations, arranged alphabetically by designer's name, date from the period 1945-65.

1345. SCENOGRAFIA ROMANEASCA--QUADRIENALA DIN PRAGE--1971
(STAGE-DESIGN OF RUMANIA--PRAGUE QUADRENNIAL--1971).
[Bucharest: Rumanian Center of the International Organization of Sce-
nographers and Theatre Technicians and the Office for Organizing Art
Exhibitions, 1971]. Unpaged [60 p.]. Paperbound. Illus.

Text and captions in Rumanian, French, and English. Brief
introduction and fifty-three pages of illustrations.

1346. Schalcher, Traugott. "Siegfried Buermann, spanische Buehnenbildner
(Siegfried Buermann, Spanish Scene Painter)." GEBRAUCHSGRAPHIK
(INTERNATIONAL ADVERTISING ART) 14 (June 1937): 18-23. Illus.,
part color.

English and German text. Brief commentary and twelve illustrations.

1347. Shergold, N.D. A HISTORY OF THE SPANISH STAGE FROM MEDI-
EVAL TIMES UNTIL THE END OF THE SEVENTEENTH CENTURY. Oxford: Clarendon Press, 1967. 654 p. Illus. Biblio.

The best source of information on Spanish scenery in public
performances and at court during this period. Well illustrated.

1348. Shergold, N.D., and Varey, J.E. "A Problem in the Staging of AU-

TOS SACRAMENTALES in Madrid, 1647–48." HISPANIC REVIEW 32 (1964): 12–35.

Detailed analysis of evidence to show that in 1647 the number of AUTOS SACRAMENTALES presented in Madrid on Corpus Christi day was reduced to two, and that the number of CARROS, or pageant cars, was increased to four.

1349. "Stan White on Designing for the Theatre." CANADIAN ART 20 (July–August 1963): 232–37. Illus.

Includes twelve illustrations of White's designs for the Ottowa Little Theatre.

1350. Strike, Maurice. "The Designer's Dilemma." CANADIAN THEATRE REVIEW, no. 1 (Winter 1974): 45–48. Illus.

Commentary on the problems of working as a stage designer in Canada. Illustrated with a design by the author.

1351. Strzelecki, Zenobiusz. "Contemporary Polish Stage Design." WORLD THEATRE 6 (1957): 119–26. Illus.

Twentieth-century design in Poland, including discussion of the work of Karol Frycz, Wincenty Drabik, Tadeusz Kantor, Jan Kosinski, and Jerzy Toronczyk.

1352. Szydlowski, Roman. THE THEATRE IN POLAND. Warsaw: Interpress, 1972. 176 p. Paperbound. Illus., part color. Biblio.

Chapter on modern Polish stage design, pp. 95–109, plus illustrations.

1353. Tharrats, Juan–Jose. ARTISTAS ESPANOLES EN EL BALLET [Spanish artists of the ballet]. Barcelona: Argos, 1950. 52 p. Illus., part color.

Text in Spanish. Concerns the ballet designs of Pablo Picasso, Jose Maria Sert, Juan Gris, Pedro Pruna, Joan Miro, Mariano Andreu, Juan (Joan) Junyer, Salvador Dali, Esteban Frances, and others.

1354. Trumper, Bernardo. "Contemporary Scene Design as Seen by a Chilean Designer." INTERSCAENA 4, no. 4 (Autumn 1970): 1–8. Illus.

General remarks on the functions of scenery and lighting in the modern theatre, with brief discussion of some of the author's work in Chile.

1355. Villaurrutia, Xavier. "Hope and Curiosity: Experimental Theatre as a Source." THEATRE ARTS 22 (1938): 607–9. Illus.

Brief sketch of experimental theatre in Mexico in the 1930s, mentioning a number of stage designers and reproducing two settings by Agustin Lazo.

1356. _____. "Mexican Painters and the Theatre." WORLD THEATRE 1, no. 3 (1951): 36–40. Illus.

Brief notes on theatre work by Diego Rivera, Jose Clemente Orozco, and other Mexican painters, c. 1925–50.

1357. Whittaker, Herbert. "Stage Designer Theatre's Step-Child." CANADIAN ART 22 (May–June 1965): 41–47. Illus., part color.

Survey of the designer's place in the Canadian theatre, suggesting that he has been shabbily treated.

1358. Winkler, Konrad. "Stanislaw Sliwinski: Stage Designer and Man of the Theatre." STUDIO 110 (November 1935): 294–95. Illus.

Brief commentary and four illustrations of the work of this Polish stage designer.

1359. Woodrow, Ernest A.E. "Theatres. [Parts] XX–XXI." BUILDING NEWS 64 (14 April 1893): 500–501; (26 May 1893): 695–98. Illus.

Describes and criticizes the Asphaleia system of stage construction at the Budapest Opera House.

1360. Wren, Robert M. "Grooves and Doors on the Seventeenth- and Eighteenth-Century Dutch Stage." THEATRE RESEARCH / RECHERCHES THEATRALES 7 (1965): 56–57. Illus.

Proscenium doors and grooves for sliding wings, at the Schouwburg Theatre in Amsterdam. Informative illustrations.

1361. Zimmerman, L.I. "Marc Chagall: His Lessons for the Theatre." EDUCATIONAL THEATRE JOURNAL 14 (1962): 203–8.

Explicates Chagall's unconventional designs and links the artist's style to his Hassidic Jewish background.

Chapter 16

AESTHETICS

1362. Bellman, Willard F. "Aesthetics for the Designer." EDUCATIONAL THEATRE JOURNAL 5 (1953): 117-24.

Draws on the ideas of Appia, Craig, Robert Edmond Jones, and Suzanne Langner.

1363. Brockett, Lenyth Spenker. "Theories of Style in Stage Production." Ph.D. dissertation, Stanford University, 1954. 315 p.

1364. Brown, John Russell. "Theatre Illusion." INTERSCAENA-ACTA SCAEN-OGRAPHICA 3 (Spring 1973): 1-7.

Concerns scenic illusion and anti-illusion in the contemporary theatre.

1365. Caldwell, George Rollin. "A Quantitative Investigation of Audience Response to Theatrical Settings." Ph.D. dissertation, Bowling Green State University, 1974. 189 p.

1366. Carter, Huntly. "Dramatizing the Theatre." FORUM 52 (July 1914): 60-69.

Discusses the search for dramatic unity in the work of Wagner, Craig, and Reinhardt.

1367. Cole, Wendell. "Scene Types in Action." PLAYERS 25 (October 1948): 6-8. Illus.

Describes and illustrates six styles of setting.

1368. Corson, Richard. "A Garland of 'Isms.'" THEATRE ARTS 29 (1945): 728-30. Illus.

Offers definitions of selectivism, impressionism, expressionism, and similar terms applied to stage design. Cites examples of American productions.

1369. De Valois, Ninette. "Modern Choreography: Decor and Costume." DANCING TIMES, April 1933, pp. 9-11.

Remarks on the need to integrate design with other elements of the ballet.

1370. Hewitt, Barnard [W.]. "Expression in Stage Scenery." In STUDIES IN SPEECH AND DRAMA IN HONOR OF ALEXANDER M. DRUMMOND, pp. 54-66. 1944. Reprint. New York: Russell & Russell Publishers, 1968.

Historical sketch of scenic forms as expressive elements; speculation about the development of new scenic forms employing expressive light, sound effects, and motion pictures.

1371. _____. "The Theatre and the Graphic Arts." Ph.D. dissertation, Cornell University, 1935.

1372. Hewlett, J. Monroe. "Scenery and Stage Decoration: Tradition, Composition, Scale." AMERICAN ARCHITECT 112 (1917): 225-31. Illus.

Unusual discussion of baroque easel paintings as sources of pictorial composition for stage designers.

1373. Honzl, Jindrich. "The Mobility of Theatrical Sign." INTERSCAENA 3 (Winter 1969): 37-50. Illus.

A review of twentieth-century stage design in terms of changing "signs."

1374. _____. "Spatial Problems of the Theatre." INTERSCAENA 4 (Spring 1970): 1-10. Illus.

Survey of theatrical environments and production style from the late nineteenth century to about 1930, ending with a plea for a nonpictorial, dynamic conception of theatrical production.

1375. Johansen, Waldemar. "The Adaptation of Modern Painting to Stage Design." PLAYERS 19 (February 1943): 8-10, 26. Illus.

Examines the techniques of modern painting as aids in teaching and understanding stage design.

1376. _____. "Notes on Abstract Art in the Theatre." THEATRE ANNUAL 4 (1945): 29-32.

Identifies the characteristics of abstract stage designs.

1377. Jones, Robert Edmond. THE DRAMATIC IMAGINATION. New York:

Duell, Sloan and Pearce, 1941.   157 p.

Deals with stage design in a more inspirational than informational manner--and succeeds in being inspiring.

1378.   Josal, Wendell John.   "A Semiotic Approach to the Aesthetic Problem of the Duality of Stage Design as a Spatial and Temporal Art."   Ph.D. dissertation, Northwestern University, 1961.   255 p.

Applies Susan K. Langner's semiotic aesthetic theory to stage design.

1379.   Kumbatovic, Filip K.   "On the Problem of Audio-Visual Unity of Text and Action in the Theatre."   In INNOVATIONS IN STAGE AND THEATRE DESIGN (see item 57), pp. 158–65.

Analyzes stage design in relation to "happenings," on the one hand, and rich technical possibilities on the other.

1380.   Kurth, Henry.   "A Projection towards Stage Architecture."   THEATRE ANNUAL 20 (1963):   72–88.

Theoretical argument for a simplified architectural stage.

1381.   Mitchell, Lee.   "The Space Stage Defined."   THEATRE ARTS 20 (1936): 530–36.   Illus.

Space staging is "a method of attack in which we conceive the action of the play in terms of the relationships of the characters to one another, in space."   Illustrated by the author's own designs.

1382.   Mitchell, Roy.   "Dynamic Scene: The Theatre of the Wheel."   THEATRE ARTS 14 (1930):   49–59.   Illus.

Theoretical discussion of a projected unit setting formed by a staircase in the shape of a helix.

1383.   _____.   "Towards a New Scene Convention."   AMERICAN MAGAZINE OF ART 24 (January 1932):   28–34.   Illus.

Here and in an earlier article, AMERICAN MAGAZINE OF ART 22 (March 1931):   194–96, Mitchell condemns the picture-frame stage and promotes new conventions.

1384.   Pickett, Warren Wheeler.   "An Experiment in Response by Different Temperament Types to Different Styles of Set Design."   Ph.D. dissertation, University of Michigan, 1969.   132 p.

1385.   Russell, Douglas A.   "Problems of Design: Shakespeare's Plays."   PLAY-

ERS 50 (February–March 1975): 70–76. Illus.

Largely theoretical.

1386. Schechner, Richard. ENVIRONMENTAL THEATER. New York: Hawthorn Books, 1973. x, 339 p. Illus. Biblio.

Discusses the scenic principles of this type of theatre.

1387. Stevens, Thomas Wood. "The Stage without a Curtain." THEATRE ARTS 22 (1938): 145–50.

Concerns the function of scenery in presentational productions.

1388. Volbach, Walther R. "Time and Space on the Stage." EDUCATIONAL THEATRE JOURNAL 19 (1967): 134–41.

Chapter 17
MANUALS AND TEXTBOOKS
OF CONTEMPORARY PRACTICE

1389. Adix, Vern. THEATRE SCENECRAFT. Anchorage, Ky.: Children's Theatre Press, 1956. 309 p. Illus. Biblio.

1390. Ashworth, Bradford. NOTES ON SCENE PAINTING. Edited by Donald [Mitchell] Oenslager. New Haven, Conn.: Whitlock's, [1952]. 47 p.

1391. Bay, Howard. STAGE DESIGN. New York: Drama Book Specialists Publishers, 1974. 218 p. Prof. illus.

1392. Bell, Stanley, et al. ESSENTIALS OF STAGE-PLANNING. London: Muller, 1949. xi, 111 p. Illus. Biblio.

1393. Bowman, Ned A. HANDBOOK OF TECHNICAL PRACTICE FOR THE PERFORMING ARTS. Wilkinsburg, Pa.: Scenographic Media, 1972. [34], 169 p. Unpaged indexes. Illus. Biblio.

At head of title: NED A. BOWMAN'S INTER-GALACTIC SERIAL SHOP COOKBOOK. Published in ring binder, in paper binding, or as loose sheets. Leaves perforated for inter-filing with later parts. This first part is devoted to makeup and plastics.

1394. Bryson, Nicholas L. THERMOPLASTIC SCENERY FOR THEATRE. New York: Drama Book Specialists/Publishers, 1972. 104 p. Illus.

Volume 1: Vacuum Forming of Thermoplastics.

1395. Buerki, F.A. STAGECRAFT FOR NONPROFESSIONALS. 3d ed. Madison: University of Wisconsin Press, 1972. xii, 131 p. Paper-bound. Illus.

1396. Burris-Meyer, Harold, and Cole, Edward C. SCENERY FOR THE THE-ATRE. Rev. ed. Boston: Little, Brown and Co., 1971. 537 p. Illus. Biblio.

1397. Corey, Irene. THE MASK OF REALITY: AN APPROACH TO DESIGN FOR THEATRE. Anchorage, Ky.: Anchorage Press, 1968. 124 p. Illus., part color. Biblio.

1398. Cornberg, Sol, and Gebauer, Emanuel L. A STAGE CREW HAND-BOOK. Rev. ed. New York: Harper & Row, 1957. 291 p. Illus.

1399. Dolman, John. THE ART OF PLAY PRODUCTION. Rev. ed. New York and London: Harper & Bros., 1946. 440 p. Illus. Biblio.

1400. Etheridge, Ken. SCENIC DESIGN FOR AMATEURS. Edinburgh: Albyn Press, 1947. 64 p. Paperbound. Illus.

1401. Forman, Robert. SCENE PAINTING. London: Pitman, 1950. viii, 40 p. Illus., part color.

1402. Friederich, Willard J., and Fraser, John H. SCENERY DESIGN FOR THE AMATEUR STAGE. New York: Macmillan, 1950. 279 p. Illus.

1403. Gassner, John W. PRODUCING THE PLAY. Rev. ed. New York: Dryden Press, 1953. 933 p. Illus. Biblio.

Includes sections on "Designing the Play," by Mordecai Gore-lik, pp. 301-54; "Lighting the Play," by Abe Feder, pp. 355-78; and incorporates Philip Barber's THE NEW SCENE TECHNI-CIAN'S HANDBOOK (first published in 1928), pp. 671-879.

1404. Gillette, Arnold S. AN INTRODUCTION TO SCENIC DESIGN. New York: Harper & Row, 1967. viii, 210 p. Illus. Biblio.

1405. _____. STAGE SCENERY: ITS CONSTRUCTION AND RIGGING. 2d ed. New York: Harper & Row, 1972. 445 p. Illus. Biblio.

1406. Hake, Herbert V. HERE'S HOW! A BASIC STAGECRAFT BOOK. Rev. ed. Evanston, Ill.: Row, Peterson, 1958. 128 p. Illus. Biblio.

1407. Helvenston, Harold Finley. SCENERY: A MANUAL OF SCENE DE-SIGN. Stanford, Calif.: Stanford University Press, 1931. 111 p. Illus.

1408. Jones, Eric. STAGE CONSTRUCTION FOR SCHOOL PLAYS. London: Batsford, 1969. 88 p. Illus.

1409. Joseph, Stephen. SCENE PAINTING AND DESIGN. London: I. Pit-man, 1964. xii, 132 p. Illus. Biblio.

1410. Kenton, Warren. STAGE PROPERTIES AND HOW TO MAKE THEM. London: I. Pitman, 1964. vii, 119 p. Illus.

1411. Melvill, Harald. DESIGNING AND PAINTING SCENERY FOR THE THEATRE. London: Barrie and Rockliff, 1963. 98 p. Illus.

1412. Motley [pseud.]. THEATRE PROPS. New York: Drama Book Specialists/ Publishers, 1975. 128 p. Illus. Biblio.

1413. Napier, Frank. CURTAINS FOR STAGE SETTINGS. London: F. Muller, 1937. x, 146 p. Illus.

1414. _____. NOISES OFF: A HANDBOOK OF SOUND EFFECTS. London: F. Muller, 1936. x, 117 p. Illus.

1415. Nelms, Henning. SCENE DESIGN: A GUIDE TO THE STAGE. New York: Sterling Publishing Co., 1970. 96 p. Illus.

1416. Parker, Wilford Oren. SCENO-GRAPHIC TECHNIQUES. 2d ed., rev. and enl. Pittsburgh: Carnegie Institute of Technology, 1964. 85 p. Illus.

1417. Parker, Wilford Oren, and Smith, Harvey K. SCENE DESIGN AND STAGE LIGHTING. 3d ed. New York: Holt, Rinehart and Winston, 1974. x, 597 p. Illus. Biblio.

1418. Payne, Darwin Reid. DESIGN FOR THE STAGE: FIRST STEPS. Carbondale: Southern Illinois University Press, 1974. 352 p. Illus.

1419. Pektal, Lynn. DESIGNING AND PAINTING FOR THE THEATRE. New York: Holt, Rinehart and Winston, 1975. 412 p. Illus., part color. Biblio.

1420. Philippi, Herbert. STAGECRAFT AND SCENE DESIGN. Boston: Houghton-Mifflin Co., 1953. 448 p. Illus.

1421. Selden, Samuel, and Rezzuto, Tom. ESSENTIALS OF STAGE SCENERY. New York: Appleton-Century-Crofts, 1972. 278 p. Illus. Biblio.

1422. Smith, Andre. THE SCENEWRIGHT: THE MAKING OF STAGE MODELS AND SETTINGS. New York: Macmillan Co., 1926. vii, 135 p. Illus.

1423. Southern, Richard. PROSCENIUM AND SIGHT-LINES: A COMPLETE

SYSTEM OF SCENERY PLANNING AND A GUIDE TO THE LAYING OUT OF STAGES FOR SCENE-DESIGNERS, STAGE-MANAGERS, THEATRE ARCHITECTS AND ENGINEERS, THEATRICAL HISTORY AND RESEARCH WORKERS AND THOSE CONCERNED WITH THE PLANNING OF STAGE FOR SMALL HALLS. 2d ed. London: Faber and Faber, 1964. 235 p. Illus.

1424. _____. STAGE-SETTING FOR AMATEURS AND PROFESSIONALS. London: Faber and Faber, 1937. 272 p. Illus. Biblio.

1425. Stahl, LeRoy. THE SIMPLIFIED STAGECRAFT MANUAL. Minneapolis: T.S. Denison & Co., 1962. 218 p. Illus.

1426. Stell, W. Joseph. THE THEATRE STUDENT: SCENERY. New York: Richards Rosen Press, 1969. 256 p. Illus. Biblio.

1427. Stern, Lawrence. STAGE MANAGEMENT: A GUIDEBOOK OF PRACTICAL TECHNIQUES. Boston: Allyn and Bacon, 1974. x, 323 p. Illus.

1428. THEATRE CHECK LIST: A GUIDE TO THE PLANNING AND CONSTRUCTION OF PROSCENIUM AND OPEN STAGE THEATRES. Prepared by and Published for the American Theatre Planning Board. Middletown, Conn.: Wesleyan University Press, 1969. 71 p. Paperbound. Illus.

1429. Warre, Michael. DESIGNING AND MAKING STAGE SCENERY. London: Studio Vista; New York: Reinhold, 1968. 104 p. Illus. Biblio.

1430. Welker, David Harold. THEATRICAL SET DESIGN: THE BASIC TECHNIQUES. Boston: Allyn & Bacon, 1969. xi, 349 p. Illus.

1431. Wyatt, Jenifer. STAGE SCENERY. London: H. Jenkins, 1957. 93 p. Illus.

1432. Zinkeisen, Doris. DESIGNING FOR THE STAGE. London and New York: Studio, [1938]. 79 p. Illus., part color.

Chapter 18

PERIODICAL ARTICLES ON CONTEMPORARY PRACTICE

SEE ALSO items 40, 42, 45–47.

1433. Adducci, Alexander F. "Our Poisoned Scene Shops." EDUCATIONAL
THEATRE JOURNAL 23 (1971): 109–16.

Describes the health hazards associated with the use of such
chemical substances as solvents, polyurethane foams, and aero-
sol products.

1434. Arnold, Richard. "Modernizing the Scene Shop." PLAYERS 43 (August–
September 1968): 188–91. Illus.

Discusses space flexibility, storage flexibility, and new equipment and materials.

1435. Billings, Alan G[ailey]. "The Use of Plastic Film." PLAYERS 46
(December–January 1971): 65–67. Illus.

Brief discussion of the scenic use of polyethylene film.

1436. Dahlstrom, Robert A. "Polyethylene Piranesi." PLAYERS 44 (August–
September 1969): 254–57. Illus.

Describes the making of architectural elements out of polysty-
rene.

1437. Lounsbury, W[arren]. C. "Have You Tried Fiber Glass?" EDUCATIONAL
THEATRE JOURNAL 16 (1964): 240–41.

Concerns the use of fiber glass in making scenery and props.

1438. Molyneux, William. "Opera Scenery Can Be Built on a Shoestring."
MUSICAL AMERICA 74 (15 February 1954): 28, 166–67. Illus.

Suggests fragmentary, stylized sets, home-built.

1439. Stock, William H.   "The Method of Multi-Vanishing Point Perspective."
       EDUCATIONAL THEATRE JOURNAL 17 (1965):   346-53.

       Describes a mechanical system of transferring a ground plan
       to a perspective view.

1440. Stock, William H., and Grubbs, Robert.   "MLL--a New Base for Scene
       Paint."   EDUCATIONAL THEATRE JOURNAL 16 (1964):   237-39.

       Describes experiments with a base called Mixing Latex Liquid,
       tested against the usual glue-water base.

1441. Sturcken, Frank W.   "A Sound System Design for Legitimate Theatre."
       EDUCATIONAL THEATRE JOURNAL 16 (1964):   230-36.   Illus., diags.

1442. "Theatre Design: Stage Scenery."   ARCHITECT'S JOURNAL 140 (26
       August 1964):   513-25.   Illus.

       A practical guide for architects.   Appended is a glossary of
       technical terms used in the British and American theatre.

Part III

STAGE LIGHTING AND PROJECTED SCENERY

Chapter 19

GENERAL HISTORIES

SEE ALSO items 1498, 1503, 1549, 1589.

1443. Applebee, L.G. "The Evolution of Stage Lighting." JOURNAL OF
THE ROYAL SOCIETY OF ARTS 94 (2 August 1946): 550-63. Illus.

Sketch of the history of stage lighting, mainly concerning
twentieth-century developments. Undocumented and not always
accurate.

1444. Bergman, Goesta M. THE LIGHT IN THE THEATRE. Totowa, N.J.:
Rowman & Littlefield. About 300 p. Illus. Biblio.

Announced for publication in 1977; title tentative. A history of
stage lighting from the Middle Ages to the present, by an able
scholar. The first book-length study of the subject in English.

1445. Burch, Roger Bruce. "The Design of Electrical Lighting Control Systems
in the United States." Ph.D. dissertation, University of Illinois (Urbana-
Champaign), 1972. 206 p.

Examines American lighting control systems from the introduction of electricity to 1971.

1446. Byrne, Muriel St. Clare. "Lighting, Stage: History." In OXFORD
COMPANION TO THE THEATRE, edited by Phyllis Hartnoll, pp. 559-
69. 3d ed. London: Oxford University Press, 1967.

1447. Hartmann, Louis. THEATRE LIGHTING: A MANUAL OF THE STAGE
SWITCHBOARD. New York: D. Appleton and Co., 1930. 151 p.
Illus. Biblio.

An informative book by David Belasco's lighting technician.
Describes nineteenth-century gas equipment, the development
of electrical instruments, and the author's techniques of stage
lighting. An appendix transcribes the complete light plot for
Belasco's production of Molnar's MIMA.

1448. Lawrence, W[illiam]. J[ohn]. "Perfecting Stage Lighting." NEW YORK DRAMATIC MIRROR, 24 February 1917, p. 5. "Solving Lighting Problems." NEW YORK DRAMATIC MIRROR, 3 March 1917, pp. 5, 7.

   A two-part article on the history of stage lighting in the United States, discussing the development of gas lights, electric lights, dimmers, and special electrical effects.

1449. Rosse, Herman. "Light in the Theatre." CHAPTER ONE 4 (December 1957): 1-3. Illus.

   Sketchy history of stage lighting in the nineteenth and twentieth centuries, with good illustrations.

1450. Unruh, Delbert. "Composition in Light--Aesthetic and Functional Considerations." THEATRE DESIGN & TECHNOLOGY, no. 38 (October 1974): 17-22. Illus.

   Examines sculpture by Bernini, paintings by Tintoretto and Rembrandt, and stage designs by Appia.

Chapter 20

BEFORE 1900

SEE ALSO items 1443-50, 1507.

1451. "Application of the Electric Light in Theaters." SCIENTIFIC AMERICAN SUPPLEMENT 16 (10 November 1883): 6535-36. Illus.

> Details of the lighting equipment in the temporary theatre at the International Exhibition of Electricity in Munich, Germany --an important "model" installation. Well illustrated.

1452. Bangham, P. Jerald. "A Method for Analyzing Prompt Book Notations for Evidences of Gas Lighting Practices." OSU THEATRE COLLECTION BULLETIN 8 (1961): 34-41.

> Examines three promptbooks and tabulates notations about intensity, special effects, instruments, and color.

1453. Barlow, Anthony D. "Lighting Control and Concepts of Theatre Activity." EDUCATIONAL THEATRE JOURNAL 25 (1973): 135-46. Illus.

> Examines theatres from the seventeenth to the nineteenth centuries in order to identify how auditorium and stage lighting was related to social and aesthetic functions of the playhouse.

1454. Bissing, H. "Electricity on the Stage." ELECTRICAL WORLD 30 (3 July 1897): 3.

> Compares the arc lamp to the limelight for stage use.

1455. _____. "The Switchboard for Stage Lighting." ELECTRICAL WORLD 31 (19 February 1898): 246-47. Diags.

> A brief primer of stage lighting for engineers.

1456. Brokaw, John W. "An Inventory of Gas Lighting Equipment in the Theatre Royal, Hull, 1877." THEATRE SURVEY 15 (1974): 29-37.

An extensively annotated transcription of the inventory, raising some interesting questions about early lighting equipment.

1457. D_____, J.E. "Scenery and Decoration of Theatres: Lighting the Stage." BUILDER 5 (1847): 281.

Describes a precocious experiment in abolishing footlights and lighting the stage from the auditorium ceiling and from above and behind the proscenium.

1458. "The Electric Light at the Theatre." BUILDER 42 (7 January 1882): 10.

Discusses the need to change old scene-painting styles to accommodate new electric lighting.

1459. "Electric Lighting at the Covent Garden Theater." SCIENTIFIC AMERICAN 81 (30 September 1899): 211.

Brief but informative.

1460. "The Electric Lighting of the Grand Opera at Paris." ENGINEERING (London) 32 (21 October 1881): 417-19. Illus.

Swan lamps were installed as footlights. The rest of the article refers to house lighting.

1461. Ezekiel, Margaret. "All the Lighting of the House is Done by Electricity." THEATRE DESIGN & TECHNOLOGY, no. 27 (December 1971): 24-27. Illus., diags.

Technical description of Samuael Gardiner's electric ignition system for gas lights, patented c. 1870.

1462. Goodman, Lawrence P. "More Light on the Limelight." THEATRE SURVEY 10 (1969): 114-20.

Note about the first stage use of the limelight (by William C. Macready) in 1837.

1463. Guest, Ivor. "Babbage's Ballet." BALLET 5 (April 1948): 51-56. Illus.

Discusses Charles Babbage's 1845-46 project for using lights to color neutral costumes and scenery in a ballet in London.

1464. Held, McDonald Watkins. "A History of Stage Lighting in the United States in the Nineteenth Century." Ph.D. dissertation, Northwestern University, 1955. 311 p.

1465. _____. "Special Lighting Effects on the Late Nineteenth-Century

American Stage." BULLETIN OF FURMAN UNIVERSITY (FURMAN STUDIES) 33 (1950): 61-77.

Sunlight, fires, lightning, shimmering water, etc., accomplished by limelight and electric lamps.

1466. Lathrop, George Parsons. "Stage Scenery and the Vitascope." NORTH AMERICAN REVIEW 163 (September 1896): 377-81.

Suggests that motion picture projectors such as Edison's Vitascope can be used to project theatrical scenic effects such as waterfalls, ocean waves, and moving panoramas.

1467. Lawrence, W[illiam]. J[ohn]. "Early English Stage and Theatre-Lighting (1580-1800)." In "THE STAGE" YEAR BOOK 1927, pp. 9-22. London: Carson & Comerford, 1927. Illus.

A well-reasoned study, drawing on literary, dramatic, and iconographic evidence to identify the instruments used and the methods by which effects were achieved.

1468. _____. "First Use of Limelight on the Stage." NOTES & QUERIES, s. 7, 8 (1889): 225-26.

First used by William C. Macready in 1837-38, in London.

1469. Lee, Briant Hamor. "Pierre Patte, Late 18th Century Lighting Innovator." THEATRE SURVEY 15 (November 1974): 177-83. Illus.

As early as 1781, Patte proposed to light the stage from the front, from the sides, and from above, with lens-and-reflector instruments. He also advocated removing footlights.

1470. Legge, Brian. "Stage Lighting in the 19th Century." TABS 26 (September 1968): 17-23. Illus.

Mainly concerns gas and electric lighting in English theatres.

1471. "The Lighting of Theatres." BUILDER 19 (3 August 1861): 521.

Ventilated footlights at the Paris Opera.

1472. "The Lighting of the Savoy Theatre." ENGINEERING (London) 33 (3 March 1882): 204-6. Illus.

Detailed report on the first electric lights (stage and auditorium) in a London theatre. Reprinted in TABS 20 (September 1962): 29-32.

1473. "A Lighting Plot for Irving's MERCHANT OF VENICE." EDUCATIONAL THEATRE JOURNAL 24 (1972): 265-68.

Transcription of a rare printed plot from the 1890s or early twentieth century. Lists instruments, color media, and intensities.

1474. "Lighting the Stage: New Theatre in Paris." BUILDER 9 (28 June 1851): 406.

Describes an unnamed new theatre in Paris with a circular stage, curved backdrops, no footlights, and reflectored lights above the stage. Equipped by one Barthelemy.

1475. "Living Pictures." ELECTRICAL WORLD 25 (12 January 1895): 45-48. Illus.

Use of electric lights in tableaux vivants recreating old-master paintings.

1476. Morinni, Clare de. "Loie Fuller, the Fairy of Light." DANCE INDEX 1 (1942): 40-51. Illus.

Includes discussion of this dancer's experiments with light, beginning around 1890.

1477. Mullin, Donald C. "Lamps for Garrick's Footlights." THEATRE NOTEBOOK 26 (1971-72): 92-94. Illus.

Illustrates and describes a late nineteenth- or early twentieth-century spring candlestick similar to a type of footlight lamp that Garrick may have imported from France for Drury Lane, c. 1763.

1478. Schooling, William. "Colour-Music: A Suggestion of a New Art." NINETEENTH CENTURY 38 (July 1895): 125-34.

Proposes a color organ of the kind invented by Wallace Rimington about the time this article was published.

1479. Stoker, Bram. "Irving and Stage Lighting." NINETEENTH CENTURY AND AFTER 69 (May 1911): 903-12.

Excellent description of Henry Irving's gas lighting equipment, his experiments with electrical lighting, his development of new color media, and his efforts to perfect an "art" of stage lighting.

1480. Willis, Richard A. "The Joys of Gas Lighting." THEATRE DESIGN & TECHNOLOGY, no. 17 (May 1969): 4-7. Illus.

Brief survey of stage lighting in America in the nineteenth century, covering both gas and electricity.

1481. Wilstach, Claxton. "Electricity on the Stage." GODEY'S (November 1896): 518-23. Illus.

Sciopticon projectors, electrically operated "explosions," light bulbs in costumes and props, and similar special effects.

1482. _____. "Light and Sound on the Stage." GODEY'S 133 (August 1896): 183-89. Illus.

Electrically operated special effects (lightning, sunrise, wind, etc.).

1483. Wolcott, John R. "The Genesis of Gas Lights." THEATRE RESEARCH / RECHERCHES THEATRALES 12 (1972): 74-87. Illus.

Describes the development of gas as an illuminant, both in England and in the United States, and its application to lighting the Chestnut Street Theatre in Philadelphia in 1816.

1484. Woodrow, Ernest A.E, "Theatres. [Parts] XLII-XLIV." BUILDING NEWS 67 (28 September 1894): 422-23; (26 October 1894): 566-69; (9 November 1894): 638-40. Illus.

Discussion of theatre lighting (gas and electric) for architects. Generally refers to British practice. Excellent illustrations of lighting instruments.

Chapter 21
1900 TO 1950

SEE ALSO items 1443-49, 1473, 1479, 1574, 1589, 1591, 1592, 1594.

1485. [Bentham, Frederick P.]. "Fifty Years in Stage Lighting." TABS
22 (March 1964). viii, 119 p. Illus.

Entire issue devoted to a history of the first fifty years of
Strand Electric and Engineering Company, one of the world's
leading designers and manufacturers of stage lighting and control equipment. The author's technical references may occasionally bewilder the layman, but he provides a fascinating
behind-the-scenes view of the development of stage lighting.

1486. Bentham, Frederick P. "Twenty-Five Years of Stage Lighting Equipment."
TRANSACTIONS OF THE ILLUMINATING ENGINEERING SOCIETY
(London) 26 (1961): 79-94. Illus.

Describes "the development of stage lighting equipment (dimmers and control excluded) in Britain during the past 25 years,"
with comparisons to German and American practices.

1487. Blackall, Clarence H. "The American Theater--VIII: Theater Lighting."
BRICKBUILDER 17 (July 1908): 133-38. Illus.

A veteran theatre architect discusses instruments, color media,
switchboards, and special effects.

1488. Bogusch, George E. "Norman Bel Geddes and the Art of Modern Theatre Lighting." EDUCATIONAL THEATRE JOURNAL 24 (1972): 415-
29. Illus.

The author finds that he cannot confirm Geddes's claim to have
invented the high-powered lensed spotlight and other new devices. He examines a number of Geddes's productions, attempting to demonstrate that he "used lighting to unify expressionistic
productions."

1489. "The Boston Opera House." ELECTRICAL WORLD 55 (12 May 1910): 1197-1202. Illus.

Technical description of stage lighting and electrical equipment in this theatre.

1490 Bragdon, Claude. "Artificial Lighting for Out-of-Doors." THEATRE ARTS 1 (1916-17): 188-92. Illus.

Gas and electric lighting for open-air performances.

1491 ———. "Decorative and Theatrical Lighting." TRANSACTIONS OF THE ILLUMINATING ENGINEERING SOCIETY 19 (1924): 888-901.

Remarks on stage-lighting techniques, with examples from his own productions for Walter Hampden and from other American productions.

1492 ———. "Harnessing the Rainbow." In his THE ARCH LECTURES, pp. 116-26. New York: Creative Age Press, 1942. Illus.

A brief sketch of the history of color organs and suggestions for their future development.

1493. "Broadway to Have a New 'Theater of Color.'" CURRENT OPINION 71 (November 1921): 612-13.

Describes an experimental lighting system developed by an Italian, Achille Ricciardi, in which constantly changing colored light is achieved by a moving strip of gelatin color medium.

1494. Cerny, Frantisek. "Lighting that Creates the Scene and Lighting as an Actor." In INNOVATIONS IN STAGE AND THEATRE DESIGN (see item 57), pp. 126-45. Illus.

Concerns Emil F. Burian and Miroslav Kouril's production of Wedekind's SPRING'S AWAKENING in Prague in 1936, in which they used a lighting and projection system called the "Theatergraph."

1495. Curtis, Augustus D., and Stair, J.L. "Recent Applications of Color in Lighting." TRANSACTIONS OF THE ILLUMINATING ENGINEERING SOCIETY 15 (1920): 678-92. Illus.

Includes discussion of stage lighting, pp. 684-87, with remarks on new striplights and balcony-rail lights. Good illustrations.

1496. Dean, Basil. "Recollections and Reflections." TABS 20 (December 1962): 5-23. Illus.

Recollections of his experiments and innovations in stage light-

ing, beginning around 1920. Valuable information on early
lighting equipment and techniques in England, Germany, and
the United States.

1497. "The Exploring Eye." ARCHITECTURAL REVIEW 137 (March 1965):
201-3. Illus.

Brief remarks on the career of Mariano Fortuny y Mandrazo,
inventor of new lighting techniques in the early twentieth
century.

1498. Fagan, J.B. "The Art of Stage Lighting." ILLUMINATING ENGINEER
(London) 12 (1919): 118-33.

Brief sketch of the history of stage lighting, remarks on the
work of Gordon Craig and Mariano Fortuny, and a description
of the author's own cyclorama system at the Royal Court Theatre, London.

1499. Feeney, James M. "New Method of Stage Lighting." LIGHTING
JOURNAL 3 (October 1915): 217-19. Illus.

Technical description of the new system of lighting at the
Belasco Theatre, New York, equipped with "X-ray" reflectors
in a hood over the apron.

1500. Feher, Erwin [M.]. "Images of Light in the Theatre." THEATRE
CRAFTS 4 (September 1970): 20-23, 42-43. Illus.

A brief but informative history of projected scenery.

1501. Fox, Edward Lyell. "Dramatizing Electricity." GREEN BOOK ALBUM
7 (June 1912): 1120-26. Illus.

Miscellaneous notes about lighting for special effects in recent
American productions.

1502. Fuchs, Theodore. HOME-BUILT LIGHTING EQUIPMENT FOR THE
SMALL STAGE. New York and Los Angeles: Samuel French, 1939.
xii, 39 p. Illus.

1503. _____. STAGE LIGHTING. Boston: Little, Brown, and Co., 1929.
viii, 500 p. Illus. Biblio.

A comprehensive textbook that provides valuable documentation
of technical equipment and practice in the early twentieth century. Includes a chapter on the history of stage lighting;
technical discussion of electricity, light, and color; and detailed descriptions of instruments, dimmers, and color media.

1504. Gressler, Thomas H. "Lighting a Show with John Murray Anderson."
PLAYERS 51 (October–November 1975): 28–31.

Anderson, working with his electrician Carlton Winckler, was
"one of the first practitioners of artistic lighting design in the
1920's."

1505. Groom, H.R. Lester. "Stage Lighting." ILLUMINATING ENGINEER
(London) 19 (April 1926): 101–5, 116–19. Illus.

Discussion of available equipment and its uses.

1506. Hamilton, John L. "Designing a Practical Lighting Control Board."
PLAYERS 15 (March–April 1939): 9–10, 36. Illus.

Of some historical interest. Related articles by the same author appear in PLAYERS 17 (January 1941): 13, 28; and 17
(February 1941): 9–10.

1507. Hartmann, Louis. "Lighting Effects on the Stage." TRANSACTIONS OF
THE ILLUMINATING ENGINEERING SOCIETY 18 (1923): 419–33.

Practical discussion of his work as David Belasco's lighting
technician. Added commentary on early American stage lighting by a former gas-boy, William Hall.

1508. Izenour, George C. "Revolution in Light." THEATRE ARTS 31 (October 1947): 73–75. Diag.

Describes an electronic-console lighting control system devised
by the author and installed in the Yale University Theatre.

1509. _____. "Science and the Contemporary Theatre." In TEN TALENTS
IN THE AMERICAN THEATRE, edited by David H. Stevens, pp. 198–
223. Norman: University of Oklahoma Press, 1957.

An autobiographical sketch, with particular attention to the
research on stage lighting that led to the opening of his theatre technology laboratory at Yale.

1510. Jones, Bassett. "Mobile Color and Stage Lighting." ELECTRICAL
WORLD 66 (1915): 245–49, 294–97, 346–49, 407–9, 454–56. Illus.

An important series of technical articles by an engineer who
developed new types of lamps and improved color media for
stage lighting. Well illustrated with light plots and photographs
of instruments.

1511. _____. "The Possibilities of Stage Lighting Together with an Account
of Several Recent Productions." TRANSACTIONS OF THE ILLUMINAT-
ING ENGINEERING SOCIETY 11 (1916): 547–72. Illus.

An informative and well-illustrated account of Jones's installa-
tions in theatres, ballrooms, and outdoor theatres.

1512. Klein, Adrian B. COLOUR-MUSIC. London: Crosby Lockwood, 1926.
303 p. Illus. Biblio.

Also published in several later editions. Reviews the history
of color organs and similar devices, then describes current
techniques, including Klein's own color projectors. Brief
chapter on stage lighting.

1513. [Kliegl, Herbert A.]. "Stage Lighting." ILLUMINATING ENGINEER-
ING 51 (January 1956): 113-22. Illus.

An excellent brief history of twentieth-century stage lighting
in America, with good illustrations. (The article is unsigned,
but the author's name is listed in the annual index.)

1514. "Klieg-Light Kliegl." NEW YORKER 33 (13 July 1957): 20-21.

Interview with John H. Kliegl, co-founder of the well-known
stage lighting firm, who provides a sketch of its history.

1515. Kobler, John. "The Whole Thing Is All with Lights." NEW YORKER
23 (15 November 1947): 38-53. Port.

A profile of Jacob Buchter, chief electrician of the Metropolitan Opera House, New York, since 1920. Biographical data
and much information on lighting equipment and special effects.

1516. Kook, Edward F. "What Is Good and Sufficient Lighting?" THEATRE
ARTS 15 (1931): 619-22. Diags.

Describes and diagrams a standard lighting layout for the amateur theatre.

1517. "The Long-Forgotten Magic Lantern: Boris Aronson Expands the Scope
of the Slide Projector." INTERIORS 108 (December 1948): 84-95.
Illus., part color.

Experiments in projecting images onto a variety of abstract
scenic shapes onstage.

1518. Lucklesh, Matthew. "Color Effects for the Stage and Displays." In
his COLOR AND ITS APPLICATIONS, pp. 274-78. New York: Van
Nostrand, 1915.

Describes a method of changing scenery or parts of scenery
by altering the color of the light.

1519. _____. "Light and Shade in Stage-Craft." In his LIGHT AND SHADE
AND THEIR APPLICATIONS, pp. 186–89. New York: D. Van Nostrand
Co., 1916.

   Discusses the expressive potential of light and shade as used
   in the New Stagecraft.

1520. _____. "Stage-Lighting." In his THE LIGHTING ART: ITS PRACTICE
AND POSSIBILITIES, pp. 180–88. New York: McGraw-Hill Book Co.,
1917.

1521. McCandless, Stanley R. "Electrical Layout of the Yale Theatre."
AMERICAN ARCHITECT 131 (20 March 1927): 365–68. Illus.

1522. _____. "Glossary of Stage Lighting." THEATRE ARTS 10 (1926): 627–
42.

   Definitions of terms identifying instruments, accessories, light
   placement, control equipment, and electrical operation. A
   useful documentation of lighting practices in the 1920s.

1523. _____. "Lighting as Part of the Course in Play Production." PLAYERS
8 (March-April 1932): 7–8.

1524. _____. "Lighting the Legitimate Theater." ARCHITECTURAL FORUM
57 (September 1932): 279–86. Illus.

   A technical presentation for architects.

1525. McCandless, Stanley R., and Ehrhardt, Louis. "The Procedure for Lighting a Production" and "The Application of Lighting to the Stage." In
OUR THEATRE TODAY, edited by Herschel L. Bricker, pp. 287–312 and
313–29, respectively. New York: Samuel French, 1936.

   A brief primer of stage lighting--theory and practice.

1526. McCandless, Stanley R., and Wolff, Fred. "The Problem of the Switchboard." PLAYERS 23 (January-February 1947): 55–56.

1527. Moses, Montrose Jonas. "David Belasco and the Psychology of the
Switchboard." In his THE AMERICAN DRAMATIST, pp. 111–34. 2d
ed., rev. Boston: Little, Brown and Co., 1917.

   A survey of Belasco's career and a description of his lighting
   methods.

1528. Murray, Donald Louis. "The Rise of the American Professional Stage
Lighting Designer to 1963." Ph.D. dissertation, University of Michigan,
1970. 365 p.

1529. Neuburger, A. "Modern Stage Illumination." SCIENTIFIC AMERICAN SUPPLEMENT 69 (16 April 1910): 244-45. Illus.

Mariano Fortuny's system of reflecting light off colored surfaces onto a sky dome.

1530. "New System of Lighting Control." PLAYERS 4 (January-February 1930): 5.

Description of a new General Electric control board installed in the Chicago Civic Opera House. Equipped with self-synchronous motors and thyratron tubes to reduce the size of the console.

1531. Oenslager, Donald [Mitchell]. "Let There Be Light." THEATRE ARTS 31 (January 1947): 46-52. Illus.

Discusses light in nature, in the pictorial arts, and on the stage. Lists twelve technical innovations that must be made to improve stage lighting. For a reevaluation of this article, see item 1582.

1532. Pichel, Irving. "Lighting." THEATRE ARTS 9 (1925): 614-24. Illus.

Discusses equipment, especially switchboards and dimmers, and some of the functions of stage lighting.

1533. _____. MODERN THEATRES. New York: Harcourt, Brace and Co., 1925. xi, 102 p. Illus. Biblio.

Includes chapters on "Problems of Stage Lighting" and "Lighting Equipment." Largely refers to American practice.

1534. Pollock, Arthur. "Illumination and the Drama." DRAMA 4 (1914): 93-109.

Detailed discussion of current practices and available instruments.

1535. Porter, Charlotte. "The New Stage Art: Fortuny." DRAMA 4 (May 1914): 292-301.

Enthusiastic account of Mariano Fortuny's sky dome, setting it in the context of the aims of the New Stagecraft.

1536. Powell, Alvin Leslie, and Rodgers, Alston. LIGHTING FOR THE NON-PROFESSIONAL STAGE PRODUCTION. New York: Krieger Publications, 1931. 39 p. Paperbound. Illus.

A well-illustrated manual by two General Electric engineers. Dated, but of some historical interest.

1537. Rae, F.B. "Stage Lighting by Zones." ILLUSTRATED WORLD 27 (August 1917): 875-76. Illus.

Describes an amateur performance lighted only by spotlights equipped with reflectors.

1538. Reeves, H.H. "Construction and Installation of Stage Lighting Equipment." GENERAL ELECTRIC REVIEW 17 (April 1914): 412-22. Illus.

Useful technical description of instruments and their installation.

1539. Ridge, Cecil Harold. STAGE-LIGHTING FOR "LITTLE" THEATRES. Cambridge, England: W. Heffer & Sons, 1925. 98 p. Illus. Biblio.

One of the first modern books on stage-lighting practice. Issued in several later editions.

1540. Rimington, A[lexander]. Wallace. COLOUR MUSIC: THE ART OF MOBILE COLOUR. New York: Stokes, n.d. [c. 1912]. 205 p. Illus., part color.

Describes his color organ and the uses of mobile color music.

1541. Rosse, Herman. "Magic Lanterns." CHAPTER ONE 7 (April-May 1960): 1-2, 5-6, 8. Illus.

A somewhat episodic historical sketch of color organs and projected scenery, by a designer who himself experimented in this field. Well illustrated.

1542. Rubin, Joel Edward. "The Technical Development of Stage Lighting Apparatus in the United States, 1900-1950." Ph.D. dissertation, Stanford University, 1960. 338 p.

A pioneering study of American lighting technology, drawing largely on previously unexploited sources such as the catalogs of manufacturers of stage-lighting equipment.

1543. Scales, Robert Roy. "Stage Lighting Theory, Equipment, and Practice in the United States from 1900 to 1935." Ph.D. dissertation, University of Minnesota, 1969. 512 p.

1544. Selden, Samuel, and Sellman, Hunton D. STAGE SCENERY AND LIGHTING: A HANDBOOK FOR NON-PROFESSIONALS. New York: F.S. Crofts & Co., 1930. 415 p. Illus. Biblio.

A popular textbook, issued in several later editions. This first edition may be of some historical interest.

1545. Sellman, Hunton D. "Recent Developments in Stage Lighting Control."

THEATRE ARTS 25 (1941): 543-44.

Notes on autotransformer, electronic-reactance, and experimental electronic dimmer systems.

1546. Sheringham, George. "The Lamp-Lighter." ENGLISH REVIEW 36 (1923): 146-53. Illus.

Nontechnical discussion of a prismatic colored-light projector developed by Adrian B. Klein.

1547. Stainton, Walter H. "Color Music." In STUDIES IN SPEECH AND DRAMA IN HONOR OF ALEXANDER M. DRUMMOND, pp. 67-77. 1944. Reprint. New York: Russell & Russell, Publishers, 1968.

Informative sketch of the history of color organs and similar instruments for projecting mobile color.

1548. Stein, Donna M. THOMAS WILFRED: LUMIA--A RETROSPECTIVE EXHIBITION. [Washington, D.C.: Corcoran Gallery of Art, 1971]. 102 p. Paperbound. Illus., part color.

Catalog of an exhibition concerning Wilfred's career, especially his work with color organs.

1549. THEATRE LIGHTING PAST AND PRESENT. Mount Vernon, N.Y.: Ward Leonard Electric Co., 1923. 62 p. Paperbound. Illus.

Well-illustrated survey of the history of stage lighting, especially gas and electricity (pp. 7-30), plus an illustrated catalog of Ward Leonard dimmers.

1550. Thomas, Frank D. "The Realism of Modern Stage Effects." GREEN BOOK ALBUM 5 (May 1911): 1006-11.

Describes the use of colored motion pictures as backgrounds to stage boats, trains, etc.

1551. Turner, W.J. "Modern Stage Lighting." LONDON MERCURY 7 (1922-23): 649-51.

Critique of a new German lighting system, the Schwabe-Hasait system, noting that it does little more than create realistic atmospheric effects.

1552. Violett, Ellen. "Name in Lights." THEATRE ARTS 34 (December 1950): 24-27. Illus.

Sketch of the career of lighting designer Jean Rosenthal.

1553. Walker, John A. "The Functions of Stage Lighting in the Changing

Concepts of Stage Design." Ph.D. dissertation, Cornell University, 1952. 215 p.

1554. Wallace, John J. "The Impossible in Stage Lighting Is Achieved." SCIENTIFIC AMERICAN 133 (September 1925): 154-55. Illus.

David Belasco's "practical elimination of direct lighting from his stages," replacing it with diffused light from instruments equipped with reflectors.

1555. Wechsburg, Joseph. "The Right Light." NEW YORKER 36 (22 October 1960): 49-84. Port.

Profile of Abe H. Feder, the lighting designer. His theatrical activities are discussed on pp. 70-72.

1556. Wilfred, Thomas. "Prometheus and Melpomene: How They Met as Equals." THEATRE ARTS 12 (1928): 638-41. Illus.

Discusses his use of the Clavilux color organ in a production of THE VIKINGS AT HELGELAND at the Goodman Memorial Theatre, Chicago.

1557. Wilkins, Harold T. "Scenic Wonders of the Theater." POPULAR MECHANICS 45 (January 1926): 67-71. Illus.

Description of lighting and electrical equipment at Drury Lane Theatre, London, and elsewhere.

1558. Yeaton, Kelly. "A Pool of Light: Suggestions for Lighting Central Staging." PLAYERS 25 (April 1949): 152-54. Illus.

Describes and illustrates several "formulas."

1559. Young, Stark. "The Color Organ." THEATRE ARTS 6 (1922): 20-32. Illus.

Description and appraisal of Thomas Wilfred's Clavilux, a machine for presenting mobile patterns of colored light. Biographical note on Wilfred, p. 62.

Chapter 22

AFTER 1950

SEE ALSO items 1485, 1486, 1513, 1528.

1560. Abbott, Stanley. "Arena Lighting: An Analysis of Four Methods."
THEATRE ANNUAL 22 (1965–66): 76–87. Diags.

Three-, four-, and five-instruments-per-area methods, as well
as the central-peripheral method.

1561. Arnott, Brian. "THE ARCHITECT AND THE EMPEROR OF ASSYRIA:
A Scenography of Light." DRAMA REVIEW 17 (June 1973): 73–79.
Illus.

Discusses a production at the National Theatre of Great Britain
in 1971, designed by Victor Garcia and Michel Launay; lighting by David Hersey.

1562. Bock, Fred Clinton. "A Scheme for Arena Theatre Lighting-Grid Design in Terms of Grid Spacing, Walkway Space, and Masking by Louvres."
Ph.D. dissertation, Ohio State University, 1966. 172 p.

1563. Bonnat, Yves. "The Lighting of Open-Air Performances." WORLD
THEATRE 9 (Summer 1960): 149–57. Illus.

1564. Bristow, Charles. "Lighting an Opera." OPERA 14 (April 1963): 220–
26. Illus.

General discussion by a lighting designer.

1565. "Concerning Projected Scenery: The Technicians Reply." WORLD THE-
ATRE 3, no. 4 (1954): 48–59. Illus.

Joel E. Rubin, Leland H. Watson, and Ernest Klausz respond
to an article by Walter Unruh (see item 1597). They discuss
instruments, screens, and the subject of back projection vs.
front projection.

1566. Corathiel, Elisabethe H.C. "Richard Pilbrow." THEATRE WORLD 59 (November 1963): 28-30. Illus.

A profile of this British lighting designer.

1567. Corry, Percy. "Stage Lighting--1966." DRAMA, n.s. 83 (Winter 1966): 42-44.

A survey of available equipment and techniques.

1568. "The Designer Talks: Richard Pilbrow in Interview with Robert Water-house." PLAYS AND PLAYERS 18 (October 1970): 22, 24. Illus.

Interview with a British lighting designer.

1569. Dewey, Walter S. "More Flexibility from the Front." EDUCATIONAL THEATRE JOURNAL 11 (1959): 23-28. Illus.

Calls for more frontal lighting from the auditorium and stresses the need to plan for it before construction.

1570. Eaton, Quaintance. "Painting with Light." OPERA NEWS 30 (2 April 1966): 28-31.

Concerns projected scenery in operatic productions.

1571. Feder, Abe H. "Theatre Form through Light." JOURNAL OF THE AMERICAN INSTITUTE OF ARCHITECTS 34 (October 1960): 81-83.

Comments on lighting stage and auditorium, by a well-known lighting designer.

1572. Feher, Erwin M. "The Electric Environment." INTERSCAENA-ACTA SCAENOGRAPHICA 2 (Spring 1972): 16-21.

Considers the sources and nature of a curriculum for a course in lighting technology at the Ontario College of Art.

1573. _____. "The Vivian Beaumont Theatre and Its Stage Lighting Facilities." INTERSCAENA 2 (Spring 1968): 40-48.

1574. Goodman, Saul. "Meet Jean Rosenthal." DANCE MAGAZINE 36 (February 1962): 19-23. Illus.

Brief sketch of the career of this American lighting designer.

1575. Graham, Robert. "On the Development of a Lighting Score." IMPULSE 1952, pp. 13-18.

A primer of stage lighting for dancers.

1576. Howard, George T. "Automation or Mechanization." EDUCATIONAL THEATRE JOURNAL 10 (1958): 250-53.

Noting that automated lighting changes are impossible in live theatre, the author proposes that every instrument be mechanized so that its position, intensity, beam size, etc., can be remotely controlled.

1577. Hrbas, Jiri, ed. NEARLY ALL ABOUT THE MAGIC LANTERN. Translated by Oldrich Albrecht. Prague: Czechoslovak Film Institute, 1968. 187 p. Illus.

A collection of articles about the Laterna Magika.

1578. Jacobson, Robert. "New Light on Festival Opera." SATURDAY REVIEW 53 (12 September 1970): 80-81. Illus.

Brief remarks on new opera productions, heavily dependent on lighting, designed by Josef Svoboda, Luciano Damiani, Rudolf Heinrich, Jean-Pierre Ponnelle, and Guenther Schneider-Siemssen.

1579. Kirby, Michael. "The Uses of Film in the New Theatre." TULANE DRAMA REVIEW 11 (Fall 1966): 49-61. Illus.

Mainly concerns American experiments of the 1960s.

1580. Kook, Edward F. "Images in Light for the Living Theatre." Sponsored by the Ford Foundation, 1963. 248 p. Illus. Biblio. Mimeographed.

A study of scenic projection: historical notes, present uses, instruments, optical principles, potential. Letters from scenic and lighting designers in Europe and America in response to a questionnaire about their use of projected scenery, pp. 48-200. Technical data on some available projection machines, pp. 208-43. Good bibliography.

1581. "Laterna Magika." Edited by Erika Munk. TULANE DRAMA REVIEW 11 (Fall 1966): 141-49. Illus.

Excerpts from Czech publications concerning Josef Svoboda's multimedia presentations at the Brussels World's Fair and in Prague.

1582. "Let There Be Light." THEATRE DESIGN & TECHNOLOGY, no. 25 (May 1971): 16-22, 26. Illus.

A panel discussion involving Donald Oenslager, Fred Wolff, William Warfel, and others in a review of lighting progress since 1947.

1583. MacKay, Patricia. "A CHORUS LINE: Computerized Lighting Control Comes to Broadway." THEATRE CRAFTS 9 (November–December 1975): 6–11, 26–29.

   An account of the lighting of the first Broadway show to employ computerized lighting control. Includes an illustration of Tharon Musser's lighting plot.

1584. Nickolich, Barbara E. "The Nikolais Dance Theatre's Uses of Light." DRAMA REVIEW 17 (June 1973): 80–91. Illus.

   Discusses lighting in Nikolais productions from 1956 to 1972, particularly SOMNILOQUY (1967). Good illustrations.

1585. Palmer, Richard H. "Style in Lighting Design." EDUCATIONAL THEATRE JOURNAL 19 (1967): 142–48.

   Lighting design for realism, formalism, surrealism, etc.

1586. Planer, Paul. "Projected Opera Settings." OPERA NEWS 18 (15 February 1954): 4–5. Illus.

1587. Read, John B. "Light on the Matter." DANCE AND DANCERS 22 (February 1971): 17–21. Illus.

   A British lighting designer discusses his career, stressing his work for the dance.

1588. Rosenthal, Jean. "The Art and Language of Stage Lighting." THEATRE ARTS 45 (August 1961): 17–19, 78.

1589. Rosenthal, Jean, and Wertenbaker, Lael. THE MAGIC OF LIGHT. Boston: Little, Brown and Co., 1972. ix, 256 p. Illus. Biblio.

   A combination autobiography and manual of stage-lighting practice, with a chapter on the history of stage lighting and a list of Rosenthal's productions.

1590. Rubin, Joel E. "The Projected Setting: A Symposium." EDUCATIONAL THEATRE JOURNAL 6 (1954): 260–67.

   The participants were E.F. Kook, Thomas Wilfred, Paul Planer, Peggy Clark, Stanley McCandless, John Asby Conway, and Paul F. Wittlig.

1591. _____. "Theatre Lighting: A New Era of Technological Development." JOURNAL OF THE AMERICAN INSTITUTE OF ARCHITECTS 36 (August 1961): 78–81. Illus. Biblio.

   Brief sketch of the history of twentieth-century lighting and a description of current developments and possibilities.

1592. Sargeant, Winthrop. "Please, Darling, Bring Three to Seven." NEW YORKER 31 (4 February 1956): 33-59. Port.

An informative profile of Jean Rosenthal, the lighting designer.

1593. Skelton, Tom. "Handbook of Dance Stagecraft." DANCE MAGAZINE 29 (October 1955)-31 (March 1957). Illus.

Series of sixteen articles largely concerned with lighting for the dance: color, placement, intensity, equipment, etc.

1594. Smedberg, George. "Postwar Developments in Stage Lighting." EDUCATIONAL THEATRE JOURNAL 5 (1953): 253-58.

More intense lamps, more efficient arc spotlights, more flexible autotransformer dimmers, and so on.

1595. Thayer, David. "Flexibility and Preset Control Boards." EDUCATIONAL THEATRE JOURNAL 13 (1961): 30-33.

Granting the many advantages of pre-set control boards, the author objects to the loss of spontaneity they require.

1596. _____. "Notes on Lighting Design for the Elizabethan Stage." EDUCATIONAL THEATRE JOURNAL 11 (1959): 222-28.

Advocates simplified lighting for Elizabethan-style platform stages.

1597. Unruh, Walther. "Projected Scenery." WORLD THEATRE 2, no. 4 (1953): 22-29. Illus.

Discusses methods and equipment.

1598. Versteeg, Robert. "A Multi-Media Production of ROMEO AND JULIET." EDUCATIONAL THEATRE JOURNAL 21 (1969): 259-74. Illus.

Description of a production at Louisburg College, North Carolina, in which three multi-planed slide screens were used to show projected images.

1599. Waterhouse, Robert. "A Light Paint." PLAYS AND PLAYERS 19 (October 1971): 24-25. Illus.

Brief discussion of projected scenery, with particular reference to Patrick Robertson's designs for DANTON'S DEATH at the New Theatre, London.

1600. Watson, Lee. "Color Concepts in Lighting Design." EDUCATIONAL
THEATRE JOURNAL 10 (1958): 254-58.

Rejects the theory that the stage should be lighted with a
warm color from one side and a cool color from the other.
Proposes alternatives.

1601. Weiss, David W. "The New Design Problem: Multi-Media Effects."
PLAYERS 45 (August-September 1970): 264-67.

Assesses the use of projections, motion pictures, and light displays in stage productions.

1602. Wilfred, Thomas. "The Designer Enters the Ring." PLAYERS 30 (November 1953): 28-29. Illus.

Describes plans for his "Heptarena," an arena theatre in which
the spectators sit within a ring of projected scenery.

1603. _____. "The Projected Setting." EDUCATIONAL THEATRE JOURNAL
6 (1954): 136-44. Illus.

Discusses direct-beam and lens projectors, image plates, and
instrument placement, then goes on to describe his system of
projected scenery for arena staging.

Chapter 23

MANUALS AND TEXTBOOKS
OF CONTEMPORARY PRACTICE

1604. Bellman, Willard F. LIGHTING THE STAGE: ART AND PRACTICE.
2d ed. New York: Chandler Publishing Co., 1974. 495 p. Illus.
Biblio.

1605. Bentham, Frederick. THE ART OF STAGE LIGHTING. London: Pitman, 1968. 466 p. Illus.

1606. Bongar, Emmet W. THE THEATRE STUDENT: PRACTICAL STAGE LIGHT-
ING. New York: Richard Rosen Press, 1971. 124 p. Illus. Biblio.

1607. Corry, Percy. LIGHTING THE STAGE. London: Pitman, 1954. 157 p.
Illus.

1608. Goffin, Peter. STAGE LIGHTING FOR AMATEURS. 4th ed. London:
J.G. Miller, 1960. 158 p. Illus.

1609. Jones, Tom Douglas. THE ART OF LIGHT AND COLOR. New York:
Van Nostrand Reinhold, 1972. 119 p. Illus., part color.

Theory and practice of light machines and color organs.

1610. McCandless, Stanley R. A METHOD OF LIGHTING THE STAGE. 4th
ed., rev. New York: Theatre Arts Books, 1958. 143 p. Illus.

1611. _____. A SYLLABUS OF STAGE LIGHTING. 11th ed. New Haven,
Conn.: n.p., 1964. 135 p. Illus. Biblio.

1612. Ost, Geoffrey. STAGE LIGHTING. London: H. Jenkins, 1957. 96 p.
Illus.

1613. Parker, Wilford Oren, and Smith, Harvey K. SCENE DESIGN AND
STAGE LIGHTING. 3d ed. New York: Holt, Rinehart, Winston,
1974. x, 597 p. Illus. Biblio.

1614. Pilbrow, Richard. STAGE LIGHTING. New York: Van Nostrand Reinhold, 1970. 151 p. Illus., part color. Biblio.

1615. Rubin, Joel E[dward]., and Watson, Leland H. THEATRICAL LIGHTING PRACTICE. New York: Theatre Arts Books, 1954. 142 p. Illus. Biblio.

1616. Sellman, Hunton D. ESSENTIALS OF STAGE LIGHTING. New York: Appleton-Century-Crofts, 1972. 228 p. Illus. Biblio.

1617. Warfel, William B. HANDBOOK OF STAGE LIGHTING GRAPHICS. 2d ed., rev. and enl. New York: Drama Book Specialists/Publishers, 1974. 41 p. Illus.

1618. Wehlburg, Albert F.C. THEATRE LIGHTING: AN ILLUSTRATED GLOSSARY. New York: Drama Book Specialists/Publishers, 1975. 62 p. Spiral bound. Illus.

1619. Wilfred, Thomas. PROJECTED SCENERY: A TECHNICAL MANUAL. New York: Drama Book Shop, 1965. 59 p. Illus. Biblio.

1620. Williams, R[ollo]. Gillespie. THE TECHNIQUE OF STAGE LIGHTING. 2d ed. London: Pitman, 1960. 198 p. Illus.

1621. Wilson, Angus. STAGE LIGHTING FOR THE AMATEUR PRODUCER. London: Pitman, 1960. 89 p. Illus.

INDEXES

Author Index

Subject Index

Person (as Subject) Index

AUTHOR INDEX

This index is alphabetized letter by letter and references are to item numbers. Included are all authors, editors, compilers, illustrators, contributors, and translators whose works are cited in this bibliography. Additional references appear in the Person (as Subject) Index for authors who are the subject of biography, or whose works are the subject of analysis.

A

Abbott, Claude C.   448
Abbott, Stanley   1560
Abercrombie, Lascelles   503
Abrahams, Doris   834
Abril, Manuel   1336
Adami, Giuseppe   805
Adams, John C.   272
Adams, Richard G.   1
Addis, Denise   773
Adducci, Alexander F.   1433
Adelsperger, Walter   357
Adix, Vern   1389
Adler, Dankmar   925
Akers-Douglas, Eric   1298
Akimov, Nikolai   826
Alarma Tastas, Salvador   1299
Albright, H. Darkes   886, 892
Alden, John   921
Aleotti, Giovanni Battista   98
Alexandre, Arsene   827
Allen, Patricia   635
Allen, Ralph G.   306-13
Allen, Walter J.   358
Allevy, Marie Antoinette   620
Altman, George   2
Amberg, George   116, 970-71, 1300, 1313

American Society of Scenic Painters   926
American Theatre Planning Board   1428
Amery, Colin   449
Amundsen, Gerhard   700-703, 1301
Anderson, John   973
Appen, Karl von   707
Appia, Adolphe   144, 887-92
Applebee, L.G.   1443
Apthorp, William F.   691
Archer, William   273, 359-60
Ardoin, John   975
Armfield, Maxwell   1078
Armistead, Horace   976
Armstrong, William A.   361-62, 412
Armstrong, Will Steven   1265
Arnold, Richard   1434
Arnold, Richard Lee   927, 977-78
Arnott, Brian   1561
Arnott, J.F.   363
Arnott, Peter D.   195
Aronson, Boris   979, 1043
Arrington, Joseph Earl   928
Ashbolt, Allan   1302
Ashworth, Bradford   1390
Association of Finnish Stage Designers   1303

Author Index

Author Index

Author Index

Hagen, Claude L. 1107
Hainaux, Rene 151-54
Hake, Herbert V. 1406
Hale, Edward E. 155
Hall, Roger Allan 56
Hamar, Clifford E. 914
Hamblin, Junius N. 380
Hamilton, Clayton 156, 510-11, 1108-11
Hamilton, John L. 1506
Hammack, J. Alan 15-16
Hannon, Daniel Leroy 937
Harbron, Dudley 381
Harker, Joseph 261
Harris, Augustus 382
Harshbarger, Karl 512
Hart, Jerome 1112
Hartmann, Louis 1447, 1507
Hartnoll, Phyllis 1446
Harvey, E.T. 938
Hashim, James 221
Hastings, Baird 157, 655-57, 849
Hatch, Robert 1113
Hatton, Joseph 383
Hawley, James 610
Hawley, James A. 384
Hawley, James Abgriffith 280
Hays, David 157
Held, McDonald Watkins 1464-65
Hellman, Geoffrey T. 1114
Helvenston, Harold Finley 1407
Herf, Estelle 513
Herkomer, Hubert von 385-86
Herman, Henry 387
Hersh, Burton 1115
Herstand, Theodore 514
Hewes, Henry 1116
Hewitt, Barnard W. 99, 388, 515, 891-92, 1370-71
Hewlett, J. Monroe 1117-18, 1372
Heymann, Henry 250
Hickenlooper, George 789
Hicks, Lee Roy 1119
Highfill, Philip H., Jr. 325
Hild, Stephen Glenn 1120
Hill, Derek 850
Hillestrom, Gustaf 1323
Hippely, Edward Charles 611
Hirschfeld, Kurt 717
Hitchman, Percy J. 516-17

Hoctin, Luce 658
Hodge, Francis 57
Hodges, Cyril Walter 281
Hoelscher, Eberhard 718
Hoermann, Helmuth 692
Hoffmann, Ernst T.A. 693
Holme, Geoffrey 138, 159
Hont, Ferenc 1324
Honzl, Jindrich 1373-74
Hood, Hugh 1325
Hopkins, Albert A. 107
Hopkins, Arthur 1140
Hoppe, E.O. 518-20
Horanyi, Matyas 1326
Horner, Harry 1121-22
Horton, Percy 521
Hosley, Richard 222
Hotson, Leslie 282
Houghton, Norris 851, 1123-25
Hourmouziades, Nicolaos C. 202
Howard, Deborah 852
Howard, George T. 1576
Howe, Samuel 1126
Hrbas, Jiri 1577
Hubbard, Hesketh 522
Hume, Samuel J. 144, 1127
Hunningher, Benjamin 158, 1327
Hunter, Frederick J. 17, 1128-31
Hunter, Jack Worth 108, 389-90
Huston, Hollis W. 391
Hyllested, Mogens 523

I

Ilko, Donald Wilson 1132
Innes, C.D. 719
Irvine, St. John 503
Isaacs, Hermine Rich 1133-34
Isaacs, Jacob 283
Izenour, George C. 1508-9

J

Jackson, Allan Stuart 326-27, 392, 610, 940, 1135
Jackson, Peter 524
Jacobson, Robert 1578
Jacquot, Jean 95
Jaffe, Irma B. 90
Janosa, Lajos 1343

Author Index

Lee, Ming Cho 1043, 1163
Leeper, Janet 162, 536-37, 726, 897
Legge, Brian 1470
Leitner, Margaret 1164
Lerche, Frank Martin 918
Lerminier, Georges 662
Leverton, Garrett H. 943
Levinson, Andre 830, 859
Levy, Julien 1075
Lewis, Cecil 563
Lewis, Virginia E. 944
Leyda, Jay 860
Lieberman, William S. 663
Lingg, Ann M. 1165
Lissim, Simon 664-65, 828, 861
Lister, Raymond 666, 861
Little, Alan M.G. 204-6
Lloyds, Frederick 400
Lobanov, Nikita D. 828, 862
Logan, Olive 109-10
Loney, Glenn M. 253, 667, 735, 863, 1334-35
Loomis, Laura H. 224
Louchheim, Aline 1166
Lounsbury, Warren C. 37, 919, 1437
Lowrey, Edward W. 1167
Luckiesh, Matthew 1518-20
Luzzati, Emanuele 811

M

MacArthur, Roderick 668
McCalmon, George 288
McCandless, Stanley R. 1016, 1521-26, 1610-11
McClure, Theron Reading 784
McConnell, Frederic 1168
McCullough, Jack W. 945
McDermott, John Francis 946
McDowell, John H. 67-69, 99, 163, 289-90, 334, 1169
MacFall, Haldane 538-39
Macgowan, Kenneth 164-66, 737, 1078, 1170-74, 1212
MacKay, Patricia 1583
MacKaye, Percy 947
MacLeod, Joseph 813
McManaway, James G. 291
McNamara, Brooks 70-71
Mahelot, Laurent 615

Mahnken, Harry 1175
Mahnken, Janine 1175
Mann, Dorothea Lawrance 1176
Mannes, Marya 1177-78
Manson, George J. 948
Marchi, Mariano Vellani 811
Marker, Frederick J. 401
Marker, Lise-Lone 949
Marks, Claude 540
Marks, Samuel M. 1179
Marlis, Alan Philip 402
Marsh, John L. 950
Marshall, Francis 167
Marshall, Herbert 541, 864
Marshall, Thomas F. 951
Marston, Richard 952
Martinez Sierra, Gregorio 1336
Marussig, Guido 811
Matkovic, Marijan 1337
Matthews, James Brander 7, 72-73
Matz, Mary Jane 814, 898
Mayer, David III 403
Mayor, Alpheus Hyatt 24, 86, 96, 775, 785-86
Melchinger, Siegfried 727
Meldon, Charles 88
Meltzer, Charles Henry 1180
Melvill, Harald 1411
Melvill, Harry 827
Merchant, W. Moelwyn 404
Mercier, Jean 899
Merkling, Frank 815, 1181-82
Messel, Oliver 542, 645
Meyer, Annie Nathan 865
Meyerhold, Vsevolod 866
Middleton, Herman David 1184
Mielziner, Jo 1185-87, 1212
Miesle, Frank Leland 335
Miles, Bernard 543
Miller, Charles James 544
Miller, Harry Tatlock 545
Miller, James H. 20
Miller, William E. 292
Mitchell, Lee 1381
Mitchell, Roy 1382-83
Moderwell, Hiram K. 168, 900, 1190, 1252
Mohler, Frank C. II 787
Moholy-Nagy, Laszlo 716
Moiseiwitsch, Tanya 546
Molnar, Farkus 716

Author Index

Author Index

SUBJECT INDEX

References are to item numbers. This index is alphabetized letter by letter.

A

Absurd, Theatre of the 160
Act drops. See Curtains, drop
Altar decorations, baroque 90, 802
American Ballet Theatre 972
American Society of Scenic Painters
 926
Angle perspective 759, 764, 771,
 795
Aquatic drama 392
Arena stage 3, 547, 1155, 1558,
 1560, 1562, 1602-3
Argentina 1311
Armbruster Scenic Studio 915-16, 1135
Asphaleia system 114, 694, 733, 925,
 968, 1359
Auditorium Theatre, Chicago, stage
 machinery 925, 968
Australia 1302

B

Ballet design 23, 50, 88, 116, 118-
 19, 125, 142, 145-47, 167,
 179, 192-93, 428, 443, 450,
 454, 460, 554, 597-98, 635,
 637, 656, 663, 810, 834, 972,
 1353, 1369. See also Ballets
 Russes; Ballets Suedois; Dance; and
 the names of particular designers.
Ballets Russes 78, 116, 120, 135,
 162, 165, 180, 185-87, 454,

560, 599, 637, 834-37, 845-
 46, 848-49, 852, 858, 862,
 873, 1190
Ballets Suedois 673
Bauhaus 716
BEN HUR 927, 961, 1074
BLACK CROOK 934
Blackfriars Theatre, London 283,
 292, 300
Booth's Theatre, New York 931-32
Borders 65, 418, 435
Boston Opera House, electrical
 equipment 1489
Bourgeois Galleries 1078
Box sets 62, 67, 372, 389, 391
 399, 444, 622, 630
Brazil 1342
Bridges, stage 405, 447, 583, 941
Bristol (England), Theatre Royal,
 stage machinery 352-53, 394,
 425
Bulgaria 1319

C

Canada 1318, 1325, 1328, 1332,
 1349-50, 1357, 1572
CASTLE OF PERSEVERENCE 227,
 233
Chat Noir cabaret, Paris 632
Chestnut Street Theatre, Philadelphia
 967, 1483
Chicago Civic Opera House, stage
 equipment 996, 1530

261

PERSON (AS SUBJECT) INDEX

References are to item numbers. This index is alphabetized letter by letter.

Person (as Subject) Index

Person (as Subject) Index

Neppach, Robert 713
Neu, Thea 473
Nicholson, Peter 362, 412
Nijinsky, Vaslav 1142
Noguchi, Isamu 498, 1080
Novotny, J. 249

O

O'Brien, Timothy 459, 473
O'Connor, John 422
Odinokov, Vladimir 1006
Oenslager, Donald M. 86, 1037,
1048, 1069, 1124, 1202, 1245,
1282
O'Hearn, Robert 1069, 1080, 1181
Olah, Gustave (Gusztav) 1298, 1317
Oliviera, Pernambuco de 1342
Oman, Julia Trevelyan 459
O'Neill, Eugene 76, 1082, 1276
Orlik, Emil 706, 745
Orozco, Jose Clemente 1356
Ott, Paul 713
Otto, Teo 717

P

Papon, Louis 608
Parigi, Giulio and Alfonso 789
Parks, Gower 473
Parrish, Maxfield 1046
Pasetti, Leo 703
Patte, Pierre 1469
Pember, Clifford 1262
Penna, Nilson 1342
Peruzzi, Baldassare 758, 776
Peters, Rollo 1045, 1192, 1262
Phelps, Samuel 366, 411
Physioc, Joseph A. 1050
Picasso, Pablo 180, 637, 650, 663,
1353
Pignon, Edouard 670
Pilbrow, Richard 1566, 1568
Piper, John 473, 531, 602
Pirandello, Luigi 813
Pirchan, Emil 705, 730, 739
Piscator, Erwin 137, 149, 711, 719,
723
Pitcher, William John Charles. See
Wilhelm, C.

Pixerecourt, Guilbert de 621
Pizzi, Pier Luigi 814
Planer, Paul 1590
Platt, Livingston 1045, 1152,
1223, 1262-63, 1267-68
Plersch, Jan 1330
Poel, William 581
Pogany, Willy 1262
Polunin, Vladimir 533
Pomarede, Leon 946
Ponnelle, Jean-Pierre 667, 1578
Porter, William T. 938
Pozzo, Andrea 90, 768
Prampolini, Enrico 812
Pratt, John 1293
Pride, Malcolm 473
Pruna, Pedro 1353
Pugin, Augustus W.N. 402

Q

Quaglio, Carlo 1330
Quaglio, Lorenzo 98
Quaglio family of stage designers
815

R

Raban, Josef 249
Rabinovitch, Isaac 826, 847, 850
Radok, Alfred 137
Ramon, George 534
Rauschenberg, Robert 1080
Reimann, Walter 713
Reinhardt, Max 127, 140, 156,
168, 708, 737, 749, 750, 752-
53, 813, 1226, 1366
Reinking, Wilhelm 715
Resnik, Regina 1138
Reynolds, James 998, 1228
Ricciardi, Achille 1493
Rice, Peter 473
Richards, John Inigo 333, 344
Richter, Gerd 718
Ricketts, Charles 461, 470, 496,
502, 587
Rimington, Alexander Wallace
430, 1478
Rinfret, Jean-Claude 1069
Ritman, William 1153